Accountability in Higher Education

Edited by

PETER SHELDRAKE
RUSSELL LINKE

Educational Research Unit,
The Flinders University of South Australia

Sydney
George Allen & Unwin
London Boston

Cover design by Dennis Jones
Index compiled by E. Zalums

National Library of Australia Cataloguing-in-Publication data:

Accountability in higher education.

Index
ISBN 0 86861 121 2

1. Educational accountability—Australia—Addresses, essays, lectures. 2. Higher education and state—Australia—Addresses, essays, lectures. 3. Education, Higher—Australia—Aims and objectives—Addresses, essays, lectures. I. Sheldrake, Peter Francis, ed. II. Linke, Russell Dean, joint ed.

379.15'0994

Library of Congress Catalog Card Number: 79-83555

Set in 9 pt. Times Roman on 10 pt. by the University Relations Unit, Flinders University.
Printed in Hong Kong

Contents

Accountability in Higher Education

Foreword

The poet T. S. Eliot once said of Shakespeare: "Never has a man turned so little knowledge to such great account". A modern Eliot might wryly comment in opposite terms on the present state of higher education—that never has an institution turned so much knowledge to so little account.

Accountability has become in recent years a dominant feature of tertiary education, indeed of education as a whole, in Australia. If the 1960's can be portrayed as a period of expansion during which education was an increasingly favoured activity, then the so-called "steady state" of more recent times has been characterised by a growing disfavour with education and an increasing demand that educationists make reasonable account of themselves. This is not to say that educationists have not been accountable in the past—indeed, in fiscal terms the various institutions have been held to account for many years. Rather it seems the public, government, and other interested parties have become concerned to have a fuller accounting of what we are doing and where we are heading.

There are, in particular, two major features of the recent developments in higher education that point to concerns over accountability. The first, which perhaps has created the greater attention, at least in the public communication media, is to do with expenditure. Federal revenues for tertiary education have more than doubled in the past decade and while the proportion of Federal funds spent on tertiary education is quite modest compared with that in many other advanced industrial societies, the actual amount of money being spent is nevertheless quite considerable. Since 1976 there has been a marked curtailment of expenditure, and this has been associated with, among other things, a number of serious questions about the value of money being spent. In particular two questions have been increasingly asked: is the money being made available used in the most efficient and effective way possible?; and is the nature of educational provision by institutions appropriate to the needs of students? With increasing unemployment and concern over the appropriateness of qualifications, and over the longer term issue of the changing nature of industrial society, the role of educational institutions and the form and content of higher education becomes increasingly salient in the cost accounting of government expenditure.

At the same time a second change has been evident, which is to do with the nature of the student population. During the past decade the number of students participating in higher education has increased dramatically, as a result both of the general increase in 17-22 year old students, and in particular of the increasing participation rate among females. Both of these processes have rapidly levelled off. The participation rate among females in higher education is now marginally above that for males, and the most recent predictions suggest that we may well find the total number of people in the 17-22 year old group begin to fall in the last decade of this century. There have, of course, been a number of other changes in the student population, in particular the increase in proportion of students entering higher education only after spending a period of time in the work force. However it is unlikely that these changes will offset sufficiently the general slowing down in the number of new students entering higher education.

All the authors contributing to this book have addressed themselves in one way or another to these general issues, which have already been carefully documented elsewhere (Hore, Linke and West, 1978). Indeed, it is with this context in mind that the present book was initially planned. It began with the opportunity provided through an annual meeting of the Higher Education Research and Development Society of Australasia being held in Adelaide, for which the editors commissioned a number of papers on the general theme of accountability in higher education. These papers were presented in draft at that annual meeting, and in the light of relevant comments and questions from participants were subsequently revised for presentation in this book. The papers have been designed to reflect the three fundamental levels at which the notion of accountability in higher education may be considered: the system, the institution and the individual.

Chapters one to three deal with accountability at the system level. The first of these, by Hyde, reviews the overall nature of the post-secondary education system in Australia, then identifies some of the major themes concerning accountability at that level. This chapter acts as a backdrop to the three succeeding chapters dealing respectively with the Federal, State, and community perspectives on tertiary education. Chapter two, by Chippendale, examines the Federal response to and interest in accountability, and charts both the existing ways in which accountability is ensured and the possibility of future developments in this area. Following this analysis, Hall and Willett examine accountability at the State level, focusing on the emergence of State post-secondary education coordinating bodies and their implications for institutional accounting. The final paper in this group, by McDonell, then reverts to the theme of community accountability first heralded by Hyde.

Chapters five to seven examine the institutional perspective. Again these are introduced by a chapter which reviews the institutional perspective as a whole, by Ramsey and Howlett, followed by two which look at academic accountability at the institutional level, firstly in relation to resources and secondly to courses and programs. The chapter by Burke and McKenzie deals with what is perhaps the most familiar area of accountability in higher education, that of accounting for the use of resources, although in doing so the authors have broadened the frame of reference conventionally used in this area. By contrast, Johnson and Harman then look at academic accountability as it applies specifically to the teaching activities of higher education institutions.

Chapters eight and nine deal with the implications of accountability at the individual level. The first of these, by Patching, serves both to complement the preceding two chapters and to provide in turn a more general review of accountability at the individual level. The next chapter by Niland then serves to relate aspects of individual accountability to the purposes of higher education, with particular reference to vocational education, and refers back to institutional and system wide levels of accountability with a focus on the area of manpower planning.

Finally, Nilsson, in reviewing the preceding nine chapters, picks up the concepts of accountability and responsibility as they are used both in theory and in practice, and subjects both to a characteristically precise analysis.

Each of these papers, in their various ways, are addressed to the dominant concern of this book, which is to provide a detailed analysis of the meaning and practice of accountability in higher education. And accountability in higher education is not just another passing fashion among academic educationists, but a development whose sources lie in the general economic climate of the nation and in the changing nature of the student population. Thus our concern is not to suggest simply that accountability is likely to be an important issue in the future, for there is overwhelming evidence that this is already the case. Rather our purpose in this book is to present a number of constructive and practical ways by which the higher education sector can respond to the inevitable pressures for accountability, and indeed to initiate appropriate procedures before other, less desirable methods are imposed.

Chapter One

The Structure of Higher Education in Australia

J. Hyde

Higher education in Australia includes two systems of institutions within the tertiary sector—universities and colleges of advanced education. Tertiary education itself corresponds with post-school education, and it is usually acknowledged by educational commentators that technical and further education (TAFE) is included in this sector because of its post-school nature, not because of the educational level of its courses. Generally speaking, institutions in higher education, that is, universities and colleges of advanced education, offer courses which lead to awards above that of associate diploma, although there is some overlap at this level with TAFE.

Within higher education itself there is some dispute over the overlap in level of courses in the two systems. On the one hand, the universities are concerned to maintain unfettered their traditional leadership on the educational ladder and are particularly concerned at the alleged encroachment by colleges of advanced education into what they consider to be their fields of interest. There is also some feeling that, in areas of overlap, college courses are inferior, rather than simply different in emphasis. On the other hand, colleges of advanced education have alleged that the universities have expanded courses in professional and vocational areas, more properly the province of the colleges. In addition, there are some in the colleges who believe that many university courses are vocationally irrelevant and, as a result, a waste of public funds. This dispute in part can be seen in terms of different notions of accountability in universities and colleges.

Institutions

Universities. There are at present nineteen Australian universities. At the time of the Murray Report in 1957 there were nine, of which six were the well established State universities. One of the others, the Australian National University, was involved only in research, and two, the NSW University of Technology and the University of New England, had been established within the preceding ten years. There were also university colleges at Canberra (part of the University of Melbourne) and Newcastle (NSW University of Technology), and the University of New England had been until 1954 a college of the University of

Sydney. Since 1957, ten new universities have been established, of which three were upgraded from university colleges and one was the result of an amalgamation of two colleges of advanced education. The Australian National University absorbed the Canberra University College to form a comprehensive teaching and research institution.

It is widely accepted that universities are more than training institutions (and in fact it is often argued that training is not a proper role at all for them) but that they have a more comprehensive role in the education system. This includes not only high level training for the professions—engineers, medical practitioners, lawyers—but also general studies in the humanities, social sciences and sciences, and research into all areas of academic enquiry. But this in itself does not describe a university. Many see institutional autonomy and academic freedom, both individual and institutional, as essential preconditions for the survival of the institution as a valuable resource to society, arguing that a high standard of research and scholarship depend on them.

Of course the issue is not as clear cut as that. As soon as we begin to look more closely a number of questions arise—for instance, are autonomy and academic freedom inseparable?, and to whom should universities be accountable? The Committee on Post-Secondary Education in Western Australia—the Partridge Committee (1976)—described universities in relation to coordination:

> *The universities cannot be considered to be merely components of a State system of post-secondary education. They belong also to an Australia-wide system, and indeed to an international community of universities. Within this system, there is very free communication and exchange of ideas and persons; their activities are deeply influenced by traditions maintained within that wide community; and, very importantly, their standards both in teaching and research are exposed to the scrutiny and judgement of sister universities elsewhere in Australia and throughout the world. While it is essential that they should be responsive to interests and needs of their own local community, it is equally important that they should be free to respond to intellectual and educational movements flowing in from universities and other institutions all over the world. Because of their history, their endowment and the high intellectual levels they are expected to maintain, they have the responsibility for providing an intellectual or academic leadership that no other type of institution is so well fitted to assume. We would fear that an attempt to place them under the close control of a local academic authority might impair their capacity to provide such leadership.*
> (para. 8.19: p. 154)

There has developed within most universities an extensive committee system to ensure internal accountability. Thus universities have established a range of committees below their Councils whose function it is to look at departmental, faculty and general issues. Membership of the committees is drawn widely from the university community, and faculty and general committees often have representatives of the 'community at large' among their membership. University councils are also broadly based, with members from both inside and outside the university. Finally, a senate or convocation plays an upper house role in relation to the council, and membership of this body usually includes automatically all graduates of the university, and members of staff with university level academic qualifications.

Colleges of Advanced Education. The Martin Report of 1964 was the starting point for a period of rapid growth in higher education in Australia. In fact, in the advanced education sector, which the Report created in its recommendations for high level or tertiary non-university institutions, there have been two phases of expansion since 1965. Initially, contrary to the recommendations in the Report, the Government did not intervene in teacher training. It did, however, establish the Commonwealth Advisory Committee on Advanced Education, which became the Commission on Advanced Education. By 1971 there were 43 colleges of advanced education, which included the central institutes of technology, agricultural colleges and new institutions. In 1974 the Labor Government, extending previous developments under Liberal Education Ministers, particularly Gorton and Fraser, began complete funding of higher education, including teachers' colleges. As a result a second increase in the number of colleges of advanced education occured, as teachers' colleges were upgraded or underwent changes of name. By 1976 there were 83 colleges in Australia, although through amalgamations and the creation of Deakin University from two colleges, this number fell to 73 in 1977 (Australian Bureau of Statistics, 1977).

The difference in the roles of colleges of advanced education and universities was seen in the Martin Report (1964) as a difference of emphasis rather than level:

> *The objective of the education provided by a technical college is to equip men and women for the practical world of industry and commerce; teaching them the way in which manufacturing and business are carried on and the fundamental rules which govern their successful operation. The university course, on the other hand, tends to emphasize the development of knowledge and the importance of research; in doing so it imparts much information which is valuable to the practical man, but which is often incidental to the main objective.*
>
> (para. 5.137: p. 165)

As the system has developed, colleges have been more clòsely coordinated by boards of advanced education, institutes of colleges and the like, than have been universities. In theory there have been possibilities for exception to this with the NSW Higher Education Board and the W.A. Post-Secondary Education Commission and their predecessors. In practice, however, these seem to have played a low-key role in relations between universities and the Australian Universities Commission, especially since the advent of complete Federal funding in 1974. Even so, there has been increasing concern in universities that the colleges are involved in upward academic drift into areas traditionally (in Australia) university based. While the theoretical differences between the two types of institutions (although converging) remain, there is considerable overlap in courses, with perhaps the exception of the humanities, and to a lesser extent social sciences and general sciences. The main practical difference, it seems, occurs in the areas of autonomy and academic freedom.

As with the universities, colleges of advanced education have widely based committee structures which provide for some self-accountability and community presence in their decision making. College councils too, are structured similarly to those of universities.

Coordination

Constitutional power for education in Australia is considered to lie with the States (see the detailed discussion of this in the chapter by Chippendale elsewhere in this book). Since 1942, however, the Federal Government has become increasingly involved in education, particularly through the amendment in 1946 to Section 51 of the Constitution giving power to the Commonwealth to legislate 'with respect to the provision of benefits to students.' As yet the scope of Commonwealth power has not been legally tested. H. V. Evatt (Tannock and Birch, 1973), the author of the amendment, believed it gave the Commonwealth full Constitutional power over education: 'direct power and responsibility reside in this Parliament.' (121: see also Chapter 2) Tannock and Birch (1973) support the view, and Birch (1975) contends that

> *The [High] Court would not seem to support contentions like 'education is a State's right' and has implied that in exercise of its powers ... the Commonwealth may validly pass laws with an education component.*
>
> (p. xi Introduction)

Even so, *de facto* power lies with the States, although the Commonwealth influence has continued to grow, particularly in higher education. The Commonwealth has tended to exercise its influence by the power of the purse, especially since 1974 when complete Commonwealth funding over Section 96 Grants began. Smart (1976: 236) points out that Commonwealth expenditure increased in real terms more than seven times between 1964-5 and 1975-6. In 1964 there had been only two Commonwealth agencies, while by 1975 six new authorities had been established.

The States, under their assumed Constitutional responsibility, have established most universities and colleges of advanced education; universities under their own Acts, and colleges either under separate Acts or under a blanket college Act. Although universities were State funded, most States interfered little in their operations. Colleges on the other hand, either evolved from technical colleges, agricultural colleges, teachers' colleges or were newly established after the Martin Report. They have been subject to various forms of State control, from Public Service Department control to boards of advanced education. The continuation of coordination has been encouraged by the evolving Federal funding system for colleges. Increased pressures have arisen for universities to become publicly accountable in a similar manner at State level, particularly as the colleges have gained political leverage.

Commonwealth. The Australian Universities Commission was first established in the early 1940's and formally established after the 1944 Walker Report. It was established in its present form in 1959, after the Murray Report. Following the Martin Report, which recommended the establishment of an Australian Tertiary Education Commission to coordinate universities, colleges of advanced education and teachers' colleges, the Commonwealth Advisory Committee on Advanced Education, which later became the Australian Commission on Advanced Education, was established. The roles of the two Commissions were to investigate and advise the government on the levels of funding for universities and colleges, on a triennial basis, with a view to promoting the balanced development of each system.

The Commissions undertook their tasks with some zeal but with little coordination between themselves. As a result, the triennial report for 1976-78 recommended funds of $3.5 billion. Smart points out that:

> *It appears that these staggering figures led the Prime Minister to decide that a Tertiary Education Commission (TEC) must be established to coordinate and rationalise the funding and development of the university and college sectors.*
>
> (1976:247)

The Government suspended the triennium, and set about establishing the Tertiary Education Commission. With the 1975 suspension of Parliament the Bill lapsed. The subsequent Liberal Government went along with plans to establish a Tertiary Education Commission, but included also the Technical and Further Education Commission (TAFEC).

The role of the new Tertiary Education Commission (TEC) is substantially a telescoping of the roles of the three former commissions. In fact it coordinates the recommendations of three Councils which correspond with these three previous bodies. Its main functions are to make decisions on cross-sectoral matters, or on recommendations which may change the balance between the sectors. However its most difficult tasks are not its relations with the various sectors, or institutions, but its relations with Government. As Harman (1977: 10) has suggested, there appears to have been a shift in power from the commissions to the Department of Education and Cabinet. This has nowhere been more effectively illustrated than in the change in the flow of information between the Commissions (and now the TEC) and the Government. As Harman points out:

> *The commissions no longer ask institutions in any meaningful way what they need, and they in turn tell the government what the needs of institutions are nationally. Instead the Government simply informs each commission how much it has to distribute for one year at a time (not three), [by way of "Guidelines"] and then lets it carve this amount up among institutions.*
>
> (1977: 11)

This is especially evident in the recent TEC Report (1978) in which the Commission in its effort to comply with the Guidelines—without criticism, unlike the Schools Commission—had to reject some of the advice of its expert Councils in relation to recommendations for tertiary education.

This shift in power is in fact a result of the frictions which existed between the commissions, and which still exist to some extent between the Councils of the TEC. The power of the Department of Education is such that it has a branch whose major task is to review recommendations of the TEC, which is meant to be a direct source of advice to the Minister free of the type of political direction characterised by a government department. But even in Government departments there has been a shift of power, illustrated in the siting of the Williams Committee secretariat in the Department of the Prime Minister and Cabinet, and not in the Department of Education.

State. Machinery for coordination at the State level varies considerably between States. In New South Wales, the Higher Education Board is charged with coordinating the activities of universities and colleges of advanced education. It is, in fact, very much an advanced education coordinating body for it has not initiated any action for coordinating the universities. In advanced education the Board acts much the same as the boards of advanced education in other States, dealing with course approval, accreditation and college submissions to the TEC. In the case of the universities, it has the power to require submissions to be made through it, although it has never exercised this power; it is aware of university submissions, but offers advice only when requested by the TEC. It has nevertheless become very influential. New South Wales also has a powerful Ministry of Education through which the Higher Education Board reports to the Minister. In addition, the recent Hagan Report (1978) stresses that higher education should be seen as an integral part of the State education system, and as such recommends that the HEB be required to consult with a new State Education Commission over development and establishment of institutions, rationalization and duplication, acquisitions and such other matters as directed by the Minister, before submitting State Reports (p. 25). Although the Report does not propose to draw the HEB under its authority, the position of the Board, the new State Education Commission and the Ministry could have some interesting implications for higher education.

In Victoria the advanced education system has been split between the Victoria Institute of Colleges and the State College of Victoria (based on former teachers' colleges). This has caused some problems in developing a coordinated system and there has recently been an inquiry into the relationship between the two bodies; this effectively forestalled action by either body which might have affected the other until the larger Post-Secondary Inquiry—the Partridge Committee—could report. The Partridge Committee has recommended the establishment of the Victorian Post-Secondary Education Commission encompassing universities, colleges of advanced education and TAFE, complemented by the dissolution of the VIC and SCV, and the establishment of a Council on Advanced Education and a Board of TAFE. The Report envisaged that the universities would retain their independence and autonomy in the new system (Partridge 1978). However the Government developed the recommendation and introduced a Bill to the State Parliament which placed the universities under the same close control as other tertiary institutions. During the period immediately after this the universities succeeded in having the Bill amended, and the final legislation restored much of their autonomy. One exception however, is that universities will now have to seek approval for the establishment of new courses from a State body. Until now, the State Advisory Council on Tertiary Education—a representative body—has been the only apparatus for coordination of all higher education institutions. This is an *ad hoc* committee, and its effectiveness has been somewhat limited.

In Queensland the college system has been coordinated by the Board of Advanced Education, which is responsible for accreditation, course approval, budget approval and planning. There is also a Board of Teacher Education which is required to collaborate with the BAE. Recently the Government established an *ad hoc* representative Joint Advisory Committee on Post-Secondary Education in an attempt to coordinate post-secondary education, including the universities.

South Australia, like Queensland, has a Board of Advanced Education which exercises similar substantial coordination in the college sector. The universities are not required to collaborate with other institutions, although recently under the pressure of common interest while faced with an Enquiry into Post-Secondary Education—the Anderson Committee—the vice-chancellors joined the directors of the colleges on an informal committee concerned with collaboration. The Karmel Report recommended the establishment of a Tertiary Education Committee encompassing both universities and colleges of advanced education which was not established. However the Board of Advanced Education has some of its recommended powers, and the South Australian Council for Educational Planning and Research has some others, including among its functions those of promoting coordination, cooperation and rationalisation. The Anderson Enquiry (1978) has recommended the establishment of the Tertiary Education Authority of South Australia to coordinate the whole post-secondary sector, and the present BAE is likely to be subsumed by TEASA. The Committee's recommendations have recognised the traditional place of universities in the education system, and in the short term at least conditions will remain almost unaltered for them, with the exception of course approval requirements. In the longer term, however, the implications of an embracing body may become more apparent.

The Report of the Committee on Post-Secondary Education in Western Australia—the Partridge Report—also recommended the establishment of an overarching Western Australian Post-Secondary Education Commission. Previously, the W.A. Tertiary Education Authority was charged with overseeing higher education. Like the NSW Higher Education Board, however, it was concerned mainly with the colleges and undertook the functions of a board of advanced education. The Partridge Committee (1976) noted that

> ... the [W.A.] Tertiary Education Commission has not attempted to intervene seriously in the discussions between the Universities Commission and the universities. Our impression is that the [W.A.] Tertiary Education Commission has operated only marginally in relation to the universities ...
> (para. 8.16, p. 153)

The Report recommended the abolition of the W.A. Tertiary Education Commission; the Government, however, amended the W.A. Tertiary Education Commission to become the W.A. Post-Secondary Education Commission, bringing TAFE under its control. It also recommended the repeal of the W.A. Teacher Education Authority which was the coordinating body for the teachers' colleges. Recently this was approved, with the four advanced education colleges becoming autonomous institutions.

Coordinating arrangements in Tasmania, as in most of the other States, are in a period of change. However the problem is simpler than elsewhere, as the University of Tasmania and the Tasmanian CAE are the only higher education institutions at present, although the establishment of the Australian Maritime College may have some effect on higher education there. The Report of the Committee on Post-Secondary Education in Tasmania (1976) recommended the establishment of a three man advisory committee with no financial powers, which would report to the Minister on coordination of post-secondary education and its development, and the establishment of a Coordinating

Committee for Technical and Further Education, also to report to the Minister, but charged with collaboration with the advisory committee. The Tasmanian Government appointed two Committees to investigate the recommendations of the Karmel Report—the Cosgrove Committee to advise on the mechanism of implementing the restructuring recommendations, along with any misgivings, and the Kearney Committee to advise on appropriate coordinating machinery and specific details of sectoral matters. The report of the latter recommended the establishment of the Tertiary Education Commission of Tasmania (TECT), an overarching but advisory body. It has no real power, but might become influential through its functions of advising the State Minister of Education and the federal Tertiary Education Commission.

The situation in the Australian Capital Territory and the Northern Territory is somewhat different from that in the States. The ACT has one university, the Australian National university, and one college of advanced education, Canberra CAE. The Darwin Community College is a multi-level tertiary institution serving the Northern Territory. These institutions receive their funding directly from Federal Government revenue, submitting proposals to the Australian Treasury along with Australian Public Service departments at the time of drafting the federal Budget. They are also subject to the Commonwealth Tertiary Education Commission along with other tertiary institutions.

Pressure Groups

One of the main pressures for accountability in higher education has come from the increasing numbers and strength of concerned interest groups. These range from industrial and student groups through to professional and executive bodies. There is not enough space in this discussion to list exhaustively and describe all pressure groups, but a reasonably representative cross section of these will be considered. The groups examined are the Australian Vice-Chancellors' Committee, the Federation of University Staff Associations and the University of Adelaide Staff Association, and the Australian Union of Students. There will also be a short discussion of professional associations in relation to higher education.

Australian Vice-Chancellors' Committee (AVCC). The AVCC is a pressure group consisting of all the Australian Vice-Chancellors (as its name implies). Two other groups have been modelled on it, and their roles and functions are substantially similar in relation to the colleges of advanced education. These are the Conference of Directors of Central Institutes of Technology (DOCIT) and the Australian Conference of Principals of Colleges of Advanced Education. DOCIT's membership is made up of directors or principals of major multi-purpose colleges: there is one from each State with two additional members from Victoria and the principal of the Canberra CAE. The membership of the Conference of Principals is open to directors or principals of all Australian colleges of advanced education. There are 68 members, from the total of 73 colleges of advanced education, and these include all the members of DOCIT.

The aims of the AVCC are to provide a forum for discussion of items of common concern, to formulate advice to councils/senates on these issues, to publicise or take appropriate action on its findings and decisions, and to collect and disseminate information to the universities which may be of interest and concern. Its articles of incorporation include these and additional objects: to liaise internationally; to print, publish and promote material of interest; and to disseminate career information to students and graduates. In order to undertake these functions the Committee maintains an office in Canberra, published a now defunct journal, has an executive Standing Committee and sub-committees on teaching, research, finance and building, staff, students, and statistics, and a Steering Committee on Research and Experiment into Educational Matters.

Although the AVCC has considerable influence it is in fact a committee of nineteen individuals. It is not accountable to the universities, nor has it, except in some minor matters, the power to act for them. The Chairman's Report for 1967-70 recognises this fact:

> *It must be emphasised ... [that] the AVCC has no power to act on behalf of the universities: authority continues to reside ... in each university's governing body. Unless each Vice-Chancellor has obtained the prior approval of his governing body, the most the AVCC can do in regard to taking united action on an issue is to make recommendations to individual Councils or Senates.*
>
> (para. 10.1.3)

However, some controversy has arisen lately with the AVCC entering into industrial negotiations independently of the universities.

Federation of Australian University Staff Associations (FAUSA). Although individual staff associations in universities have retained their own identities, they are represented nationally in a federation which has become one of the most influential pressure groups in higher education. Staff associations in colleges of advanced education have followed the lead of their university counterparts and established the Federation of Staff Associations of Australian Colleges of Advanced Education (FSAACAE). FAUSA acts as both an industrial body and a professional association. As such it plays important roles in industrial negotiations with individual universities (in association with the local staff association), the Academic Salaries Tribunal, and the Commonwealth Government. It has also spent a good deal of effort in making submissions to the various education inquiries in recent years. As a professional association it has been involved in promoting its concept of 'the university' and liaising with international and other national bodies with similar aims. An agenda for an executive meeting selected at random illustrates the breadth of FAUSA's interest: items included a report on a meeting with the Federal Minister of Education; discussion on a draft report on senior support staff; salaries; superannuation; a discussion of tertiary education, mainly concerned with the NSW Higher Education Act; science policy; research funding; industrial registration; tax concessions; a discussion on the role of Education Research Units; consideration of a report of the Committee on the Status of Women Academics; and discussion centering on a proposed Association of Australian Universities.

FAUSA aims at promoting accountability in universities not only through industrial means but also as a professional body. As such it seeks to protect industrial as well as academic and ethical standards. Individual staff associations have considerable importance within their own institutions.

Nationally, of course, their opinions are reflected through FAUSA, but locally, active members are often to be found as activists of governing bodies and other important committees within the university. At a local level, individual staff associations tend to act more as industrial bodies than professional associations, as would be expected.

Some agenda, selected at random, concerning meetings of the University of Adelaide Staff Association included the following items: finance for tertiary education; study leave; ratification of FAUSA Capitation Fees; maternity leave; petition concerning the Australian Broadcasting Commission; meeting with the Australian Union of Students; and a request from another staff association for information on departmental government.

The Australian Union of Students (AUS). AUS is the most overtly political of the various pressure groups in higher education. It is a national organisation representing students who are members through the affiliation with AUS of their local Students' Associations or Student Representative Councils. Originally, AUS membership was restricted to universities, but in 1970 the eligibility was widened to include colleges of advanced education and teachers' colleges. Because of its diverse membership it is difficult for it to act as a trade union or professional body, hence its more political role. It derives a good deal of strength in promoting accountability from an increasingly articulated concern by students for the content and relevance of their education, and for a widening of provision to enable greater access to higher education by students from backgrounds under-represented in universities and colleges of advanced education.

There has been some upheaval in AUS over the past few years with legislative attempts at blocking its sources of funding. Even given its problems, the Union has continued to be recognised as an important source of opinion. It takes part in discussions with governments, institutions and other bodies concerned with higher education policy making and has submitted extensively to the various educational inquiries. It also represents Australian students internationally.

Professional Associations. While the aim of many professional associations in higher education is fairly narrowly placed within specific disciplines, the effects of their demands and actions can be somewhat more far reaching. For instance, the recent compliance by higher education authorities to the demands of engineering associations for the addition of an extra year onto first degree courses, when faced with the threat of non-recognition of existing awards and ineligibility of subsequent graduates for membership of the associations, has placed a considerable extra expense on higher education funds. It has also led to similar demands from other associations. Another current campaign is that of nursing associations to have nurse education conducted at first degree level. This proposal has met with somewhat stronger opposition from Governments and higher education authorities, although some institutions are understandably in favour of it. It seems that the arguments in both cases, although couched in educational terms, may well be more economic than educational.

Higher Education and Accountability

In this section I propose to discuss more generally the notion of accountability in higher education. Its aim is to put into perspective the roles and functions of the groups and systems discussed earlier. As a socialist critique it departs from some of the premises which have been prevalent in writings on Australian higher education in the past.

Demands for increased accountability in higher education have occurred in two definable stages. The first, during the period of rapid expansion, accompanied increased demand for places in higher education, and its most vocal foci were in student demands for a voice in governance, assessment, course design and the like, and in staff demands for the end of professorial board rule. At the same time, although less vocally, general community demand for a voice in educational policy making and governance increased, although this was directed more at primary and secondary education than at higher education. These demands appeared to be a reflection of the awareness of potential for personal autonomy that education fostered in a great number of people, who in turn attempted to restructure the education system to push back the limits to personal autonomy that are inherent in it.

The second and current stage followed almost immediately from the first, but is based on the pragmatism of economics while the first was based in ideology and educational philosophy. It has been generated by political demands for financial accountability and is part of a wider political demand with its roots in the economic system. This stage is an attempt to head off growing demands from the earlier stage for personal liberation which would endanger the hierarchical structure of education, itself a reflection of society at large.

The attempt to institutionalise demands for educational accountability and convert them to demands for fiscal accountability has been noted elsewhere. D'Cruz (in Chippendale and Wilkes, 1977) notes that:

> *Accountability in education is an appealing concept that can catch the interest of the public, especially the legislators who have to meet the increasing outlay of public money on education. In the United States, for example, the evidence is that in the current climate of economic crisis, with many state legislatures and state education agencies pressing for what is seen as money-saving accountability, the situation [that is centralised control] 'has reached crisis proportions in at least 30 states and is spreading fast to all 50'.*
> (p.201)

D'Cruz notes that it is the economic crisis (following a period of rapid growth which blurred the significance of State control) which has given government an opportunity to control financially developments in educational philosophy. Few would deny that governments have rights to fiscal accountability from higher education. In Australia, as well as elsewhere, education is highly political. Institutions in higher education are established by statute and funded almost entirely from the public purse, while ultimately pragmatic decisions based on political needs shape structures for sectoralisation and coordination. Hudson (1976) suggests that:

> *Governments are the only agencies which can act for the community as a whole. They have a clear responsibility to promote leadership in the investment the nation makes in its future as well as in providing immediate services which are beyond the scope of the market to provide.*
> (p. 48)

This again is undeniable. But as Wood, himself a politician, points out (in Chippendale & Wilkes, 1977):

> *The point at issue is **to what extent** governments should use their authority and **to what extent** education is accountable to governments.*
> (p. 105, emphasis added)

It should be recognised that, especially in our system of representative government, government cannot necessarily be equated with community. It represents majority choice at a specific time, and cannot reflect the opinion of all the myriad of communities at any time. It is important that community opinions should be reflected in the participation of interested individuals in the governance and control of institutions which directly influence them. Demands for community accountability do not deny the role of government, but rather question to what extent government participation should be in democratic control of institutions and the system. Johnson (in Chippendale and Wilkes, 1977) correctly notes that institutions are not only accountable to governments but also to press scrutiny; to professional associations into which graduates go; to each other to maintain a parity of standards and mutual acceptability; and to the international community of institutions for the quality of their scholarship and research.

The dangers of equating too closely government and community lie in over-coordination and over-bureaucratisation. This in turn inhibits institutional initiatives reflecting local or regional needs, and rapid responses in meeting these needs, as institutions increasingly respond to the pressures and directives of central authorities which have, at least in the past, tended to encourage conformity within easily recognisable boundaries which promote simplified or similar patterns of administration.

On the other hand, the dangers in under-coordination lie in upward academic drift, especially as demands for status from articulate members of the local community—that is often staff and some business interests—are accommodated. The results are often similar to over-coordination, that is, institutional rejection of its original rationale which includes serving a wide cross-section of local and regional demands and needs.

It is also appropriate that demands for accountability must consider the rights of minority groups to have access to higher education and ideologies other than the dominant ones. Bureaucratic control, essentially directed at fiscal accountability, tends to view and expect educational results to be quantifible and easily relatable to economic factors and results. Bureaucratic attitudes are in large part transferred to government thinking and thus play a major role in political decision making. While including government as one part of community, and acknowledging its legitimate right to one form of accountability, it is unwise to assert that a strong governmental role in higher education is synonymous with community involvement. This unfortunately has been the case in some of the literature on community and education. For example Batt suggests that the strong governmental intervention in advanced education constitutes, with the nature of college councils, staff and students, a pronounced community reference.

> *One of the factors to emerge early in our study of non-metropolitan colleges of advanced education was that community reference was most pronounced*

in the life of the colleges. To start with the colleges had been established by governments and their ultimate objectives set by the community acting through governmental agencies. They were funded almost entirely by governments. They were governed by councils composed largely of community representatives and were coordinated by government bodies. In the final analysis the most important questions relating to the colleges would be settled in ministerial cabinets by representatives of the people at large. Colleges were required to demonstrate sufficient community demand for graduates in the courses they wished to offer and standards were set through accreditation procedures by official government agencies. In the colleges themselves staff and students were members of the outside community as well as members of their college, and the college programmes appeared to be overwhelmingly oriented to providing competence for life in the community outside.

(1976:39)

Another problem in the discussion of government and community in education has been the transference of overseas ideas, and often uncritical acceptance of overseas prescriptions without adequately recognising the differences between conditions in Australia and other comparable countries. Brimblecombe notes that:

Australia differs from the United Kingdom and the United States in that local government has always been weak and there is no tradition of community participation in education policies and decision making processes. The idea of community involvement then is a new one to the Australian public, and to the Australian educational scene. There is at present, with few exceptions, no organization machinery established to accommodate it, nor is there a psychological or social framework for reference. Thus it will not be easy to introduce.

(1976: 7)

This is not to say that there are no useful comparisons to be made. Although community participation may not have had as strong a tradition in Australia there are many similarities between the structures that have evolved in Australia and elsewhere. In addition, demands for accountability, both community and fiscal, have not been confined to Australia but have been widespread. It is important that discussion of the issue recognises the differences and similarities between local and overseas situations.

I have noted earlier that in the United States of America demands for fiscal accountability have led to the dangers of bureaucratisation, even with the tradition of community involvement and community accountability that exists there. Bowles and Gintis (1976) offer a comprehensive and compelling critique of American education, its control in the interests of those who benefit most from the economic system, and the inherent inequalities it perpetuates as a reflection of the economic system. Karabel supports this view:

... the stratified system of public higher education, like the class bound system of secondary education before it, results in a redistribution of resources from poor to rich.

(1972:555)

Very little work offering a comprehensive critical analysis has yet been undertaken in Australia, and there has been a paucity of debate on the correlation between economic circumstance and education, and the reinforcement in each of the inequalities of the other. However Abbey and Ashenden (1976) in their review of the Bowles and Gintis work suggest that, while specific conditions may differ, many of their findings have some relevance to Australia with its similar economic system.

A central problem concerns the difficulty of making higher education more accountable, not to governments which can enforce fiscal accountability, but to individuals. In this sense accountability means personal relevance. Discussion of this issue has tended in the past to be cast in terms of an opposition between societal interest and individual aspiration. For instance, Van Lennep in an address to the OECD Conference on Future Structures in Higher Education used this concept:

> *Being by nature labour intensive, relative costs per unit [for education] are rising very fast and at the same time the increasing competing claims from various other sectors for public resources set limits to the possibilities of expansion.*

> *On the other hand, rapid changes in the employment structure and in social attitudes may frustrate individual aspirations of students and need to be taken into account.*

> (1974:12)

He went on to suggest that fundamental changes were necessary to solve these problems, and noted that most OECD member nations were reorganising post-secondary education because of the problems caused by its rapid growth. He also suggested that:

> *At the heart of this reaction [reorganisation] lie the difficulties experienced in all Member countries in establishing satisfactory relationships between the offerings of the higher education system, the aspirations of its new clients, and the needs and absorptive capacity of society for qualified people.*

> (p. 13)

This is, however, an inadequate conceptual dichotomy. Society does not act as an homogeneous unit against the aspirations of individuals. Conflict may also be understood in terms of opposing groups or classes in society and discussed within the concept of class analysis. Bowles' and Gintis' critique, for instance, in adopting this position is able to explain more adequately the inequities and contradictions which exist within the education system. From their analysis the role and interest of the dominant economic sector—the ruling class—can be seen in retaining clear control of the education system. On the other hand, analyses based on the view of society pitted against individual as suggested by Van Lennep and others, inadequately explain the widespread consolidated pressures for one position or another by groups which correspond with different classes or conflicting sections of a class.

The transition of the past 15 years to mass higher education might have been a challenge to the pre-existing hierarchy of occupations if the system were unable to absorb graduates into established career positions. Instead the transition has been accompanied by attempts to vocationalize higher education which have, in Australia, seen the development of the college of advanced education system in that direction, and the newer demands for major growth in technical education. In the case of the CAE system, current demands exceed the expectations of its authors. While the Commission on Advanced Education has consistently opposed the introduction of liberal arts courses in the colleges, and the colleges themselves have restricted many general studies courses to minor sections of programmes, the Martin Report (1964) advocated the inclusion of liberal studies in diploma programmes:

> *In technical colleges [CAE's] where the educational emphasis is on technological disciplines, there is the risk of courses becoming over specialized, the main interest being in 'training' rather than in 'education'. The Committee believes that the introduction of liberal studies in appropriately designed courses within the diploma curriculum will add to the breadth of the student's education, developing in particular his critical, imaginative and creative abilities. The unfolding of such qualities will help to ensure that young technologists are alive to the human and social reactions of their work.*
>
> (para. 6.64, p. 182)

In addition, vocationalisation of the CAE sector is increasing, as is illustrated by the most recent teacher education cutback recommendations of the various higher education inquiries. Rather than expanding opportunities for students to gain a more general education, the lack of proposals to retain student numbers is resulting in a contraction of the system. While demands for fiscal accountability and demands for community accountability are not, *a priori,* incompatible, the conflict between them in the Australian context reflects, as noted earlier, the contradictions in our system. Hudson suggests that the political economy of education is concerned particularly

> *with the decisions which relate the efficiency of the system to its other qualitative aims.*
>
> (1976:47)

However the problem arises of applying cost benefit analysis to measure efficiency in education, especially non-vocational education. While cost benefit analysis might illustrate material benefits to graduates of professional and vocational education, difficulties arise in attempting to apply it as a measure of non-vocational education where the benefits of self-satisfaction and the like may not be able to be measured in material terms.

Ashby (1973) suggests that:

> *Cost benefit analysis can doubtless suggest ways in which mass higher education can be more efficiently conducted; but it would be positively inefficient to try to increase the efficiency of that sector devoted to minority 'hand made' education.*
>
> (p. 149)

While the first part of this suggestion is correct the second part is inadequate. The grey area between vocational and minority 'hand made' education encompasses much of the university's teaching, some of the teaching of colleges of advanced education, and almost all of the further education component of TAFE. As I have suggested, cost benefit analysis is unsuitable for this area, but the fact that the grey area is being questioned points to its inadequacy and to the need for increased community accountability and relevance in education.

The reconciliation of demands for fiscal and community accountability will continue to be impossible while the two are directed toward conflicting goals. Community accountability can only be realised in a social context which includes total community accountability, not only in education but in the workplace and in leisure activities. As Mackie has suggested:

> *Educational change must be consonant with changes in the workplace; when factories and offices are changed from hierarchical, alienating structures into democratically run, egalitarian institutions, then schools [and indeed all educational institutions] will function as agencies for promoting equal opportunity for all. The school alone can never be an agent for equality in a fundamentally unequal society.*

(1976: 28)

Superficial reforms will not result in complete community accountability, even though they will increase the chances for its realisation through making individuals more aware of education's potential for themselves. As such it is an important though not exclusive avenue for social reform. However in times of economic crisis the dominance of fiscal accountability is always likely to be re-imposed. The conflict between community and fiscal accountability is emphasised during troughs in the economy and will, as they become more severe, reflect this severity. Changes in the structures of higher education will not ensure the realisation of the goals of community accountability unless these changes are accompanied by changes in the social context in which they are situated.

Chapter Two

Accountability at the Federal Level*

P. R. Chippendale

The Setting

Teachers and administrators in the academic world may be apprehensive of accountability because institutions of higher learning have a long history of muddling through and getting away with it in fairly comfortable fashion. Accountability, however, threatens to fix responsibility, to demand fundamental thinking about ends and means, and to require the development and application of sophisticated management tools to activities whose goals have been generally unclear and whose methods and procedures have been largely unexamined. Moreover it is a cherished tradition in the association of higher learning that it resists accountability to its clients, to society or to the State, and it shields itself from what it regards as crude incursions of governments and politicians, economists and other technocrats who would examine its goals, analyse its methods, unmask its mystique and demand that it render account. A pertinent question for this chapter is whether, in the contemporary socio-political setting, this tradition can be sustained in Australian tertiary education.

In the industrialised nation-states of the second half of the twentieth century education has been a major social enterprise, and the function of tertiary education has been so expanded and so elaborated that this segment of national educational systems has become a significant and costly social institution, absorbing in its own right increasing proportions of government expenditure. In this new and, in the history of western education, unique social and political setting for tertiary institutions, it would appear reasonable that national governments require institutions of tertiary education which they fund and maintain at least to render account of their efficiency in fiscal terms, if not their effectiveness in educational and social terms as well. Yet in Australian education it remains a paradox, at any rate to the layman, that accountability of tertiary institutions to the national government (which will provide funds of $169.7 million for tertiary education this year—Tertiary Education Commission, 1978: Vol 1: App. D.) is virtually non-existent. But there is already significant criticism, questioning and, in high places, proclamations on policy and planning

* The author wishes to acknowledge the assistance of Dr. J. A. Allen, Chairman of the Queensland Board of Advanced Education, who kindly commented on the draft of this chapter.

(Ibid: 17-23) which indicate that this paradox cannot be sustained for much longer. And there are other indicators of an impending accountability in the social and educational environment:

* a decline in the myth of higher education as the Aladdin's Lamp to the good life;
* the diversification and promotion by the State of new forms of post-school education which lack a tradition of autonomous government;
* a realization in society and among educators that money does not solve all problems in higher education or other social endeavours;
* the competition for the tax dollar among a variety of social projects;
* the evolution of sophisticated management techniques and an emphasis on measurement and evaluation of social services and other endeavours sponsored by the State;
* the movement for rationalisation, coordination and the centralisation of funding and control of all forms of post-school education;
* the competition for survival among tertiary institutions in an environment of declining demand, contracting resources and numerical oversupply of institutions, and a belief that the demonstrably accountable institutions have the best survival chances.

In this new and unique socio-political setting of post-school education an academic interest has developed in the idea of accountability in tertiary education in Australia, and in what accountability may mean in operational terms for the relationship of tertiary institutions to the national or federal government. Moreover, this interest has been sharpened by activities of the present Federal Liberal Government in revising and changing the policies of its Labor predecessor. In this process statutory corporations in Australia have come under government scrutiny and institutions of higher education, themselves statutory corporations, are inevitably being questioned in regard to their efficiency and accountability.

Accountability

Accountability has to do with effectiveness and efficiency. It means the responsibility to demonstrate that an organization has achieved certain ends, and responsibility to demonstrate that it has employed the most efficient means in achieving those ends. In an educational institution these issues of effectiveness and efficiency may have to do not only with educational goals, but also with social causes that governments which support tertiary education may be advancing, such as the equalisation of opportunity in education and employment for minority or disadvantaged groups.

There is now ample overseas evidence of requiring at least some degree of accountability of post-school education in both the educational and social dimensions. Despite the powerful, autonomous tradition of the higher learning, the courts and other regulatory agencies in the United States of America have come to exercise a major role in the questions of access to post-school education and in the consumer rights of the student. Moreover, the Federal Government in the United States has increasingly used its powers associated with the provision of both special and general funds to require post-school education to advance desegregation, affirmative action for minorities and women, and the provision of equal opportunity. In the U.S.A. external accountability now looms much larger than internal institutional evaluation; the power of the academic guild, which requires accountability of academics to their peers, has declined as the taxpayer and the consumer have become increasingly concerned in what tertiary institutions are doing (Allen, 1977: 5-7; Carlson, 1977).

In Australia, at least until very recent years, government, educational planners, statisticians and funding authorities have been almost exclusively concerned with inputs into tertiary education. The extent to which Australia is likely to follow the United States, where there is an increasing emphasis on educational accountability in terms of outputs, and the extent to which the Federal Government in Australia could or would require such accountability are current questions of fundamental importance.

Framework for Accountability at the Federal Level

The framework in which tertiary institutions might be held accountable at the federal level in Australia can be found in constitutional powers, legislative provisions, and administrative and policy initiatives and procedures of the Commonwealth. This framework is implicit in:

* *Section 51(xxiiiA)* and *Section 96* of the Australian Constitution;
* Commonwealth legislation which bears directly upon education in the *States Grants (Tertiary Education Assistance Act)* and the *Tertiary Education Commission Act;*
* Commonwealth legislation, which bears on only indirectly but which may influence educational policies and procedures, in the *Remuneration Tribunals Act,* the *Audit Act,* the *Trade Practices Act,* the *Ombudsman Act,* and the *Hospitals and Health Services Commission Act* (recently repealed but still of significance to this discussion);
* Detailed *Guidelines determined by the Commonwealth Government for expenditure* by the Tertiary Education Commission;
* The activities of the *Commonwealth Department of Education* in advising the Commonwealth Minister on policy issues across the whole spectrum of education.

The relevance of each of these powers and provisions requires some explanation.

Implications of Commonwealth Constitutional Powers

Under *Section 51 Amendment (xxiiiA) of the Constitution* the Commonwealth may make laws with respect to "the provision of maternity allowances, widows' pensions, child endowment, unemployment, pharmaceutical, sickness and hospital benefits, medical and dental services (but not so as to authorise any form of civil conscription), *benefits to students* and family allowances". (Australia, Constitution, Amendment xxiiA, section 51—emphasis added). Although the Commonwealth may thus provide "benefits to students" it cannot require the States or any one else to furnish these benefits and it cannot require any eligible person to accept the benefits it provides. It may, however, ensure irrespective of State laws that the benefits which it provides reach those who wish to receive them.

A glance at history in regard to Amendment xxiiiA of Section 51 is instructive. The genesis of this Amendment,carried by referendum in 1946, was in the desire of the Labor Government of the day to place beyond challenge its existing and anticipated social services, and to secure direct Commonwealth jurisdiction over its educational and quasi-educational programmes. Twelve years after the referendum, the purpose of the "benefits" part of the social services amendment was made explicit in the Commonwealth Parliament by Dr. H. V. Evatt, the Attorney-General who had drafted it. According to Evatt:

> *The whole purpose of the Constitutional Amendment was to give the Parliament power, as the occasion demanded, to make provision by legislation for benefits to students—in other words, to make educational grants, this Parliament being responsible for them. It is not therefore, a question of divided legislative power and responsibility; direct power and responsibility reside in this Parliament ...*
> (Australia, Parliamentary Debates, 6th May 1958, Vol. 19)

Commonwealth legislation under the "benefits to students" power includes provision for all tertiary living allowances, Aboriginal educational grants, and reimbursement to the States for loss of university, college of advanced education and technical college fees following the abolition of student fees for tertiary education and the assumption of responsibility for financing the tertiary sector by the Commonwealth (Beazley, 1977). The "benefits to students" power has not been used to date in ways which bring tertiary institutions into a position of social or educational accountability to the Federal Government. Nevertheless it is evidently a power of considerable significance for the Commonwealth to require accountability of tertiary institutions in regard to social causes the Federal Government may advance. The significance of the "benefits to students" power has recently been underlined by I. K. F. Birch:

> *There are some areas in which a federal government could pass laws that made specific education demands. Section 51 of the Constitution provides the Commonwealth Parliament with a wide range of concurrent powers. Among these are powers to make laws with respect to migrants, defence, and, by implication, Aborigines. It is clear that the High Court regards these powers as plenary powers and considers the Commonwealth Parliament's legislation in these areas to be valid. By Section 109 of the Constitution, state laws which are inconsistent must give way. Fairly exact requirements could be set, for example, by the Parliament on the question of the education of migrants and Aborigines. Such laws would not only have to be obeyed by and in the states but would also take precedence over inconsistent state laws.*
> (1977: 25).

Section 96 of the Constitution and its relevance for accountability in education may be well enough known. It is the constitutional means most often used by federal governments to aid education in the States, and the means whereby the Commonwealth through its States Grants Acts finances tertiary education in Australia. It empowers the Commonwealth to "grant financial assistance to any State on such terms and conditions as the Parliament thinks fit" (Australia, Constitution, section 96).

The importance of Section 96 for the accountability of tertiary institutions to the Commonwealth is underlined by Birch:

> ... *Ever since the 'Rhodes Case' in 1926, the High Court has held that the grants power can be taken at face value: and it is difficult to envisage a condition which could not be imposed in making a grant. ... Further, a grant under Section 96 is not voidable on the ground that the State Governments are being used as a pipeline to transfer funds from the federal treasury to, say, a particular school or school authority. This suggests that all the conditions so far imposed on the states with respect to grants for education purposes, including those requiring the matching of a grant* **or a process of accountability,** *are constitutionally supportable.*

(1977: 24-25—emphasis added)

Implications of Commonwealth Legislation

The most recent provisions of *States Grants Legislation* (Australia, Laws, Statutes etc., States Grants Tertiary Education Assistance Act, (No. 158), 1977) are indicative of an increasing Commonwealth control and accountability in the disbursement of funds in the tertiary sector. Previously the conditions of grants were largely limited to furnishing the Commonwealth with a satisfactory certificate of audit. The 1977 legislation goes much further: the audit statement is now to be in accordance with a form approved by the Tertiary Education Commission; a cash flow procedure is introduced for capital funding; and the Commonwealth reserves the right to transfer capital funds from one State to another, from one project to another or one sector of tertiary education to another. This reserved right to transfer capital funds would not only extend and intensify building approval procedures at the federal level, but also significantly increase the financial power and authority of the Tertiary Education Commission in regard to building programmes. The Commission would assume a position similar to that of the Commonwealth Department of Construction with respect to capital building programmes for Commonwealth departments and authorities where the funds are appropriated in the budget of the Department of Construction and not the individual instrumentalities.

The significantly increased measure of fiscal control of tertiary education by the Commonwealth, embodied in this legislation, may well foreshadow even more far reaching centralisation of control and accountability in the field of education and elsewhere. As the Chairman of the Queensland Board of Advanced Education remarked recently:

> *Quite apart from the specific application of these new principles in the funding of higher education, there is the more general question of whether this foreshadows a new approach to Section 96 Grants generally.*

> *If sustained in this case and extended to others, there will have been achieved a silent but significant revolution in a direction completely opposite to the rhetoric of 'New Federalism'.*

(Allen, 1977: 30-31).

There is no evidence to suggest that federal governments will recoil from the long-standing movement in Australian government and politics to centralise power in the Commonwealth. Given this, and the carefully considered proposition advanced by Birch, that the conditions which the Commonwealth may attach to grants for education are virtually without limit, the exercise of Section 96, through States Grants Legislation, is a powerful means for the Commonwealth to exact accountability in tertiary education at the federal level.

The States Grants (Tertiary Education Assistance) Act 1977 is complemented in Commonwealth legislation on tertiary education by the *Tertiary Education Commission Act 1977* (Australia, Laws, Statutes etc., Tertiary Education Commission Act (No. 25), 1977) which established the Tertiary Education Commission. While the States Grants Legislation has firm constitutional support in Section 96, the position of the Commission appears to be legally suspect. The constitutional validity of the Commission could possibly be derived from the "benefits to students" power of Section 51, but its existence and activities are apparently open to serious legal challenge (Birch, 1977: 25).

Under the Act, the Commission is to enquire into and advise the Minister on the necessity for and the conditions and allocation of financial assistance in respect of universities, colleges of advanced education, and technical and further education institutions. The Act also empowers the Commission to enquire into and advise the Minister on any other matter relating to tertiary institutions referred to it by the Minister or which the Commission itself considers to warrant enquiry. Moreover, the Commission is to perform its functions with the object of promoting:

(a) the balanced and coordinated development of the provision of tertiary education in Australia; and

(b) the diversifying of opportunities for tertiary education.

It is also worth noting that under the Miscellaneous provisions of the Act, the Minister, on the request of the Commission or one of its Councils, (the three advisory councils to the Commission for universities, advanced education colleges, and technical and further education institutions), may appoint a committee to assist the Commission (or Council) in relation to a specified matter. Such committees are empowered to enquire into and make reports on the matter specified in the request as the Commission or Council directs. This provision establishes significant possibilities for the Commission to initiate enquiries—but not publish the reports—on a variety of matters affecting tertiary institutions.

While the authority and means for the accountability of Australian tertiary education to the Commonwealth, as presently exercised, is in Section 96 of the Constitution and the States Grants Legislation, the methods and procedures for accountability, albeit of uncertain legal validity, can be forged by the Tertiary Education Commission; in its First Report the Commission notes that it and its Councils "essentially have a common task in seeking to achieve the most efficient use of the resources available to tertiary education" (Tertiary Education Commission, 1977: Para. 1.5, 2). The Commission (1978: Paras. 2.16-2.25, 17-21) has already recommended procedures for course approvals which require both universities and colleges of advanced education to obtain the approval of the Commission for teaching programmes within fields of study. These procedures include conditions that Commission approval will be required for:

(I) individual universities to offer courses at the UG2 (Diploma) or UG3 (Associate Diploma) levels;

(II)   individual colleges of advanced education to offer courses at the PG2 (Postgraduate Degree) level; and
(III)   any lengthening of courses in established fields of study.

Moreover, all proposals for the establishment of courses at the UG3 level, including those attracting total Commonwealth funding in specified Technical and Further Education (TAFE) institutions will require Commission approval in accordance with arrangements determined by the Commission. In the case of developments in the advanced education sector, the Commission expects its approval of a new development to precede any formal accreditation applications to State bodies. Furthermore, the Commission (1978: Para. 2.22, 20—emphasis added) recommends that:

> *Where major developments are contemplated across a whole field of study (e.g. nurse education), involve more than one sector in a significant way (e.g. teacher education, paramedical studies), where a new institution is being established or an institution is being developed in a major way, the* **Commission may issue planning guidelines relevant to the particular fields of study or institution.**

Giving notice of intent for further rationalisation, coordination and accountability in Australian tertiary education the Commission's Second Report (1978: Para. 2.23, 21) states:

> *The Commission will keep under review educational trends which involve significant alterations to the size or structure of the Tertiary Education system. It has already been concerned at the proliferation of external course offerings throughout Australia and will be giving consideration to the institution of a process which facilitates a logical and orderly development of courses offered by this mode of teaching; it will have regard to the capacity of particular institutions to mount programs of appropriate quality and to the clientele for such courses. The Commission is also concerned at the tendency to raise the level at which courses are offered. It will therefore be necessary to monitor trends in enrolments as between bachelor and diploma courses, and the relationship between UG3 and certificate course enrolments.*

The Commission contends that its recommended procedures for course approvals, "In accordance with its charter to promote the balanced and coordinated development of the provision of tertiary education and the diversifying of opportunities for tertiary education" (Tertiary Education Commission, 1978: Para. 2.22, 20) "... should help to achieve balanced and coordinated development of academic programs, while permitting universities and State advanced education authorities to have a significant degree of discretion in mounting new courses" (1978: Para. 2.25, 21).

These new arrangements, if accepted by the Commonwealth Government, would modify traditional university autonomy in developing new teaching programmes, and would bring the universities into a position of accountability to the Commonwealth which they have not previously experienced. In the advanced education sector the existing States Grants Legislation requires the Tertiary Education Commission to approve individual courses of study in colleges of advanced education for funding purposes (Australia, Laws, Statutes etc., States Grants (Tertiary Education Assistance) Act (No. 25) 1977). In effect, therefore, the new arrangements for course approvals would bring the universities into a position of accountability which appears to be less detailed but nevertheless approximate to that of the colleges, in so far as specific Commission approval would be required (under procedures based on approvals of teaching programmes in fields of study) for the universities, as well as the colleges, to move into new fields of study.

The recommended arrangements for middle level courses have some effects also on the accountability of the TAFE sector. State control of advanced education courses offered through specified TAFE institutions is maintained in that these courses require accreditation by the relevant State Board of Advanced Education. In some instances T.E.C. approval of these courses will provide a means, not existing hitherto, of obtaining total Commonwealth funding for them. At the same time, however, the specific Commission approval of courses offered through TAFE which attract total Commonwealth funding means accountability at the federal level for these aspects of TAFE activities.

All in all, the Commission's proposals on course approvals demand measures of coordination, rationalisation and accountability in tertiary education generally which are hitherto unknown in this country. It is worth emphasising that these proposals are recommended in accordance with the Commission's charter "to promote the balanced and coordinated development of the provision of tertiary education." While the Commonwealth Government and the Tertiary Education Commission may well avoid any direct initiatives which would bring about the closure or amalgamation of institutions, such closures or amalgamations could be forced by the Commonwealth withdrawing approval for existing fields of study or teaching programmes on the grounds of low cost-effectiveness. Such action could, in turn, bring Commonwealth and State Governments into direct conflict on issues of educational policy and accountability.

With less immediate importance but of significance for the possible future direction of accountability of tertiary education at the federal level is the Commission's acceptance of a recommendation of the TAFE Council to conduct evaluative studies for the whole tertiary sector (Tertiary Education Commission 1978: Paras. 4.83-4.90, 80-82). Further development in this area, together with the recommendations for effectiveness made or foreshadowed (as noted above) would bring tertiary institutions into a position of considerable accountability to the Federal Government.

Implications of Peripheral Legislation

In the framework of Commonwealth powers and provisions which may exact accountability from tertiary education the States Grants Legislation and the Tertiary Education Commission legislation are supplemented by what might be called "peripheral" acts, of which the *Remuneration Tribunals Act* has to date been of prime importance (Australia, Laws, Statutes etc., Remuneration Tribunals Act, 1973-1975). This Act provides, among other things, for an Academic Salaries Tribunal to inquire into and report to the Minister on the rates of salaries of academic staff of institutions of tertiary education *that should be used as a basis for making grants in respect of recurrent expenditure in connection with those institutions* (Remuneration Tribunals Act 1973-1975:

Part III, section 12c—emphasis added). Moreover, the *Tribunal may also inquire into, and report on, any matter that is, or is considered by it to be significantly related to its investigation into the salaries that should be paid to staff of these institutions.* While the activities of the Academic Salaries Tribunal may be rendered redundant in the future by the registration of the academic staff associations with industrial commissions, at present the recommendations of the Tribunal to the Commonwealth focus attention on issues of effective and efficient management in higher education, and on the accountability of the statutory bodies which govern and direct tertiary education in Australia (Remuneration Tribunals Act 1973-1975: part III, section 2d—emphasis added).

The important point in the present context is, as J. A. Allen states, that

> ... *the periodic reports of this Tribunal, particularly the 1976 Review, potentially have an influence in respect of universities and colleges well beyond the limited issue of salary determination. Several of the matters dealt with in this Review could affect the nature and structure of accountability generally, especially for coordinating boards and college Councils in the advanced education sector.*
>
> (1977:16)

The 1976 Review of the Tribunal raises issues of effectiveness and efficiency in universities and colleges, particularly in teachers colleges, which implicitly or explicitly demand a substantially increased measure of responsible management and accountability from college and university councils, from the State coordinating authorities in advanced education and, at least by implication, from federal and State governments. From its comments on duplication of effort and resources in Australian higher education, to its criticisms of abuse among university academics of the privilege to gain outside earnings and the failure of the colleges to make and enforce rules on such earnings, the Tribunal raises issues of accountability at all major levels of governance in Australian higher education. Moreover the issues of effectiveness and efficiency raised by the findings of the Tribunal have an important bearing on accountability relationships between college councils and their State coordinating authorities, and between the coordinating authorities and their State governments. For example, are coordinating authorities of college councils to accept responsibility for the issues of effectiveness and efficiency raised by the Tribunal; who is responsible for undertaking the corrective actions in management and administration which the Tribunal suggests, and who is the Tribunal to hold accountable in these and related matters in undertaking subsequent reviews? These questions may be irrelevant to a situation where academic staff are generally employed under industrial awards or industrial agreements but, for the moment at least, they stand. (It is interesting to note that the Tribunal's request for State coordinating authorities in advanced education to maintain strict controls over staff establishments in the colleges cannot be met in Queensland. The Queensland Board of Advanced Education has no such authority; there is in fact ambiguity in regard to where this authority rests.)

At present the application of the Commonwealth *Audit Act* (Australia, Laws, Statutes etc., Audit Act, 1901) to tertiary institutions is almost entirely limited to detailed accounting for the expenditure of funds granted to the States under the provisions of the States Grants Acts. Where funds have been misapplied, penalties may be invoked. Of considerable significance and potential for future accountability of tertiary institutions to the Commonwealth, however, is the current interest at federal level (it is also an interest of the States) in extending audit requirements (Australia, Parliament, Report of the Auditor General, 1977) so that audit reports would include an assessment of the effectiveness and efficiency of approved programmes. In due course such efficiency of approved programmes, thereby requiring accountability not only in regard to inputs, but also in terms of the outputs of tertiary institutions. also in terms of the outputs of tertiary institutions.

Of no practical impact at this time but of apparent potential significance for educational accountability is the *Commonwealth Trade Practices Act* (Australia, Laws, Statutes, etc., Trade Practices Act, 1974). The point has not been tested, but this Act may prove applicable in situations where students demand redress for the failure of an institution or its teaching staff to offer a course in accordance with the advertised course description. In addition, this legislation poses possible implications for higher education in regard to issues of professional ethics and practices, the relationship between academic courses and their acceptance by professional bodies, and any issue hinting at monopoly which may be seen by some to be not in the public interest.

In the 'peripheral' legislation the *Ombudsman Act* (Australia, Laws, Statutes etc., Ombudsman Act (No. 181), 1976) is relevant to issues of accountability for tertiary institutions in the Commonwealth Territories. Administrative actions of institutions in both the Australian Capital Territory and the Northern Territory have already been the subject of complaint and investigation by the Commonwealth Ombudsman. In the contemporary social environment it is reasonable to expect that this legislation will be increasingly important in issues of accountability for the territorial institutions.

Now only of immediate historical interest, but of continuing significance in the present framework for accountability of tertiary institutions to the Commonwealth is the *Hospitals and Health Services Commission Act 1973*. (Australia, Laws, Statutes etc., Hospitals and Health Services Commission Act (No. 211), 1973). Rarely considered in the educational context, this legislation empowered the Commonwealth Health Commission to, among other things, make recommendations to the Health Minister in regard to the education of health personnel, and with the Minister's approval to make grants for this purpose.

Major activities of this Commission included the preparation of a report and recommendations to the Health Minister on the organization and introduction of a comprehensive system of continuing education for medical practitioners, (Hospitals and Health Services Commission, 1975) and an appraisal of the proposal to establish a School of Medicine at Wollongong University (Hospitals and Health Services Commission, 1976). These activities in the field of education by a health commission, and the continuation of the Commission's ongoing activities by the Departments of Health and Social Security, raise questions of the accountability relationships between the Tertiary Education Commission and the Federal Government.

Ministerial Initiative and Direction: The Australian Department of Education

In addition to utilising its principal and 'peripheral' legislation the Federal Government may further exact accountability in tertiary education through *"Guidelines issued by the Education Minister to the Tertiary Education Commission."* The effect of government or ministerial guidelines is to bring the Commission, and hence the whole tertiary sector of Australian education, into a position of closer accountability to the Commonwealth. The procedure whereby the former Universities Commission and the Commission on Advanced Education advised government on the needs of universities and colleges on a triennial basis has given way to financing on a yearly basis, through a single Commission, within guidelines that are predetermined by the Federal Government. This mode of operation demonstrates a new emphasis on the Commission's accountability to the Federal Government for the coordinated use of resources in education, and on the accountability of tertiary institutions to the Commission for the output of graduates in relation to labour market requirements.

Before leaving the point of the relationship of the Tertiary Education Commission to the Federal Minister, particularly in regard to ministerial initiative and direction, it is worth noting that the enquiry presently being conducted by the Commission into the provision of study leave at universities and colleges of advanced education was established by the Commission on the initiative and request of the Minister (Tertiary Education Commission, Draft Report on Study Leave, 1978). The extent of requirements for accountability which may result from this, and from other possible inquiries of a similar kind, is a matter of future interest. It is also important to note that the Federal Minister may initiate enquiries, establish committees or propose legislation to the Parliament quite independently of the Commission. Specific examples of this independent action are a recent ministerial announcement of proposed amendments to legislation which would alter the operation of student unions in tertiary institutions in the Commonwealth territories, and an announcement by the Minister of a "National Enquiry into Teacher Education".

The framework for accountability in tertiary education at the federal level is completed by noting the growing significance of the *Commonwealth Department of Education* as the primary advisor to the Commonwealth Minister on policy issues across the whole spectrum of education. The emergence of the Department in this role was articulated by K. N. Jones (1977), its Permanent Head, in May, 1973, when he stated at a conference on "Accountability in Education":

We in education can expect to be called upon to account more precisely to our political masters and the community for the exercise of our stewardship, and we need to be prepared accordingly. As one step in this direction, within the Australian Department of Education we are about to establish a Planning and Review Branch, which will concern itself not only with longer term objectives but also with coordination and weighing up of demands from the greatly increased number of agencies operating in education at the national level, and also with the evaluation of the effectiveness of past and present activities.

The role of the Department in coordinating the advice of a number of agencies, foreshadowed by Mr. Jones in 1973, has been developed over the past few years (Australian Department of Education, 1977). Further development of this role, especially as it may relate to the formulation of Ministerial Guidelines for the Tertiary Education Commission, could bring the tertiary sector of Australian education into a position of fairly close and direct accountability to the permanent federal bureaucracy. As Allen (1977: 30) suggests:

> *This development [the growing significance of the Department as primary advisor to the Minister across the educational spectrum] has already proceeded some distance. Further extension of it would decrease the significance of direct access to the Minister by the Tertiary Education Commission and its capacity and responsibility for giving unfiltered advice on higher education policy. This and other political and philosophical developments suggest a possible trend in the future towards the development of comprehensive ministries at both State and Commonwealth levels.*

The possibility of further movement in this direction is reinforced by the growing importance of departments relative to statutory corporations under the two Fraser Ministries. The Tertiary Education Commission already appears to be further removed from the Minister than were the former Universities Commission and the Commission on Advanced Education. Moreover, advice to the Minister by each of the three tertiary sectors is well filtered by the present arrangements where the three councils—for the universities, colleges of advanced education and TAFE—have only an advisory role to the Tertiary Education Commission.

Implementing the Framework on Statutory Authorities

At the outset of this paper it was asserted that accountability of tertiary education institutions to the Federal Government in Australia is at present virtually non-existent. However, under the framework of federal constitutional power, legislation provisions and administrative procedures outlined above there is potential for the Commonwealth to require a high degree of accountability from the tertiary sector. Within this framework the Ministerial initiatives in establishing guidelines for expenditure by the Tertiary Education Commission, the initiatives of the Commission itself in regard to course approvals, the more stringent conditions being applied by the Commonwealth to Section 96 Grants for tertiary education and the growing importance of the Commonwealth Department are significant indicators of the movement toward increased measures of accountability. But a central problem in the practical exercise of federal power to exact extensive accountability from tertiary institutions concerns the powers and functions of the statutory corporations—the senates, councils and State coordinating authorities—which govern and manage the Australian universities and colleges of advanced education; and the powers and functions of the State departments which control and direct technical and further education.

Universities in Australia are governed by their senates or councils which are responsible for the entire management and control of institutional affairs, including internal allocation of financial resources. Moreover, having regard to any funding constraints operated by the former Universities Commission, the university council normally has the right to offer courses in any field of study. The accountability of the university to the Federal Government is minimal, and is generally limited to meeting requirements of financial audit.

Although the advanced education sector presents a less homogeneous picture the general principle holds that responsibility for the management and control of college affairs is divided between the college council, the State coordinating authority and the State Minister for Education. For the coordinating authority, which advises the State Minister on advanced education in his State, and for the colleges within the ambit of the coordinating board, the extent of parliamentary and public accountability to the State is much greater than for universities. State coordinating authorities generally have responsibility to approve college budgets, and to approve and accredit courses of study in advanced education. The latter responsibility has generally involved external assessment and accountability, reinforced by the requirement at federal level that only accredited courses will be supported with Commonwealth funds. In addition, the existing States Grants legislation, as previously noted, requires the Tertiary Education Commission to approve for funding purposes individual courses of study in advanced education. As with the universities the Commonwealth requires a satisfactory auditor's report. The central point in the accountability to the Federal Government of the colleges *vis-à-vis* the universities is that in the advanced education sector the Commonwealth funds individually approved and accredited courses.

In the Technical and Further Education sector the relevant institutions are generally controlled by State departments which are accountable through a Minister to State Cabinet and State Parliament. Accountability at the federal level is generally limited to the requirement that a satisfactory auditor's report be submitted to the Tertiary Education Commission in regard to the expenditure of public moneys provided by the Commonwealth for the purposes of technical and further education. The substantial funding of TAFE is the responsibility of the States. The Commonwealth supplements State funds for capital projects, and while it provides some recurrent funds for special programmes the Commonwealth is not substantially concerned with recurrent funding of the TAFE sector.

As yet the Federal Government has not adopted the recommendations of the recent Report of the Tertiary Education Commission referred to earlier in this chapter. Whether or not these recommendations are adopted as they stand they are indicative of the movement toward accountability of tertiary education at the federal level. As previously noted, the implementation of these recommendations would bring the three sectors of Australian tertiary education into somewhat similar positions of accountability to the Commonwealth in regard to teaching programmes which attract total Commonwealth funding. To some extent the recommendations of the TEC on course approvals would modify the autonomy of university councils, and requirements for accountability at the federal level would be somewhat more uniform across the three sectors of tertiary education. The Commission's foreshadowed recommendations on the rationalisation of external course offerings would probably have similar effects. Its recommendations on the development of evaluative studies to assess course effectiveness are much less explicit, and their possible effects on accountability can not be usefully assessed at this time. Their significance may be a matter for future study.

Conclusion

Implementation of the recent recommendations of the Tertiary Education Commission, with their clear focus on accountability, will undoubtedly encounter opposition from academics and educational administrators, governing councils and State coordinating authorities on grounds of Commonwealth violation of academic freedom and of improper and incompetent Commonwealth intrusion into the educational affairs of the States. Such conflicts raise significant questions about the nature and extent of institutional autonomy and its relationship to, on the one hand, academic freedom, and on the other hand, the accountability of the institution to the State or the Commonwealth.

The exploration of these issues is beyond the descriptive intent of the present paper. It is worth noting, however, that whatever the theoretical answers to these issues they will find their pragmatic solutions in the political ebb and flow of Commonwealth-State relations in Australia. These are an integral part of the Australian political scene, and are never static. Periods of quasi-stability are interspersed with periods of conflict and change. For the moment the Commonwealth is taking the initiative in attempting to require direct accountability from tertiary institutions. In doing so it has great resources of financial and legal power to secure its position; but it has no monopoly on these, or on the other political resources which are employed by both State and Federal Governments when Commonwealth-State conflicts and confrontations arise.

A recent study of the use of political resources in Federal-State conflicts over the operation of the Schools Commission shows that the problem of accountability in that case touched on areas where the Federal Government did not hold all the advantages. The conclusions drawn by this study (Weller, 1976: 82) may well have significance for the future operations of the Tertiary Education Commission as an instrument of the Commonwealth for exacting accountability from the States and their tertiary institutions:

> ... *The Federal Government could pressure a state to accept tied grants and could demand information as a condition of those grants. But if it tried to get too much information or demanded over-detailed accountability for its expenditure, the demands could become counter-productive, as the ancient state bureaucracies found themselves unable to meet the new demands. Control of tied grants is easier in theory than in practice, because political resources are far more complex than the discussion of tied grants often suggests. Money is not the source of all power. In considering any program that entails relations between two levels of Australian government, the availability of resources, the consequences of their use and the likely conflicts over status must be accepted as factors that reduce the effectiveness of brute wealth.*

In short, there are serious practical limitations on the use of federal legal and financial powers as a means of achieving detailed policy or of requiring detailed accountability. In the long term view it appears inevitable that these limitations will constrain the operation of procedures for accountability, which for the moment, at the federal level, loom large for tertiary institutions. The future accountability of tertiary education institutions is inevitably caught up in the ebb and flow of the status-conscious bargaining which characterises Commonwealth-State relations in this country.

Chapter Three

Accountability at the State Level

W. C. Hall
F. J. Willett

Introduction

Given the different backgrounds of the authors it is not surprising to find that we have opposing views on many issues. For example, one believes that State coordinating bodies can be of benefit to tertiary institutions, whereas the other is vigorously opposed to any kind of coordination at the State level. One believes that universities are held too little to account for their activities, whereas the other has marked reservations as to whether the need for State coordinating bodies can be deduced from any doctrine of "accountability" and whether the State is the appropriate level at which the university should be accountable.

Accordingly, we have divided the chapter into four main sections. The first and second deal respectively with present coordination at the State Level, and with the concept of accountability and its relationship to State coordination. The third examines the case for a post-secondary State coordinating body, and the fourth the case against a post-secondary State coordinating body. There is no attempt to reconcile our different points of view; indeed, there is probably no way of even reaching a mutually acceptable compromise. However, decisions will be made at a political level about the nature, range and scope of the authority of State coordinating bodies and these decisions will not be separate from decisions about the provision of resources. Doctrines of State academic responsibility—and hence of accountability at the State level—will be strongly reinforced by decisions of State financial responsibility.

Present Coordination at the State Level

The main institutions in post-secondary education are the universities, the colleges of advanced education (CAE's) and the colleges of technical and further education (TAFE). Restrictions placed on each of these groups vary, with these "restrictions" including the limitations imposed with respect to such matters as the types of courses mounted, student enrolments, staff appointments and the process of funding. However the recent formation of CAE's from teachers' colleges, agricultural colleges and State institutes of technology (and hence their change in status from wholly State institutions to the present separation of legal form from financial reality, given that the institutions are wholly funded by the Federal government through an intervening State body) has moved them closer toward the universities with regard to such controls.

Diagram 1

NEW SOUTH WALES

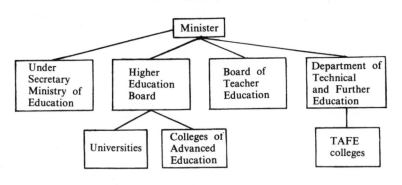

QUEENSLAND

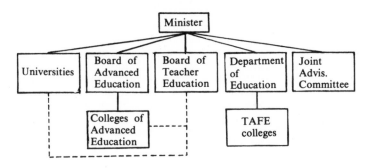

WESTERN AUSTRALIA

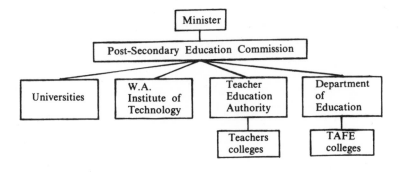

TAFE colleges have more recently been designated as tertiary institutions, and it is clear that these institutions have autonomy only in very limited areas when compared with CAE's and universities. Firm, central control dictates the staff they employ and the curriculum they teach, and the prime directing agency is a department of each State government. In the case of South Australia there is a separate Department of Further Education; in all other States, technical and further education is the responsibility of the education department, although this situation is in some cases under review. It could be argued from many international parallels that if TAFE colleges are to be regarded as "tertiary", a minimum requirement should be the separate administration of the sector along the lines of the example set by South Australia. However, even in that State fairly tight central control continues to be exercised.

No tertiary institution or part of the system is free from restrictions, even though universities are relatively autonomous at the State level, and this general authority is embodied in the State coordinating agencies shown in diagram 1 (adapted from Harman's (1978) summary) which indicates the administrative structure for post-secondary education in three Australian States. (At the time of writing the future situation in the three other States was unclear.)

Not only is the method of State coordination different in these three cases, but the coordinating boards themselves differ in composition and in their detailed terms of reference. Moreover, whereas the links between Ministers and boards and between boards and CAE's are strong ones, the links between Ministers and universities are relatively weak. State coordination in the other three States is likely to show similar differences from these existing structures. One of the principal differences between the way universities are administered and the administration of other areas of post-secondary education is that universities have a direct link with the federal Universities Council, whereas CAE's and TAFE colleges must work through the appropriate State coordinating body. The legal powers of a State coordinating body will remain limited in relation to the universities while this direct link with the Tertiary Education Commission exists, although as Hyde indicates in Chapter One the powers may be still quite effective. Universities continue to argue that whereas CAE's and TAFE colleges are State institutions, they themselves are national and even international in their outlook, although this argument is not necessarily shared by those outside the universities.

The situation of the CAE's is somewhat different, and effective State control has existed for some time. Thus State boards of advanced education are established with a requirement to perform a number of functions, including:
(1) approval and accreditation of courses;
(2) collecting statistical information;
(3) analysing and coordinating financial submissions to the Advanced Education Council;
(4) forward planning.
Existing boards have been criticised for their incompetence at forward planning, lack of consultancy, their secrecy and the absence of stated criteria for decision making. They do not directly interfere with the intellectual business of CAE's (although course accreditation committees do have influence in this regard), with academic affairs, with administrative arrangements or with the employment of staff. This lack of interference by State boards in academic and

staffing areas compares markedly with the role held by the Victorian Institute of Colleges. The present State coordinating bodies have certainly had the legal and organisational potential to be powerful coordinators and rationalisers, but most have to date been weak in this regard. The situation in Victoria, for example, is seen by many to be a complete shambles. And although the South Australian Board of Advanced Education (1977) produced a major report on the coordination of colleges of advanced education none of the important rationalisation recommendations were put into effect, even those which did not relate to the final recommendations of the subsequent Anderson Enquiry (Anderson, 1978). Recently, of course, the recommendations of the Anderson Enquiry, which overlap with some of those made earlier by the Board of Advanced Education, have been published and have now seen enactment. However there has at least been some coordination, and courses are now carefully scrutinised before being accredited rather than gaining approval merely on the basis of internal acceptability to the institution.

In recent years universities in New South Wales and Western Australia have been subject to some degree of State coordination, although in New South Wales (and apparently in Western Australia) this seems to have had little effect. However the extent of State control over universities has been increasingly under scrutiny, and in Victoria the second reading of legislation to establish a Post-Secondary Education Commission attempted to make some significant changes. The draft bill reads:

21. *(1) A university shall not—*   *Obligations of universities*

(a) *make any representations in writing to any body established under the law of the Commonwealth seeking the provisions of public moneys to assist it in carrying out its functions;*

(b) *offer a new course of study;*

(c) *establish a new faculty or school or department of a faculty or school; or*

(d) *confer or award any new kind of academic award or distinction—*

unless it has given at least four weeks' notice in writing to the Commission of its intention to do so and the Commission has not within four weeks after being given notice of the university's intention, given notice in writing to the university that it considers that the submission should not be made or that the proposed action should not be taken.

(2) The Commission may from time to time after consultation with the council of a university determine the staffing establishment of that university.

(3) Notwithstanding anything in any Act a university shall not employ any person except in accordance with the establishment determined by the Commission.

22. *The Governor in Council may make regulations for or with*   *Regulations*

respect to any matter or thing authorised or required to be
prescribed by this Act.

As is well known, the final version of the Bill was considerably modified and
the control of the Victorian Post-Secondary Education Commission on the
universities now appears substantially the same as in New South Wales and
Western Australia.

The Concept of Accountability and its Relationship to State Coordination

Arguments on accountability are bedevilled by major semantic and perceptual
differences which reflect critically upon the general standard of discussion with
respect to educational policy and organization in Australia. Notions such as
"accountability" appear to be used with private, flexible definitions.
Accountability defines a relationship which is interdependent with other
relationships such as "responsibility" and "authority", but which is not
synonymous with either.

There are two different categories of behaviour required of any institution or
individual. Firstly, there are those behaviours which are required by prescription
and which are binding, for example, the obligation on all Australian educational
institutions to conform to specific requirements about the audit of their
accounts. These prescriptions set up relationships of authority of a clear cut and
formal kind. Secondly, institutions and individuals are also expected, in all
levels of work, to behave in ways that require them to make judgements; to act
with discretion. It is this category of behaviour that sets up relationships of
accountability: the institution or the individual is accountable for the quality of
judgements made. Responsibility is a measure of the degree of accountability
and may best be quantified as the time interval between tests of the goodness of
judgment. In this sense a person whose decisions are checked frequently, for
example a clerical assistant, is less responsible than one whose decisions are
untested (or untestable) for years, for example, a chief executive.

Clearly there are a mix of prescribed and accountable elements in the roles of
both institutions and individuals. It is also clear that roles with a relatively high
prescribed content (e.g., on a mechanized assembly line), have less status than
those with a relatively high accountability content. Something of this argument
can be sampled by considering the present perturbation over the status of
medical practitioners, particularly as their relationship with the State through
Medibank and Government dominated hospital services sharply increases the
proportion of prescribed behaviour (such as form-filling, fee-conforming, etc.)
in their total role. Responsibility also has status implications.

In the light of this there is obvious difficulty in relating any discussion of the
utility of State coordinating boards to the idea of accountability. Most of the
case for subordinating universities to State coordinating bodies is an argument
in favour of increasing the proportion of prescribed behaviour required of the
university, and hence it is clearly an argument about status, not accountability.
The first section of this chapter implies that universities have too much freedom,
that the TAFE sector has too little, and that the position of the CAE's is just
right. This is misleading. Later in this chapter it is argued that some changes

should also be made in the CAE-State Board relationship. Clearly a case could be argued for all institutions to rest, for instance, at the level of restriction currently applied to TAFE colleges. There are both university and college systems in the industrialized world which have come close to that level of control, and arguments could be based on results as well as theory. What we should recognise, however, is that we have an argument exacerbated by real differences in status: that while colleges are "coordinated" and universities are not there are two tiers—and TAFE makes three.

However the notion of accountability defined above does have a bearing on the question of the proper relationship of the university (and the colleges, for that matter) to State coordinating bodies. Necessarily, that definition poses the question "accountable to whom?", and provides an answer in terms of the superordinate body or bodies which define institutional function, measure performance and, consequently, provide resources. The Australian university, in these terms, is accountable to a variety of agencies for the quality of its discretionary behaviour. It is directly accountable to the nation through bodies such as the Tertiary Education Commission and the Federal Government. It draws its financial resources from government at this level and much of the target setting, which influences its discretionary behaviour, is done with greater effectiveness at this level.

The logic of locating the target setting function of universities at the national level provided one of the basic thrusts behind the Murray Report (1957) and the formation of the Australian Universities Commission in Australia, and behind the establishment of the University Grants Commission in Britain. It is also one of the major forces behind the awkward attempts in the United States of America, in a rather different federal system, to give the national government influence in university policy making.

The location of responsibility for planning teacher supply at the State level, with only recent and partial national involvement, does not give one confidence that the summation of six or seven State level decisions on targets in a relatively simple area reflects the true national need. By far the greater part of any university's output in terms of graduates or research is more closely addressed to national needs—however poorly defined—than to State needs. To believe otherwise is to believe that federal intervention in the direction and finance of higher education has been simply an exercise in central government aggrandisement.

The university is not solely accountable to the nation or the national government, however, for it draws some resources from and is directed in part by the international university community. This is a somewhat nebulous notion and one that might well be treated with scepticism, if not derision, by those with a limited knowledge of universities. But the relationship of accountability with the world-wide university community is both real and important.

There is a dense and complex network of personal and institutional communication links which measure the work of each institution and its component parts against criteria which the university community as a whole believes to be valid. This system is open to the question "who elected them to judge?", but even this objection should not void the fact that judgement occurs, and that the judgement affects the ability of the university to recruit good staff and good students. As Professor Partridge noted in the Report of the

Committee of Inquiry into Post-Secondary Education in Western Australia:
the universities of Australia 'belong to an international community of
universities'.

(1976: 154, see also Chapter One)

In a small, new, and self-consciously innovating university the impact of
internationality and the international market-place of ideas is vidid and
immediate. One small illustration is an analysis made in early 1977 of the source
of the highest degree of the then 120 members of the academic staff of Griffith
University. Highest degrees were awarded by:
19   Australasian universities;
19   North American universities;
15   British and European universities;
11   universities from other areas, including Africa and Asia.
There is little substance in the broad argument that the universities have to be
made accountable to State boards because they are accountable to no-one else.
There is an argument, which demands attention, that universities are
accountable at two levels and that their responsibility is carried over a long time
period. One might then properly deduce that there is a legitimate field of inquiry
into what aspects of university activities could be usefully defined as
accountable at State level and in what areas their responsibility (i.e., their time
span of decision) might be reduced with advantge to the system of higher
education as a whole.

This discussion must be developed, however, within more than one
assumption about the real role of the State. If the State were the real resource
provider and the prime targetting agency, then it would necessarily have more
salience: under present circumstances coordinating bodies appointed by and
reporting to State governments, although far from wholly accountable to such
governments, may be convenient but lack a persuasive rationale.

The Case for a State Coordinating Body

Notwithstanding the arguments made above there remains an urgent need for
coordination at the State level. Two brief examples illustrate this need: the first
is drawn from South Australia and the second from Queensland.

The South Australian Institute of Technology recently introduced a course in
Library Studies. They attracted a well qualified staff to present a professional
course that many people would agree should be taught in a CAE rather than in
a university. Nevertheless the University of Adelaide also decided that it should
have a Library Studies Unit to teach a course which in many respects was
similar to that proposed by the Institute. Needless to say, there were vigorous
protestations by the University about the distinctiveness of their course when it
was suggested that there might be some similarity between it and that mounted
by the Institute. Clearly a State coordinating body could have resolved the
matter. Such a body would almost certainly have refused to accredit or to fund
the university course, and because most academic decisions are ultimately based
on financial considerations that would have been the end of the Adelaide
adventure. Interestingly enough, the University of Adelaide itself has now
scrapped the Library Studies course because of lack of funds.

The second example concerns the struggle by Griffith University to become a viable, independent institution. A State coordinating body could deal with the matter quite simply by transferring two or three of the University of Queensland's professional courses to its sister institution. The University of Queensland has steadfastly refused to do this, although Volume I of the 1978 Report of the Tertiary Education Commission instructs both institutions to discuss the problem (and this is, in fact, taking place). Similar problems have arisen involving Murdoch University and the Western Australian Institute of Technology, and the West Australian Post Secondary Education Commission will have to tackle them even if its initial concerns have avoided this particular issue.

In examining the case for coordination at the State level the following purposes are advanced:
(1) to determine which areas of education should be the responsibility of particular institutions;
(2) to coordinate capital and recurrent expenditure submissions to the Tertiary Education Commission;
(3) to undertake forward planning at the State level;
(4) to monitor the quality of post-secondary education.

Coordination of all three higher education sectors is important so that inter-institution and inter-sector rivalry, and the propping up of weak institutions by others within that sector (with the consequent waste of resources), do not take place.

The Report on Coordination of Colleges of Advanced Education in South Australia (1977) suggested that there were six ways in which post-secondary education could be rationalised:

*(a) (i) by the formation of a Board of **Post-Secondary Education** (which would incorporate the college sector, the universities and the Department of Further Education);*

*(ii) by the formation of a Board of **Post-Secondary Education** (not incorporating the activities of the three sectors but acting as a coordinating body with clearly defined functions, for example, the rationalisation of courses at the interfaces between the three sectors and the presentation of a State view of relative priorities in post-secondary education to State and Federal funding authorities);*

*(b) (i) by the formation of a **Board of Advanced and Further Education** (which could coordinate the activities of the college sector and the Department of Further Education, but allow the universities to continue as at present);*

*(ii) by the formation of a **Board of Advanced and Further Education** (whose functions could include the rationalisation of courses at the interface between the advanced and further education sectors and the presentation of a State view of relative priorities in advanced and further education to State and Federal funding authorities);*

(c) by the formation of "interface" committees to deal with problems of overlap between the university/college sectors and college/D.F.E. sectors with special reference to the introduction of new and revised courses where the possibility of unnecessary duplication may occur;

(d) by **freely exchanging** *information at the forward planning stage;*

(e) *by employing an* **independent referee;**

(f) *by government control (there have been departments established under a Minister of State, for example, in Canada and the Under-Secretary in New South Wales).*

(1977: 123-4)

Although the Committee favoured procedure (c) they recognised that without legislative power interface committees may not be effective.

Diagram 2

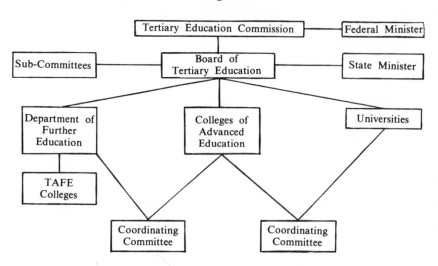

(Most TAFE Colleges are too small to be viable, independent units.)

Diagram 2 indicates a likely form that an 'ideal' structure might take. In this case the Tertiary Education Commission would handle decisions at the "wholesaling" level and the (State) Board of Tertiary Education would concentrate on "retailing". It is important that the Board of Tertiary Education should be free from sectional political influences and so its composition and terms of reference would be of crucial importance. Such a structure would shift much of the decision making back to the States (the reverse has been true in recent years); it would place CAE's on the same footing as universities and would allow for effective dialogue between the three sectors of tertiary education. Of course universities would resist such a structure for the reasons given in the Carnegie Commission's Report into the Governance of Higher Education (1973):

(1) independence gives rise to diversity;

(2) institutional independence leads to freedom to innovate;

(3) academic freedom depends upon institutional independence.

However, as the Carnegie Report points out, these reasons do not stand up to close scrutiny. "Academic freedom" is the most favoured argument and this is generally linked with "autonomy". In fact the two are almost independent. As an example of this, in West Germany there is almost complete absence of university autonomy but, as Bowden (1967) points out, academic freedom remains:

The finances of every German university are controlled in detail by a senior official of the government called a Kurator, who lives in the university offices with the bursar. Estimates have to be prepared in extraordinary detail and approved by the state government before the university can spend a penny. The annual estimates for the University of Aachen, which I have seen, were as big as a couple of volumes of the London telephone directory. Once estimates have been approved it is impossible for a professor to change an order for a gross of pen nibs to a similar order for paper clips without asking the man from the ministry, whose operations can sometimes be a great nuisance to the academic staff. Despite the very complicated structure of academic committees with their senates and rectors, financial power is firmly in the hands of the government whose representative has to be consulted and satisfied throughout the year.

Nevertheless, despite all this, and despite the fact that German university professors are all civil servants, German universities and their staff preserve a degree of academic freedom and individual autonomy which is in some ways more absolute than anything we know in England. Every professor reigns supreme in his own department and cannot be coerced by anybody. He is appointed for life and he can study and lecture about any subject in which he is interested, whether it is of the slightest importance to his students or not.

(1967: 30)

What is needed is a distinction between on the one hand, *system structures* and *system processes,* and on the other hand, *autonomy* and *academic freedom.*

The CAE's face many and varied constraints, both structurally, (for example they do not have a direct link with the national TEC) and in terms of processes (their courses must be approved and accredited), both of which affect institutional autonomy but neither of which need have any great effect on academic freedom. So often in the popular debate on academic freedom these variables become mixed, with the result that principles of academic freedom are not, in fact, under discussion.

The Case Against State Coordinating Bodies

Although examples have been given to illustrate the general need for coordination different opinions may be held as to the persuasiveness of both the examples and the arguments. The first, the case of Library Studies in South Australia, could be seen as clear evidence of the effective, if slow, working of the present system—by what agency was the University of Adelaide led to believe that it had inadequate funds? In the second case, the problem of finding the best fit of activities between two universities in Queensland falls squarely within the remit of the national Universities Council. It is not obvious, whatever weight one gives to these examples and however much one accepts that they indicate a need for coordination, that any case is made for coordination at the State level.

Unless, and until, the States move to restore themselves to the central financial and political role in higher education they are not very meaningful entities with respect to the planning of higher education in Australia. Even if the States did reassume the dominance that was theirs before the Murray Report the political and economic factors might well be at odds with the concepts of national and international need. It is possible to argue for a "small is beautiful" solution to the organization of higher education in Australia but the planning units would be small and the overlapping inefficiencies high: anyone wanting to make this argument has to read the Murray Report and to press their argument in the light of that document. To date the only area of higher education in which there has been an effective State-related market is teacher education. The former teachers' colleges were at one time specific agencies of the State carrying out State-determined and State-limited roles. Since 1974 these institutions have slowly gained some autonomy but still see their major function as the preparation of teachers, in State terms. Historically, the former teachers' colleges have been creatures of the State: it is taking much time and effort to free them from that narrowly defined vision of their role. This historical accident, however, provides little basis for the plea that all other institutions should be levelled to the dependency of the former teachers' colleges.

One can understand the restlessness of the institutes of technology with their national, and sometimes international roles and relationships in a system dominated by such principles. No canting phrases about "retailing" and "wholesaling" can obscure the reality that for many institutions of higher education the State is not an effective horizon—it is not the market or the community they serve; it is not the group capable of criticism or praise; it is not the source of funds and people.

Admittedly the students who enter universities and DOCIT institutions are most frequently residents of States. But do we want more forces supporting this reluctance of Australian students to travel outside their local metropolis? And if one wishes to press the "small is beautiful" argument, why settle for State coordination rather than coordination at the level of city or shire council?

The point was made earlier that planning in higher education needs to be at the level at which the institutions interact with the external world. It is cumbersome to coordinate at lower levels for then the system must require another coordinating sub-system—a system for coordinating the coordinators. Such duplication of effort is fine for educational bureaucrats but the cost/reward equations are not likely to be positive. There are, of course, some areas of overlapping courses—institutions do plan developments in the same field—and therefore a host of other, marginal inefficiencies. But the national system established through the TEC and its likely successors have the powers and capacities to cope with the majority of such problems without setting up enlarged State apparatuses.

It has been argued in the previous section that freedom and autonomy are independent variables, and West Germany's experience and practice have been suggested as a model. A statement by Bowden (1967) was cited that "German universities and their staff preserve a degree of academic freedom and individual autonomy which is in some ways more absolute than anything we know in England. Every professor reigns supreme in his department and cannot be coerced by anybody". This statement is so unreal as to be troubling; does it really reflect adequately on the system in which the government, directly, makes all professorial appointments; a system in which, although tenure is difficult to break, the Minister can at his discretion issue a "Berufsverbot" forbidding any professor to teach? Freedom is not easily divisible and the power of a German professor to be a departmental tyrant is not necessarily a force for good.

The argument of force adduced is one that, for obvious reasons, is difficult to deploy. The coordinating body is introduced with the suggestion that "it (the State coordinating body) would place CAE's on the same footing as universities". The history behind the relationship of some CAE's to the State has already been explored; it is sad that the frustrations of that relationship can be assuaged by sharing misery with other more fortunate institutions. It is strongly argued that there are functional differences, not those of status or prestige, between institutions such as universities and DOCIT colleges and the institutions which have, and effectively retain, their monolithic relationship to a single market—the State Education Department.

Refutation of the case for State coordination does not require an examination of whether the statement cited earlier from the Carnegie Commission's Report into the Governance of Higher Education is accurate or meaningful. It rests on a simpler proposition; that the outputs of institutions of higher education are evaluated by a range of publics in a range of markets. It would be foolish to attempt to plan, coordinate and control such outputs at political levels which are out of touch with these publics and markets.

Chapter Four

Accountability at the Community Level

J. A. McDonell

It is difficult to describe how an educational institution, let alone a whole higher education system, might be held to be accountable, other than in quite indirect ways, to "the community". But niceties of this kind do not inhibit individual members of the community or particular groups within the community from criticising the policies and practices of such institutions and, by implication, calling on them to account for what they have been doing and why. A main issue, it seems, in dialogue between institutions of higher education and the community which supports them is the extent of their responsiveness to community needs.

In what follows, then, the term "accountability" will, unless the context indicates otherwise, refer to this question of responsiveness—to the needs of individuals, to the needs of various groups of people or to the needs of whole communities. If certain needs are evident or perceived and if the functional aims of an institution and the resources at its disposal are such that it could reasonably meet such needs, the question of whether the institution is attempting to do so is a pertinent one. The degree to which it is responsive to such needs and the effectiveness of its responses are matters on which it can legitimately be questioned and, in that sense, be held accountable.

Lastly by way of introduction it should be made clear that the author's experience of higher education has been principally gained within universities. What follows is, therefore, largely a commentary on these matters as they relate to the universities. However it is hoped that much of it has relevance to colleges of advanced education and that readers more familiar with that sector of higher education will perceive the parallels that exist, even if no substantial attempts are made here to explain them.

Institutional Roles and Constraints on Autonomy

Australian universities have for some time been primarily concerned with scholarship and the advancement of knowledge. One corollary to this research and scholarship preoccupation is the necessity to emphasise, whenever the opportunity is afforded, a university's requirement for autonomy and that of its staff for academic freedom. Some would argue that these requirements are almost incompatible with the notion of accountability to the community. If "accountability" means that decisions on lines of scholarship to be pursued or on the structure and content of courses to be offered must receive community approval in order to be sustained—or even, perhaps, in order to be put into effect in the first place—it would appear to threaten the very foundations of the concept of a university held by most academics who work in one. This view of accountability is also antipathetic to the image of academics as privileged critics of society—persons who, on the basis of their scholarly expertise are free to comment publicly on community affairs without fear of any victimisation arising from the unpopularity, in some quarters, of the opinions thus expressed. Of course it may be argued that academics are demonstrating their accountability to the community when they act as its critics; but this is hardly a view which people such as politicians, when aggrieved by this criticism, tend to support. The more direct view of "accountability", as a kind of external educational auditing process, is likely to be the one accepted by most groups in the community if they feel impelled to comment, one way or another, on a university's accountability.

It is true, of course, that universities have long since lost the full autonomy which they would like to have. The extent to which they are constrained in what they may do as institutions by various agencies of the community is discussed elsewhere in this volume. In another sense, also, arguments about autonomy and accountability based on the research and scholarship picture are arguments about what a university might be or ought to be, rather than about what it is. The community outside the university is often more realistic about the role of the university than are those within it. While the community may be tolerant of the university as a refuge for intellectuals (who are, by popular definition, not practical people and whose opinions, therefore, are unlikely to be of any practical value in helping us grapple with the problems of the real world) it has a very clear notion that the predominant role of the university is the training of professional people—doctors, lawyers, engineers, teachers, accountants and the like. The very growth of universities, aided by large injections of public finance, reflects the community's recognition of—indeed, its insistence upon—this function. The dilemma faced by the universities has been well summarised in the Report of the Committee on Open University (1974):

> ... *There is a·danger that conflict may develop between the traditional requirement that universities should seek high levels· of intellectual and professional excellence and the social aspiration that much wider opportunities should be provided for an ever increasing number to gain the benefits of a university education with the possibility of entry into the more prestigious and highly rewarded professions.* (7-8)

The colleges of advanced education, established to provide a more "vocational" stream of higher education, have been less concerned with research and scholarship roles and the related problems of academic freedom and accountability. The distinction, however, was never a convincing one, particularly in view of the many highly vocational university courses, and has become further blurred with time. Colleges created as new institutions with some degree of autonomy have, naturally enough, tended to edge their way toward the university model of an autonomous tertiary institution. What other model was available in the context of Australian society? At the time when the major push toward the establishment of CAE's emerged (in the late 1960's) the newer community colleges of North America were just beginning to establish their reputation as the fastest growing sector of higher education in that continent; they were not well known here. The polytechnics in the United Kingdom were in a state of flux and the process of upgrading several of them to university status was well under way. In Australia the only autonomous tertiary institutions known to have achieved public acceptability—in terms of recognition by the community in general and of demands to enter them from young people in particular—were the universities and the quasi-university Institutes of Technology. It is not surprising, therefore, that the CAE's tended to use university-style patterns of academic staff structure, course design and admission criteria.

All institutions of higher education are increasingly being called to account for "their" failure to match the output of graduates to the current manpower requirements of the community. It is seldom recognised (in the press and in parliaments, at any rate) that this is one area in which the institutions have to a considerable extent lost their control. Proposals for increasing or, occasionally, decreasing the numbers of graduates and diplomates in any area have, since long before current graduates began their courses, been subjected to close scrutiny by government agencies and by governments themselves. Universities and colleges are accountable for the numbers of students they enrol both at first year level and in total throughout all their courses. Clearly the auditing of student numbers is going to receive increased attention in the future and levels of funding are likely to be adversely affected if the audited numbers do not reach agreed targets; moreover one cannot foresee any compensating increase in funds if institutions should succeed, intentionally or inadvertently, in attracting more than their allotted quotas of students.

In the absence of any significant changes in the ways in which policies and funding for higher education are determined by the community through governments ,one can foresee the institutions of higher education finding themselves increasingly in an "accountability dilemma". Governments—or, more specifically, politicians—will principally concern themselves with generalised overviews. They have not the time to study the details in depth and must rely on the advice of their Commissions, Councils and public servants who, they assume, have done so. However advice from such quarters will seldom result in any radical changes. Past experience indicates that any radical suggestion is far more likely to be ignored, or even positively rejected, than to be accepted; there is little to be gained by proposing politically unacceptable changes, and all changes of a radical nature are, by definition, unacceptable to some groups with political influence. Thus governments are likely to concern themselves primarily with generalities such as the overall expenditure on education and guidelines for growth which, when implemented, will produce easing or squeezing of the constraints on each major educational sector but little structural change. The agencies of government will then be concerned with the fine tuning of the system and it is in this process that the institutions may find themselves accountable, in ever-increasing statistical detail. At the same time, however, the general community tends to hold the institutions themselves responsible for the policies under which they work; it tends to see the products of the system—their own sons and daughters emerging with various educational qualifications—and to hold the institutions accountable for the numbers and quality of these products. It is difficult to explain to the parents of a recently graduated but unemployed teacher that this situation arises from a complex of factors including general social aspirations and the decisions of previous governments, and that the particular university or college from which the teacher graduated has had very little influence over the output of such graduates.

In the "quality" of their outputs, also, universities and colleges are tending to lose their autonomy. Other institutions, such as professional associations and registration boards, have considerable influence on course content and structure. Many examples can be quoted; one which has had a very direct effect on the college system and, in consequence, on universities is the decision taken in the late 1960's by the Institution of Engineers in Australia that after 1980 the minimum qualification required for Membership of the Institution would be a 4-year degree in engineering. At the time when the decision was made a 3-year diploma, available from many colleges, sufficed as a membership qualification. Although many of these colleges may have welcomed the change as one which would enable them to upgrade their courses and become more competitive with university engineering faculties the ultimate decision was that of the professional Institution and, once made, was one which imposed on all such institutions the need to expand 3-year diplomas into 4-year degrees. Inevitably the proportion of engineering students choosing to enter university courses was affected.

Accountability—To Whom?

Both universities and colleges have seen themselves in the design of their courses as accountable for meeting the needs of external groups—other institutions, occupational and professional groups, industry and government. In this process they have more than adequately met their own institutional needs for a sufficient cadre of recruits for their future staffs. Proposals about new courses and the numbers of students to be admitted to them have, in all cases within the era of Commonwealth Commissions, included justifications for their introduction based on assessments of community needs for people with the skills which these courses were intended to develop. The design of the courses themselves has in the colleges been a matter of external accreditation, with attention being given to the total structure of the course as well as to the detail of each subject and its rationale and placement within the course.

With relatively few exceptions, higher education courses in Australia are designed with one particular class of student in view—the fulltime student coming straight from secondary school. Additionally, it is usually implicit in the design that the "normal student" is one who goes straight through the course, completing it in minimum time. All students who depart from either of these two categories are expected to modify *their* requirements and ambitions to fit the design of the course. Higher education in Australia has not accepted any serious obligation to be responsive to its students, in the sense of recognising the variability in their learning needs and setting out, within reasonable limits, to meet them.

Consider a few typical situations. At one end of the scale, the academically excellent student is seldom asked to do anything other than go along with subjects (and levels of teaching of them) designed for the large "middle group" of students. Many students could quite comfortably cope with an existing 3-year course in two years. There is usually no way of their doing so—indeed,they tend to be discouraged from making any such attempt. The institution or faculty "knows best" the rate at which students "should" progress, and deviance from this norm is unwelcome. At the other end of the scale, students coming straight from school are selected on the basis of the question "Is this student likely to succeed (or survive?) in our course?" The question "Is this a course which suits the needs of this student?" is seldom, if ever, asked. In the hectic scramble to fill quotas at the beginning of each year there is no time to enquire about the motivations underlying students' selections of the courses they apply for, or the extent to which their applications are based on a realistic understanding of the nature of the courses and a realistic self-appraisal of their own ability and potential.

"Abnormal" students, particularly adults wishing to return to higher education, tend to get more individual consideration at the point of entry. However two points can be made about such students. Firstly, their selection is still made substantially on the basis of the institution's assessment (often according to very shaky criteria) of the likelihood of the student's ability to succeed in a course which, in general, has been designed with quite a different kind of student in mind. Secondly, adult students are still regarded in this country as abnormal students, despite the fact that in some university faculties they now form more than 30% of the first-year intake. Available statistics do not always provide an age distribution by faculties, but they do give an indication of the extent of adult enrolments. Thus, at Monash University in 1977, 42% of first-year Arts admissions were students who were *not* coming straight from school; in the same year, of students enrolled in bachelor degrees at Monash, 10% of the 8,400 full-time and 58% of the 2,200 part-time students were of age 26 or more. There is little or no evidence of any modification of subject or course structures to recognise this change in the student population.

The claim that adult students tend to perform better than the middle group of students in the "normal" intake does not justify self-congratulation by the institutions. People with adult attributes who are sufficiently motivated to undertake this kind of learning task are likely to succeed even if frustrated by its inadequacy in meeting their particular needs and circumstances. The proposition that such a mismatch exists itself requires investigation. It is one which has received relatively little attention in Australia but is now much discussed in the U.S.A. A short article by Hameister and Hickey (1977) summarises many of the points which recur in the literature of adult education from that country. They point out that figures from the U.S. Department of Commerce (1975) show that, in 1974, 48.3% of the college student population were 22 years of age and above. To accentuate the dichotomy, as they see it, between traditional and "new majority" (adult) students, Hameister and Hickey have enumerated the major characteristics of each group (see Table 1).

Not all the details of this analysis would necessarily apply in Australia but there is little doubt that the general comparison would remain valid—namely, that the backgrounds, needs and motivations of "traditional" and "adult" students tend to be widely different. A recent study at Murdoch University by Knight and McDonald (1977) points in this same direction. Their survey centred on four postulates about the characteristics of adult learners put

Table 1

Dichotomy Between the Traditional Student and the New Majority

Traditional Student	New Majority
1. Continuing in school	1. Returning to school
2. Learning history strongly influenced by formal education	2. Learning history strongly influenced by informal education
3. Familiar with educational routine	3. Unfamiliar with educational routine and expectations
4. Primary time commitment to school—full-time student	4. Major time commitment to family and job—part-time student
5. Adequate communication and study skills	5. Frequent deficiencies in study and communication skills
6. Minimal work experience	6. Considerable relevant work experience
7. Micro frame of reference for a more orderly input of new ideas	7. Macro frame of reference based on life-experience which has both positive and negative implications for the learning process
8. Frequently no clear vocational goal	8. Frequently clear vocational goals, but not necessarily related to educational program
9. Educational goal is to receive a baccalaureate degree at minimum	9. Educational goal may be to receive a degree, but may also include some form of certification or licensure
10. Speed of performance and peer competitiveness affects learning activities	10. Concept mastery and accuracy of performance more important than competition—frequently viewed as threatening
11. High academic grades play significant role in obtaining meaningful employment	11. Academic grades are not significant in terms of present employment situation
12. Clear idea of how he compares with academic performance of fellow students	12. No accurate basis on which to judge his academic potential

(From: LIFELONG LEARNING: THE ADULT YEARS; December 1977)

---

forward by Knowles (1970) which, although derived from the field of non-formal adult education, are consistent with and complement the Hameister and Hickey picture of "new majority" students. Knight and McDonald found that

Knowles' assumptions had considerable validity for their survey group of 340 on-campus adult students (aged above 24 years) enrolled in undergraduate courses.

If such attributes of adult students continue to be validated, Australian higher education already has—and will increasingly have—a need to accept a much greater measure of accountability than it now does for providing educational resources which are person-centred rather than institution-centred. Similar views, in a somewhat different context, were put forward in the Report of the Committee on Open University (1974). That Committee expressed the belief that

> ... *changes in the relationship between education and society demand the adoption of a more open approach to higher education than at present obtains in Australia.*

(Para. 8.4.)

A further area in which the question of accountability to the community comes strongly to the fore is that of continuing education, which in the Australian context means education programs *outside* the range of degree and diploma courses but designed to meet perceived needs for refreshment, updating and diversification in professional areas, as well as general adult education. The need for such programs is repeatedly stressed; on all sides one finds endorsement of the principles underlying "recurrent education" which are referred to in commendatory terms in reports of all the four major education sectors (Schools, TAFE, Advanced Education and Universities). And yet little development in this area has taken place. Universities, for example, were given the green light to expand their continuing education services to whatever extent they chose to do so, *within the resources at their disposal.* In a brief period while these resources were still expanding, some small-scale beginnings in this direction were made. But since the 1973-75 triennium, when the expansionary phase in Australian higher education ended, there have been no moves by the universities to reallocate their resources in such a way as to increase the fractions directed to continuing education, despite the common agreement that continuing education is a field of expanding potential and one in which institutions of higher education should become increasingly involved if they hold themselves accountable for meeting the educational needs of the community which supports them.

Characteristics of a Responsive Institution

From what has been said above it follows that an institution responsive to the differing needs of different categories of students and to the range of individual differences, even within any one such category, would be characterised by a willingness to modify its teaching methods and curricular designs (within reasonable practical limits) to meet the learning needs of different students. Such a flexibility does not necessarily imply variability in the stated objectives of courses and the methods used to assess whether these have been attained by students. It does imply flexibility in the range of learning paths and strategies which different students may follow—and, consequently, in the rates at which they progress along these paths—in reaching these prescribed objectives.

The foregoing is concerned with the practices of an institution once it has accepted a student. However responsiveness to individual needs can begin much earlier, in the process of acceptance or selection of applicants. It is worthwhile to explore some characteristics which Australian institutions of higher education might well adopt if they are to become more responsive, in this sense, to the educational needs of the community. The extent to which they are open to adult students has already been mentioned. In the establishment of external studies over many years, principally by the Universities of New England and Queensland, access which is no longer limited by the need for day-to-day attendance on campus has been greatly increased for some categories of students. Deakin University is moving in the same direction, aided by techniques developed more recently by the Open University in the United Kingdom (which, it should be noted, owes something to the experiences and practices of Australian universities in this field).

However another dimension of openness and responsiveness to community needs is still underdeveloped in this country—namely, the willingness of institutions to admit people other than those "properly qualified" for admission and to admit them to subjects, or combinations of subjects, of their own choice. An institution which is entirely responsive to the learning needs of the adult community might well have an admissions policy along the following lines.

* Individual subjects and courses of study carry, in their descriptions, careful specifications of the principal skills and understandings which entering students will be assumed to have.

* Decisions as to whether entering students do have these skills and understandings are *their* responsibility, not that of the instituion; it will provide advice and counselling, but the decision as to whether a student is likely to be able to cope with the studies offered by the institution is his or hers—not the institution's. Thus, "likelihood of success" is not a factor which the institution attempts to judge as a criterion for admission.

* While standard courses leading to recognised professional qualifications are available, students can enter into individual learning contracts which lead them to the same endpoints but by alternative paths which are appropriate to their individual skills and experience.

* Enrolment for a single subject, a unit within a subject or any combination of subjects and units of the student's choosing is no less valued, in deciding on admissions, than enrolment in a full course. Furthermore, students are entirely at liberty to switch between part-time and full-time study or to suspend their studies for a while.

* Proper credit is given for experiential learning and for other formal studies; and, in the latter case, this credit is given freely (without argument about the relative merits of "our" subjects and "theirs"), consistent with reliance on the student's self-assessment of readiness to undertake the next educational step.

* Back-up services, such as additional bridging or reinforcing study packages for students whose skills need reinforcement in some areas, are available.

The adoption of such policies, which only relate to the standard subject-offerings of the institution, would require major changes in administrative and academic attitudes and practices. Undoubtedly they would be difficult to implement and the changes could probably be achieved only by a radical restructuring since, as we shall see later, a gradual approach to the initiation of such changes may be ineffective. However, any institution which was able to make the transition to such a new state of operation would be able to claim with some conviction that it was making its resources available to the community in ways which, to a much greater extent, matched the needs of adults in that community as they, the adults, perceived them.

It would be a corollary of such admissions policies that the institution would accept the responsibility for providing continuing education as part of its spectrum of normal teaching activities. Continuing education has a responsiveness to special needs which differ from those of standard course offerings and which often emerge quickly and die down after a while. Partly because of this, it now tends to be seen as an "extra" activity by members of staff—something beyond the range of responsibilities of their appointments and which they undertake (or choose not to undertake) for a variety of motives. Continuing education will only develop to its full potential in meeting community needs if it is, as a matter of institutional policy, regarded as a normal activity. Such a policy shift would be a necessary precursor to the devising of the new staffing, administrative and financial strategies which would then be called for.

If these changes in admissions policy and continuing education policy were put into effect, the institution would be able to make a significant contribution to training in a number of new areas without becoming unduly involved in the "education versus training" controversy. Individuals and organisations seeking training in fields which reasonably draw upon those resources and expertise which the institution possesses could arrange enrolments in any relevant subjects or, when the need arose, participate in special-purpose continuing education activities. The institution itself need not be—and possibly should not be—the certifying agency for training courses unless these are relatively brief ones, totally commissioned through its continuing education program. But it need not hesitate to offer some kind of certificate of completion for any subject or short course which it offers and which has specified objectives. Different institutions would undoubtedly play different roles in this respect; the differences would arise, though, from differences in their basic educational purposes, which would lead to differences in the resources and expertise which each is able to put at the disposal of the community, rather than from some kind of differentiation between "education" and "training" institutions. It is difficult, even now, to find any higher education institution which does not simultaneously describe itself as being concerned with the education and personal development of its students, while offering explicit training courses leading to particular professional occupations. It seems hardly worth the effort to try to separate these two functions within the one institution, let alone attempt to set up distinguishable "educational" and "training" institutions.

Another way in which the community can draw upon the resources of higher education institutions, and one which is less frequently used than it could be in this country, is through consultancy on social problems within the community. Local government authorities, ethnic groups, business associations and trade unions are examples of groups which could, with profit, make greater use of university and college resources. The best approach here is not so much one of contracting to "find" solutions for such groups to problems which face them, but rather one in which the institution behaves toward such groups as individual academics should behave toward students—as facilitators of learning. People can—and should—be helped toward finding solutions to their own problems which are, in their terms, the "best" available. They need expert advice in this process, just as they need the best available information to work with. Higher education institutions, which could provide such a back-up service, have tended to be very wary of becoming involved in public issues. They have feared the backlash from one section of the community or another from the suggestion of being associated with any particular political stance. It is arguable, however, that in times to come when the community seeks a greater level of account-ability from these institutions, they would generate more public support by being recognised as a proper resource to be approached quite freely for advice on social problems than by withdrawing into a neutral, non-contributing position. All social problems have political solutions: educational institutions are likely to serve their communities better by accepting this fact and being seen to be helpful to people who have the responsibility for dealing with such problems than by trying to avoid at all costs giving offence to any political faction.

Inducing Institutional Change—A Problem

The various education commissions have in the past endorsed several proposals for change in the role and function of educational institutions. One example— the development of continuing education services—has already been mentioned. Another concerns access. The Committee on Open University acknowledged that there are large numbers of people in the Australian community who cannot now get access to higher education but who wish to do so, and could do so if the system were infused with a greater measure of 'openness' than currently exists. The Committee rejected, on balance, the view that such a change would best be brought about by the creation of a new teaching institution with a role similar to that of the Open University of the United Kingdom. Instead it opted for the strategy of encouragement of new initiatives by established institutions. In this vein, the Committee recommended the establishment of a National Institute of Open Tertiary Education (N.I.O.T.E.) which would not itself offer courses and enrol students but would, by a variety of means, seek to stimulate universities and colleges to modify their practices and evolve new resources for the opening of access to large numbers of adults.

In the event, the government of the day and succeeding governments declined to implement this recommendation. However it seems doubtful that such a strategy for institutional change would ever work except, possibly, in an expansionary period. Then, institutions may undertake new roles in response to additional funding which enables them to add new enterprises to their repertoire without significantly affecting their existing operations. In times when total resources are fixed—or even contracting—one wonders if institutions would readily react to exhortations and moral encouragement to exercise their autonomy and re-deploy their resources in an effort to become more responsive to community needs along the lines suggested earlier. An analysis of social institutions and their reactions to change put forward by Schon (1973) strongly suggests that they will not.

Schon's thesis is of interest because it relates not only to the way institutions of higher education might have behaved in response to a hypothetical innovation such as N.I.O.T.E., but also to the ways in which they are likely to behave in the face of actual proposals for change, such as those embodied in the recommendations of the Partridge Committee (1978) and Anderson Committee (1978). Schon identifies a characteristic of any social system, be it an industrial firm, a community institution or a whole community, which he calls "dynamic conservatism"—a form of resistance to change which goes beyond simple inertia and involves a tendency to fight to remain the same. This characteristic he sees as not arising from "... the stupidity or venality of individuals within the system; it is a function of the system itself." Schon describes the strategies of dynamic conservatism in the following way.

* *An oversimplified first response to the presence of a threat is to ignore it, a response ... (described as) ... 'selective inattention'.*
* *When it is no longer possible to avoid noticing a threat, it may be possible to launch a counter-attack or even a preventive attack before the threat has materialised.*
* *When the threat cannot be totally repulsed, ... dynamic conservatism runs to strategies of containment and isolation. Allow the threatened change a limited scope of activity and keep it bottled up.* (1973: 46-7)

A further strategy is one of co-option—a process by which established social systems absorb agents of change and de-fuse, dilute and turn to their own ends the energies originally directed towards change.

* *When processes embodying threat cannot be ignored, repelled, contained or transformed, social systems tend to respond by change—but by the **least change** capable of neutralising or meeting the intrusive process.*

(Ibid: 47)

Schon goes on to point out that a consequence of this attribute of dynamic conservatism is that a social system is unlikely to make any far-reaching change through a series of small steps. Rather it tends to yield, if unable to resist change, in a sudden and massive shift from the original steady state to a new one and to resist change from this stable state in exactly the same ways as before. If this is so, "... the energy required to reach the threshold of transformation takes the form of disruption and leads to crisis" and this will be brought about in most cases by "... individuals who display irrational commitment, extraordinary energy, a combativeness which enables them to battle established interests over a long period of time, and a remarkable skill at guerilla warfare." A major point of Schon's thesis relevant to any considerations of change in higher education is this:

Recognition of dynamic conservatism explodes the myth of intervention pervasive in official rhetoric, which envisages social change as a process made up of analysis of objectives, examination of alternatives, and selection of the most promising routes to change. Quite apart from its questionable claims to knowledge, the rational myth assumes implicitly that transformation occurs in a vacuum rather than in the plenum of self-reinforcing systems. Variants of the myth assume that rational plans will implement themselves, or they leave the question of implementation to a mysterious process of sales, persuasion or politics. (Ibid: 56)

Behaviour characteristic of dynamic conservatism has frequently been exhibited in the field of higher education in Australia. The response of several universities to student unrest of the late 1960's and early 1970's followed closely the strategies described above. Many institutions faced by clear evidence for several years of a significant decline in the numbers of applicants for engineering and the physical sciences have given "selective inattention" to the problem. Anyone familiar with higher education will be able to multiply such examples, and one is therefore tempted to accept the concept of dynamic conservatism as a basis for predicting the future behaviour of higher education institutions. It seems most improbable that existing institutions will gradually, and with a minimum of fuss, accept significant changes in their accountability to the community and the consequent necessary changes in their policies and practices. For example it has been suggested in a report by Dennison (1976) and implied in many other quarters that a rational future for many colleges of advanced education would be their conversion into multi-purpose community colleges. It has been argued that institutions of this kind would be more responsive to a large set of community needs, presently not being met satisfactorily, than would the current "university-model" colleges. Suppose, for the sake of argument, that this latter proposition were correct and that the community would probably benefit by some such transformations. How would they come about? Only, it seems, by some quite dramatic upheavals within the higher education system, not by any process of gradual evolution.

An institution which is simply invited—or exhorted—to convert itself into a community college without being offered considerably increased funding at the same time is unlikely to do so; and the possibility of any one institution being offered such increased funding is remote. In an overall steady-state situation, increased funding for one institution would represent a threat to the stability of the whole system of institutions, which would then bring into play *its* strategies for resistance to change. In the absence of new funding, an institution cannot be expected to transform itself willingly, no matter how rational it may seem to the outside observer that it should do so. Arguments to the effect that it would gain positive community support from accepting new responsibilities and being responsive to the community in new ways are unlikely, it seems, to be successful in overcoming the institution's inherent dynamic conservatism. It is therefore arguable that gradual evolutionary change in response to "rational planning" is unlikely on the part of educational institutions. If this is true, significant changes in institutional practice and outlook will be difficult to achieve and the methods of bringing about desired changes need much more attention than they have hitherto received in this country.

Creating a Climate of Responsiveness

Central to the question of increasing responsiveness to community needs is the problem of identification of needs. Whose task is this? Are there differences between "needs" and "wants"—or, how does one assess the validity of propositions, from a variety of sources, that particular needs exist? Perhaps the answers lie in the deliberate generation of some kind of feedback process between the institution and the community. Elements of this process can already be seen in many institutions through the use of their physical facilities by members of surrounding communities, through summer schools in recreational education, through "community education", "extension" and "adult education" programs, and through a variety of other ventures.

In most cases, however, such initiatives tend to be seen by academic staff as peripheral to the central institutional purposes. In universities, discussions about the institution's prime concerns tend to be dominated by the research and scholarship function. The establishment of some new internal structure to promote feedback between a university and the community is therefore likely to be difficult and its maintenance is likely to be under constant threat if there is competition for scarce resources. The critical factor in enabling such a process to be sustained effectively will probably be the extent to which one or two key executives in the institution are convinced of the desirability of this approach and have sufficient persuasiveness and persistence to see that it is initiated and supported. In the few instances in Australia in which this kind of policy is evident as an institutional commitment, the personal influence of the chief executive officer or one of his immediate deputies is usually discernible.

Even where there is acceptance of such accountability to the community, the problems of identifying both "the community" and "its needs" will be ever present. There will be in general no permanent conceptual structures, such as the disciplines of traditional academic practice, available as frames of reference. One exception will arise where the community in question is the body of individual adults seeking admission to the institution at varying stages of their lives.

There it will be possible, in time, to develop reliable generalisations about adult learning—about the needs and characteristics of adults which distinguish them as learners from children and adolescents—which will provide guidance for responsive policies and practices in assisting such individuals to satisfy their perceived educational needs.

Otherwise, one is likely to be working constantly with changing clienteles. In practice "the community" will probably be a range of identifiable community groups based on sets of common interests—for example members of professional bodies, voluntary organisations or the communities of particular localities. The needs of such groups will vary widely and will not remain constant over the years. With experience it should be possible to arrive at a situation in which any one group becomes fairly familiar with the range of resources relevant to its interests which is available in, say, a particular university. In that situation, the group's own perception of its needs and of the extent to which that institution has the potential to meet them would usually provide reliable guidance for deciding whether or not the institution ought to undertake any new activity for that group. In other words, in forming a judgement as to whether any proposition represents a genuine need, the perception of a "client group" which has received the right kind of encouragement to interact meaningfully with the institution is likely to be the right one.

In this kind of feedback process the role of the institution is not simply a passive one. If the feedback is effective it is improbable that the institution would simply sit back and wait to be called upon; if it is sufficiently vigorous to enter into this kind of interaction it would begin initiatives of its own. An important role of any good teacher is that of extending the student's perception of his or her own potential and of the learning needed to achieve that potential. In the same way, a responsive institution will extend, through the activities of its departments and its individual staff members, the community's perception of its own needs. "Educating the community" is sometimes put forward as a proper function of higher education institutions. The context in which this is said sometimes implies an analogue of a teacher-centred view of the classroom—one in which the student is largely dependent on the teacher for instruction as to what he (the student) ought to learn and how he ought to go about learning it. At the level of institution-community relations the more appropriate model is a learner-centred approach to education, in which the teacher's role is one of facilitating the student's learning and extending his horizons, rather than one of direction. Interpreted in this way, education of the community would automatically become an integral component of the feedback between the community and a responsive institution.

Summary

Educational institutions which, for the most part, have seen themselves as accountable to governments and commissions are likely to find in the future increasing demands that they be accountable to the citizenry for the extent to which they are responsive to the educational needs of adult individuals and community groups. They are likely to be asked more frequently to justify the restrictions they place on the kinds of people they allow to enrol, the limitations which they place on the choices of subjects open to those whom they do admit and the limited extent to which they respond to educational needs which they could meet from existing resources but which happen to fall outside their regular degree and diploma courses. Increasing awareness of the advantages of lifelong education, increasing concern about the interface between the education system and the world of work, increasing prospects for paid educational leave and other social factors encouraging adults to contemplate a return, at least for a time, to the education system and, in general, an increasing belief that the education system should better serve the majority of the community—namely the adults, who pay for it—are likely to be the sources of increasing pressure for higher education institutions to serve a wider clientele and to account to that clientele for the ways in which they do so. Finally, it should be realised that such pressures, if they are effective in bringing about change, are much more likely to result in occasional sudden and dramatic change in some institutions than they are to produce gradual change throughout the whole educational system according to some long term, national strategy.

Chapter Five

Institutional Structures and Internal Accountability

G. A. Ramsey
J. Howlett

Introduction

The tradition that an institution of higher education should be left to go about its educational business without external interference has ended. More and more, institutions of higher education are being called to account for their activities. There have recently been enquiries into post-secondary education in virtually all States, and the National Inquiry into Education and Training established by the Prime Minister under the Chairmanship of Professor Williams was given terms of reference which implied that the whole area of post-secondary education needed a close external review. Moreover the press are increasingly questioning the levels of expenditure on higher education and the activities of higher education institutions (e.g. Samuel, 1977).

There are a number of reasons for this. Firstly, there has been a dramatic growth in the national provision of higher education. Where for decades there had only been about ten universities, in the space of ten or so years from the early 1960s this number almost doubled. Do we need them all? Can they all be making a worthwhile contribution to higher education? Secondly, there was the identification of and significant growth in an alternate higher education system, that of the advanced education sector. Questions arise about the relative effectiveness of the two sectors. This debate was further compounded by the addition in 1973 of the former State teachers' colleges, previously under the control of the Education Department, to bring the total number of institutions of higher education in 1975 to about a hundred separate, largely autonomous, degree granting institutions. The third factor was the 1972 decision to abolish all tuition fees in higher education institutions and for the total responsibility for funding to be met from Federal sources. The clients of higher education were no longer to contribute, which removed the normal 'market place' accountability at a time when the cost of higher education had reached an all time high.

Whenever changes as global as these occur, doubts are raised as to their effectiveness. For the changes to have occurred with such an impact on national spending at a time when there was a dramatic down turn in the national economy meant that higher education was to be placed under close scrutiny.

Higher education institutions now appear to the public and to politicians to be in a privileged position. Their independence is guaranteed in their charters, which seem to protect them from close examination. It is this very appearance of being protected which in times of economic down turn causes increased public demand for external accountability. Such pressures produce their own internal reaction in these institutions. Structures develop for increased internal accountability and control which, it is hoped, will answer the external criticism.

The higher education institutions, as a response to this increasing demand to be "held to account", are being pressed to provide increasing amounts of data to coordinating authorities such as State Boards of Advanced Education and the Tertiary Education Commission. The data is generally produced under the rubric of "efficient allocation of resources" both among institutions and within an institution's competing departments or areas of need. External requirements produce internal demands. A reduction in the number of staff needed produces a reduction in the student intake with its corresponding reduction in the institution's budget. Internal structures are then needed to cope with any staff redundancy which may result. Conditions of tenure are called into question. Resources previously used in educating teachers must be re-deployed. Structures that were appropriate for times when higher education was expanding begin to falter when the task is to reduce the previous level of provision.

Because of some of the factors stated above, and because of an increased public awareness of what an education system does and can do, the general perception of the role and function of higher education has changed. The larger the proportion of the population that has access to or experience of the post-secondary education system, the more the old values and traditions of the system are called into question. Where previously our education systems "used to exemplify the orthodoxy of our society's best opinions of itself" (Scott, 1978: 4), they have now become a focus for society's disenchantment. The nature and purpose of differing tertiary sectors have become increasingly unclear. "Where uniformity was once valued, diversity has become an inescapable fact of life ... Where authority was once taken for granted, it must now earn its keep" (ibid). Universities particularly find it difficult to accommodate to this change in which education has become politicised in a way which has not been experienced before, with institutions being increasingly affected by (rather than affecting) the surrounding social, economic and political environments.

It is against this background of an increasing external demand to bring education to account that this chapter on institutional structures for internal accountability is written. Internal accountability does not exist in isolation. It must be such as to provide the means to respond to external demands, whether these are Federal or State coordinating authorities, the public media, or the general community, as well as to internal needs stemming from the functions for which the particular institution was established.

Demands for accountability may require a quantitative response—how many students are there in a course; how many drop out each year; what is the cost per student place; what is the area per student provided; how many books are there in the library on the course topic; and so on? But numbers are nowhere near enough. To ask a quantitative question implies that there is a qualitative standard against which the number may be judged: a drop-out rate of 30 per cent per annum is too high; library holdings of 40 books per full-time student are too low. To reduce the drop-out rate more staff are needed, or the quality of instruction must be improved, or the academic level of the intake must be raised. These require either additional resources, a re-allocation of resources, or different resources.

There are many qualitative questions in relation to which an institution may be held to account that cannot be answered satisfactorily from a hard data base. How effective are an institution's graduates in their new employment? Should a course have more liberal studies? Is the balance of practical and theoretical subjects appropriate? Does the course meet acceptable international academic standards? Yet increasingly these are the questions about which institutions are called to account.

In a legal sense an institution need only be called to public account in terms of its own Act of Parliament and any other Acts which may relate to it. (An Ombudsman Act provides a good example of a related Act.) A Parliament has a responsibility on behalf of the public to assess how well an institution performs its functions as stated in its Act. The annual document of public accountability for an institution is its annual report and the audited statement of its accounts. The audited statement reassures the public that its funds have been spent to fulfil the functions of the institution as stated in its Act and, where Federal funds are involved, that the expenditure meets the terms of the appropriate State's Grants Act under which the grant was made. The Annual Report is intended to give the public some reassurance about the quality of the provision under the Act. Unfortunately, it is a short step from a genuine attempt at public qualitative accountability to blatant lily-gilding public relations. It is through the audited statement and the annual report that internal and external accountability formally meet; and, appropriately for most higher education institutions, this is in the most public of all arenas, the Federal or State Parliament.

External demands for accountability are reflected in the increasing parliamentary debate about education. If an audited statement were to hint at some need for institutional change in finance approval procedures, the internal accountability structure in the institution would change in response immediately. To this date, in Australia at least, we have not seen much parliamentary debate of an effective kind which is directed at the quality of the educational provision as related to the Act establishing an institution. Institutions, particularly universities, have been left very much alone. The claim that "a university must be committed to the acquisition of knowledge beyond mere reference to any needs of particular times or places ... they are not mere instruments of the State. They are not instruments of Government" (Derham, 1975: 204-205), has become a very real cry against the encroachment of Government upon areas which have previously been regarded as essential to the preservation of institutional autonomy. Yet this autonomy has always been *de facto* rather than *de jure,* to be questioned or removed whenever the legislative authority may decide. Some debate on the role of the university came recently in the Senate when the Annual Report of the Australian National University was debated and the social and economic value of research in universities was questioned. The Senate pursued the subject with delicacy and the following comment is representative of how members of the Senate saw the degree to which universities ought to be "subject to governmental interference":

This Parliament is responsible for ensuring that there is accountability. But we are not concerned with aggressive accountability, we do not operate on the basis that we require institutions to answer our queries as though they were malefactors of some sort. Rather our attitude is one of interested accountability and of saying: 'What are you doing, why are you doing it in this way and how are you going?'
(Extract from a speech made by Senator Rae, Hansard, 10 March 1978)

While the first signs emerge of Parliament questioning what institutions in the higher education sector are doing, the tenor is still very much to preserve the autonomy at least of universities, and this despite the fact that the university which provided the topic for debate is allocated the same annual expenditure as some other universities with three times the student population. The price of research compared with that of teaching is very clear at the Australian National University and it must be assumed that this is accepted by Parliament, since neither side really took up the issue. Despite the protective tone of the debate, the fact that it occurred at all suggests that annual reports may well serve as a focus for public accountability in the future.

Within an institution three types of accountability may be identified— financial accountability in which the institution must account for the allocation of its funds to support its functions, program accountability where the quality of the courses offered by the institution and research undertaken are assessed, and process accountability in which the appropriateness of procedures adopted to implement a particular activity are considered (Scott, 1978).

For program accountability to be effective, objectives for the program must be stated in such a way that they can be assessed. This is difficult, and institutions often retreat to quantitative data gathering and ignore the goal definition exercise which is paramount if criteria are to be established against which programs may be held to account. The demands of external accountability should set the minimum for an acceptable level of internal accountability, not the maximum.

For What is an Institution Accountable?

The different legislative powers of the three post-secondary sectors have already been documented elsewhere (Ramsey, 1978) and it is intended in this section to deal only with the university and advanced education sectors.

In terms of legislative authority universities have a significantly greater power of self-determination than do colleges of advanced education, despite the fact that both types of institution are governed by Councils of somewhat similar composition. The main differences in legislative authority are in the areas of course planning, development, and accreditation, and in that the colleges are required in the terms of their Acts to collaborate with State coordinating authorities in the allocation of capital and recurrent resources while universities may deal directly with the Federal Tertiary Education Commission.

It is not the purpose of this chapter to present a rationale for such differences, nor to explore the anomalies whereby experienced multi-level established colleges of advanced education are treated differently from newly formed universities. These are matters for discussion of external accountability dealt with elsewhere in this book, and while they may have some implications for accountability at the institutional level there is sufficient similarity in institutional obligations relating to courses, students, staff and finance for the two sectors to be examined together.

Accountability and Courses

An institution's responsibility to account for its courses may be explored in terms of academic "quality control". A university has the legislative authority to control and assess the academic worth of its own courses, whereas a college of advanced education does not. Nowhere is the influence on internal structures for accountability of external requirements more clearly seen than in an institution's system for assessing the worth of its courses. A university need only set up a system which satisfies itself whereas a college of advanced education must set up a system which satisfies the requirements of the State coordinating authority and conforms to the guidelines established by the National Council on Awards in Advanced Education. These external pressures on internal structures for course development and assessment have not been detrimental to colleges; indeed, the colleges have benefited from such scrutiny. However, while a course may receive accreditation for attaining a particular standard this does not necessarily ensure that it will, over the five year period of accreditation, continue to be conducted in accordance with the details stated in accreditation submissions. It is the responsibility of the individual institution to ensure this, and the integrity of each institution is relied on to ensure internal mechanisms to maintain the academic standard of its courses.

There need not be major differences between the procedures used by a university and a college of advanced education, but at present the college must meet external scrutiny. Institutions in both sectors use course committees which are responsible to senior committees of the governing body (say, the academic board) for their actions. Generally the formal procedures for ensuring that accountability criteria are met must relate to the stated objectives of a given course. In the colleges the governing body is helped in this decision at least every five years by the assessment of an external accreditation committee.

The criteria on which a university and a college of advanced education may judge the acceptability of their courses may well differ. One method might be to assess graduate performance at different periods of time—say, one, five and ten years following graduation. The college sector should be geared to the immediate needs of specific employers and industries and to manpower requirements. Educational planning for such courses should reflect strong market orientation in relation to graduate output, which should be monitored. On the other hand the university sector is often non-vocational and is more geared to a social demand approach, with employer demand and manpower planning being secondary considerations. Very little research on 'graduate performance' has been done by either sector because institutional demands for judging the quality of courses have not, as yet, required it.

In terms of courses it is not simply a matter of ensuring the quality of those which exist that is important; it is the ease (or difficulty) with which institutional structures permit a quick response to an identifiable community need. For the advanced education sector the time of response to a perceived new demand can be much longer than that for a university which, provided funds are available, has to contend only with its internal structures for approval. As a result the sector which is specifically vocational and designed to meet community need is actually slower than the university sector to respond because of imposed external accountability structures. This occurs despite the Advanced Education Council statement that "strongly emphasises that without a capacity to adjust and to provide for emerging needs the system will stultify" (Advice of the Advanced Education Council in Tertiary Education Commission, 1978: 22). The major responsibility for ensuring the quality of courses, whether internally or externally, must rely on the quality of the collegiate process in the particular institution, and in the extent to which this collegiate process accepts input from present and former students, employers and professional bodies. The quality of teaching occurring in a course should be subject to as vigorous an assessment as the quality of research an institution undertakes.

Accountability and Students

The move in recent years for funding in higher education to be formula based—that is, with an institution receiving a budget in direct proportion to the number of students enrolled—makes an institution's accountability to its students just as pertinent as it was during the period when students provided a certain amount of revenue from the fees they were required to pay. For an institution to maintain its budget allocation it must maintain its number of students. In the context of a "no growth" situation, there can be pressure to lower admission standards to maintain student numbers on entry. There can be pressure to reduce failure rates so that the drop-out rate over the period of the course is kept low, with a consequent drop in academic standards required to achieve success in a particular course.

An instituion is accountable for the quality of its courses—both to students and to the wider community; it has a responsibility to students in ensuring that "earnings foregone" are justified by tertiary study, not simply in the sense of future employability but in relation to the question of balance between what is offered by the courses and the time and effort given to them by a student. Formula funding transforms a student into an E.F.T. (equivalent full time student) index and education into a consumer good. Neither fact can be ignored, but funding exigencies and the need for courses to remain economically viable must not detract from the fundamental purpose of a higher education institution which is to educate well.

The quality of educational provision may become a secondary matter in terms of staff attraction with the avoidance of staff redundancy and the efficient allocation of resources taking so much time that the essential educational needs of students, and an institution's responsibility to be accountable to students for the educational provision, are overlooked. In times of economic downturn the students themselves may tend to lose their "consumer consciousness". In times of economic uncertainty, students are more concerned with passing examinations than questioning the nature of their learning. If they do not pass they do not get a job, and nowhere is this more clear today than in entry to the teaching profession.

While student activism has lessened significantly in more recent years, institutions continue to acknowledge an obligation to allow student participation in internal affairs. Student representation on important committees is the major means for ensuring that institutions remain accountable to their clients even if, in the light of the transience of the student population, such requirements may appear to be gestures. Nonetheless, with an increasing number of mature age students in higher education,many of them undertaking study while employed, the student voice will continue to have significant influence on the development of courses.

Institutions also acknowledge their responsibility to students in the provision of careers advisory, counselling and employment services. Unfortunately with restrictions in funding,such services, which do not relate directly to courses, may be reduced. Most higher education institutions are charged in their charters to foster a "corporate life". With changing clientele, and changing needs of students this responsibility is becoming increasingly difficult to interpret and realise.

Student unions or associations provide an important formal body which can ensure that institutions remain responsible to their clientele. The degree of autonomy granted to student unions varies from institution to institution, and one likely outcome of the present moves by the Federal Government and some State governments to curtail the powers of student associations could well be to reduce their power to make institutions remain properly accountable to their students. To say that participation in the formal decision making bodies of the colleges is a sufficient channel to ensure accountability to students ignores the fact that very few students are actually involved in such committees. Higher education institutions need both avenues. They need the participation of students on decision making bodies, and they need strong organisations which can make the institutions alert to and much more responsive to the needs of students. Few higher education institutions now deny student participation in decision making processes. Students increasingly are being appointed to staff selection committees. The work of students on committees and councils is, apart from its value in aiding effective decision making, an important learning experience for students about democratic decision making, or at least about an academic institution's practical interpretation of this.

It is a truism that the quality of an educational institution's teaching program is only as high as the quality of the academic staff. In the period of rapid expansion prior to 1975 it was difficult to find staff of appropriate quality to fill the many new positions being created as the number of institutions grew. In recent times competition among academics for fewer appointments has resulted in appointments of high academic quality in both colleges and universities. As Campbell (1976: para. 7.69) points out,

> the colleges are finding, as are the universities, that in numerous disciplines ... it is a 'buyer's market', and that new appointments of very high quality, in terms of both academic standing and experience, can be made to vacant lectureships.

Such a situation can only be of benefit to the general level of teaching in higher education institutions. On the other hand, fewer positions means a lower rate of turnover of staff and a much longer wait to achieve promotion. Reduced levels of funding with high proportions of staff in tenured positions have forced institutions to adopt stricter promotion policies and significant moves toward employing more contract staff on fixed term appointments (*Ibid.,* para 5.42). To many academic staff such a prospect is undesirable since they consider that "tenure within tertiary institutions is fundamental to the preservation of academic freedom" (Spaull, 1978: 87) and that fixed-term appointments "undermine the relationship between tenure and academic freedom and through the denial of academic freedom to some academics whose intellectual qualities are not in question, create a category of second-class academics" (*ibid*).

The present reduced requirement for teacher education (involving reductions of intakes as high as 20 per cent on those of the previous year, at least in the short term) may bring in their train staff redundancy and the need for staff to re-train to teach in new areas. While an examination of age profiles of staff suggests that early retirement would cushion the effect and that a reduction in staff student ratios in Australia (which do not yet reach those accepted in some other countries) would further cushion the effect, there will still be a need for hard decisions to be made.

In this context the recent review of study leave made by the Tertiary Education Commission is most significant, for while academic staff have a reasonable expectation that time for on-going research, the up-grading of qualifications or the retraining in new areas will be granted after a number of years of service in an institution, the Draft Report has produced a number of important findings on the nature of such provisions. These findings relate particularly to institutional and individual accountability. For example, the Report recommends that staff undertaking study leave be required to account formally for that privilege:

> *The Working Party ... considered that there was much room for improvement in administrative arrangements adopted to control staff development leave schemes in colleges and has included in its recommendations proposals which it believes will achieve a higher level of accountability in professional experience programs.*
> (Tertiary Education Commission, Draft Report on Study Leave, 1978: para. 9.18)

Similar comments are applied to universities. The Report further recommends that each college

> *publish information annually on the operation of the special studies program, including data on grants made for overseas travel purposes, and provide such other statistical data on the program to the State advanced education co-ordinating authority and the Tertiary Education Commission as is determined by the Commission.*
> (*Ibid.,* para. 9(a))

Again, a similar recommendation is made for universities. The Working Party states its belief that

> *it would be desirable for universities to make more information publicly available on the operation of their special studies programs including the general benefits to themselves and the community which result. An*

appropriate vehicle for transmission of this information would be the university annual report."

(*Ibid.,* para. 5.41).

In addition, the Working Party requires annual statistical information on the operation of study leave programs to assess the effectiveness of programs. Similar requirements are made of colleges of advanced education.

The external constraints implied by the Draft Report on Study Leave will flow over into the establishment of internal structures in higher education institutions to meet them, at least for those institutions that do not have such structures. There may well be other areas of inquiry in future. The recently announced national Enquiry into Teacher Education to be chaired by Professor Auchmuty may well determine new parameters for the training of teachers. The effect of this could again be to change institutional structures, with external demands for accountability being converted to internal controls. Academic freedom for staff members paid from government funds is only a right as long as governments leave it that way. Too often in the past in education, staff have responded to quantitative questions with philosophical answers and have given qualitative questions no answers at all. It will be the challenge to staff in the immediate future to meet the increasing external demands for accountability by ensuring that the institutional structures are adequate to meet them.

Financial Accountability

Legal accountability to government in terms of finance relates mainly to the audit function which focuses almost exclusively on resource inputs, on "balancing the books" and ensuring that funds are expended appropriately in terms of the function of the institution. Little attention is paid to internal resource allocation except where there is a significant change in expenditure on a particular item compared with the previous year. Nor in the audit function is there any judgement made on the quality of output for the amount of input. Increasingly this is an area that governments will examine in comparing the costs of courses both within and between sectors.

At the institutional level financial accountability focuses on the requirement to achieve a successful audit. Internal checks on expenditure and revenue are rigorous, with stipulated levels of authorisation and lines of responsibility clearly formalised. Without the difficulty of having to "earn" the income in the sense that a normal business does, once the budget allocation has been made, keeping within the budget is a straightforward business if appropriate controls are exercised. What is more difficult is to achieve an equitable resource allocation to meet all the competing demands for funds within an institution. Attempts to allocate resources to departments solely on the basis of student numbers is not practicable. New areas have fewer students; older areas often have larger numbers of senior staff. Different institutions have different systems for resource allocation, none of which is perfect, and there is much intuitive decision making required. Yet it could be claimed that "a budget is an accurate representation of an organisation's real preferences" (Dufty, 1976: 225).

How do institutions determine equitable resource allocation? That is, how do they order and assess their "real preferences"? Budget committees make recommendations to finance committees and work in liaison with other decision making bodies, but the appropriate model for efficient budget determination continues to be a source of debate. The "means-ends" question, for example, has considerable relevance to the notion of institutional accountability; that is, "self-justifying objectives" (Harrold, 1974: 115) such as the attainment of particular resource facilities not specifically related to overall educational goals is a good example. Unused equipment, under-employed secretaries and technicians are a tribute to this form of fund allocation.

The preparation of a satisfactory budget requires an understanding of institutional functions and aims. However, as Dufty (1976: 220) notes, "very few universities and similar organisations have specifically and operationally defined their objectives. Most statements of goals are couched in vague generalities ..." This is equally true at institutional, course and subject levels. Where aims overlap between courses, the resources should overlap or be common. For educational institutions, establishing appropriate formulas for the allocation of resources is a major exercise. Cost benefit analysis as a means for assessing policy proposals has proven difficult where the evaluation of benefits in educational institutions is concerned; cost-effectiveness and other project analysis techniques represent attempts to allocate resources in relation to important policy goals translated into "target objectives, the achievement of which can be quantitatively assessed" (*Ibid.,* 6). Such a procedure means that the least costly manner of pursuing a particular objective effectively may be selected. All such procedures represent an attempt to quantify as far as is possible the procedures for decision making on resource allocation. More recent approaches to the problem of resource allocation have centred on the Planning, Programming and Budgeting System (PPBS), a procedure by which planned expenditures are allocated to specific program objectives and which "ties resource allocation to program production, qualitative considerations and operational goals" (Burke, 1977: 396).

Budgeting systems attempt to provide an impartial means for internally distributing resources. Because of unclear goals, the lack of rigid and centralised decision making structures, and financial time-horizons (long-range planning, for example, is essential to program budgeting rationality) the development of budgeting models with direct application to tertiary education has proven difficult. Equally,

Widely-accepted norms of non-interference with educational decision-making and the highly educated and professional nature of the work-force make close supervision and input-based criteria such as class contact hours inappropriate.

(Dufty, 1976: 233)

While output measures in terms of equivalent full-time students or similar criteria are preferable, adequate monitoring of output quality is difficult; for example, how does an institution assess whether the quality of research or teaching has improved in proportion to some significant additional allocation of resources?

One important aspect of a budgeting model is that it does not fully describe the resource allocation process, which, as Dufty (1976) notes, is also affected by internal and external pressure groups. Apart from the lack of appropriate output measures it is the political nature of internal decision making systems which hampers the proper application of program budgeting.

Efficient and effective resource allocation is particularly relevant in the context of present external conditions of reduced funding. Increased demands for efficiency, for example, make more obvious the possibility of widening the options of an institution. Even such simple exercises as monitoring the excessive use of electricity, and similar economic measures, can have surprising effects, releasing funds for more appropriate areas. The concept of efficiency needs further examination by institutions; not only in the use of budgeting philosophy where applicable, but as a means for enabling an institution to use more creatively and purposively its "hidden" resources.

One such area where considerable research could be done would be to help academics use their time more efficiently in achieving course and institutional goals. Simply stated, is time spent on preparing for teaching more or less effective than time spent on assessing student work? Those institutions that can achieve a resource allocation which allows maximum flexibility are those which will remain healthy. There is much debate, for example, on what percentage of the total budget should be spent on salaries. Such figures are only guides, however, and what is important is that fixed allocations do not prohibit expenditures on items such as study leave, conference travel, student supervision, and essential student services.

Institutional Structures—Collegiate and Bureaucratic

> The complex operations of a modern college or university demand a sophisticated management information system that supplies full and correct information to those who need it when they need it and in a form they can understand. The number of people who need information and the amount and complexity of the information have taken a quantum leap in recent years. This trend will accelerate in the years ahead as ... federal and state bodies hold colleges and universities increasingly accountable.
>
> (Burke, 1977: 395)

This is a statement on the United States higher education scene which has obvious relevance for Australian higher education—namely, the need for effective administration and in consequence a growing institutional dichotomy between administrators and academics, between "bureaucratic" and "collegiate" processes. And while it is generally agreed that "governance is not an end in itself but a means to the final goal of maintaining and improving the quality of programs, activities and life on campus" (*ibid.:* 400), there is a clear demarcation between college and university staff in terms of the bureaucratic and collegiate models.

The Bureaucratic Model

Coordination of multi-level and sizable campuses requires certain bureautcratic structures, if only to implement effectively policies and decisions of a collegiate process. Demands for information related to external accountability generally come from bureaucracies such as government departments or the secretariats of coordinating authorities or commissions, and responses require a well-defined bureaucratic organisation within an institution. Often the time given for an institution to respond to a particular request is too short for the democratic or collegiate apparatus to operate. If action is to be taken at all, then the bureaucratic administrative apparatus must act. The collegiate or democratic structure can respond after the event; it is extremely difficult for it to be part of the event. The tertiary education sector is sufficiently diverse that it requires rapid goal-orientated and centralised decision-making by institutions if administration is to be efficient.

In many ways it is the responsibility of the institution's bureaucracy to act on behalf of the institution by dealing effectively with the external pressures and protecting academic staff from them so that they may get on with their teaching or research largely unaware of these day-to-day demands. As McCaig (1972: 105) points out, because

> *communication between the outside world and the (institution) is through the central administration, and as the issues are usually vital to the survival and well-being of the institution, the administration has emerged quite suddenly as a powerful member of the triumvirate of teacher, student and administrator.*

A corollary of such change has been the development of higher education administration as a profession, with the "professional administrator" continuing to replace, particularly in universities, faculty members who may reluctantly accept what they see as temporary positions.

As the collegiate and bureaucratic systems seem to move further away from each other in terms of function and attitude, so a 'dynamic antagonism' has developed between them. It is the common cry of academics, for example, that "the administration" lives in another world whose goals and interests are far removed from the essential processes of education. Furthermore, academic staff see themselves as moving further away from the real source of power, now in the hands of "the bureaucrats".

The bureaucracies found in educational institutions are not static; they do not exhibit the characteristics of Weber's ideal bureaucracy with its assumptions of goal definition, ordered hierarchies, rules and clear functional responsibility. Such rigidity and clarity do not relate to the more dynamic situation of a college or university bureaucracy—ambiguous goals, unclear technology, vulnerability to environmental relations, and the large professional staffing component differentiate them from classic bureaucracies. Equally, Weber's essentially static model does not tell us anything about informal hierarchies and informal processes of power and influence. The model does not explain change over time, nor does it inform us of the manner in which decisions are made (Baldridge *et al.*, 1977).

The Collegiate Model

The collegiate model works on a 'dynamic consensus' (*ibid.:* 11) being based on the notions of democratic participation by a 'community of scholars' with a commonality of interest. However it is also inadequate as a description of what actually occurs in tertiary institutions. As Baldridge *et al.* (1977) point out, the collegiate model is weak in that descriptive and normative visions are often confused. That is, those in favour of such a consensual model often colour what actually exists with what should be happening. More particularly, the model fails to deal adequately with the problem of conflict.

Both models represent simplifications of the processes of decision making and institutional dynamics, and because neither model has direct application to higher education some writers have favoured the term 'organised anarchy' as most applicable to higher education institutions. This term reflects a view of institutional dynamics as a system which, when carefully observed, has little central coordination or control. Alternatively a 'political' model has been proposed which takes account of the influence of external groups, the politics of interest group pressures and the adaptability and compromise which characterise institutional policy-making. Decisions "are not simply bureaucratic orders but are often negotiated compromises between competing groups" (*ibid.*: 15). This notion has led Clark (1977) to suggest that an educational institution is really a "federation of professionals".

It is not our present purpose to search for the appropriate paradigm for describing institutional dynamics. It is clear that a number of elements operate—bureaucratic, collegiate and political—which are not mutually exclusive, and that there are both formal and informal power structures within tertiary institutions. In practice, however, there is a perceived distinction between bureaucratic (administrative) and collegiate (academic) structures. There need not be polarisation of or mutual antagonism between these two structures, as both are necessary in any academic institution; different tasks and decision making processes require different approaches. What is important is for both academic staff and the administration to understand which model is operating in the particular circumstance.

One area of conflict between collegiate and bureaucratic processes is the appointment of staff. It is often stated, for example, that deans and heads of departments should be selected by staff rather than appointed by administrators.

This procedure is said to be more democratic, more likely to lead to appointments which will be more acceptable to members of the department or school and more likely to avoid an authoritarian style of administration.

(Harman and Selby Smith, 1976: 137). The question raised by such a matter is "who has the right to decide what is best, and why?" In the end, the answer to this question must be that the governing body of the institution has this right, and the decisions they make may well differ from institution to institution.

Academics often regard bureaucratic participation in such areas of decision making as an intrusion into areas in which they have little understanding. Senior administrators view such appointments from a dual stance. They accept a responsibility for the quality and competence of the academic staff of the institution and are aware of the need to satisfy internal demands for equity and efficient departmental functioning. However their interests are necessarily different; their orientation is political. The need to reconcile conflicting interests (both internal and external) may require different strategies from the procedure of democratic election. Administrators assume responsibility for the effective functioning of the system; academics need not be accountable for any area outside their own, where the accountability, at least to the present time, is limited. One consequence of democratic decision making is that no one person is ultimately responsible for the appropriateness of a decision. Most who have worked in an institution of higher education have observed a collegiate decision which is either impossible to implement or for which no volunteers can be found to undertake its implementation. Centralised decision making assumes responsibility and defines areas of accountability in a way that appears to contribute directly to the effective functioning of the total system.

There are some issues which are clearly best dealt with by the collegiate process, such as the formulation of significant policies or the determination of institutional responses to such events as institutional amalgamation, while others may be more efficiently handled by bureaucratic procedures. Such issues require a coordinated overview of the institution. Where a rapid response is required, the often lengthy procedures for democratisation cannot be properly used. Equally, bureaucratic methods "can assist in the effective and expeditious execution of decisions" (Davies, 1972: 69). While the concepts of individual professional discretion and departmental or faculty discretion denote a decentralised organisation in preference to centralised organisation, the limits of such discretions and their determination are key issues. What is required is an organisation which preserves relative academic freedom while ensuring efficiency and appropriate resource allocation.

It is not possible (nor is it desirable) to ensure democratic participation or departmental self-determination in every decision. Nor is it possible for administrators to formulate policies and ensure their effective implementation without input from, and devolution of responsibility to, academic departments. Nonetheless, collegiate decision making takes more time, and time is a valuable resource, the allocation of which should be monitored closely. It seems most appropriate that the governing body of the institution ensure that the issues decided by collegiate processes are worth the time spent on them.

As has been noted, neither collegiate nor academic properly describes the process of institutional dynamics. Informal power structures also provide a real power base. These informal structures are difficult to make legitimate, yet their effect is considerable. Appropriate monitoring of the informal structures and alerting particular individuals in the institution to impending decisions and policies helps smooth the formal policy making channels. Even in terms of collegiate decision making there is internal segmentation "by sub-college, by division and particularly by department" (Clark, 1977: 70). Increased size means increased segmentation, which means increased difficulty in campuswide coordination. Hence the institution "increasingly moves toward the means normal to large-scale organisation, to bureaucratic means" (*ibid*). Where in a small institution of two or three hundred students the academic staff of the whole institution may form the collegiate, in much larger institutions collegiate sub-groups must form and hence the whole staff can never feel and act as one. In a small institution the informal structures are much more easily identified and used. The larger the institution the more difficult it is to know whether the appropriate informal structure has been used.

Increasing external pressures and the rapid growth of many institutions, in particular those involved in recently announced amalgamations, create considerable tension within an institution, and it is particularly difficult to reconcile the conflict between "bureaucratic" coordination and goal direction with the role and power expectations of individual members of an institution. To determine appropriate methods for dealing with such conflict is a considerable task. As Davies (1972: 68) notes

> *If ... it is difficult to agree on objectives, on priorities and to measure whatever it is that the organisation is supposed to produce, it will not be surprising if we argue over the type of organisation (or organisations) most likely to satisfy the community of scholars, students and administrators within the (institution) as well as the wider public associated with it.*

In an academic institution there is a natural dynamic tension between collegiate and bureaucratic processes with the political forces providing the context within which each may operate. There is no ideal academic or administrative structure for an academic institution. The best one is that which works most effectively in a particular institution with the particular individuals involved. At best, an institution can attempt to deal with conflicting demands in decision making by using whichever processes seem at the time to fulfil the criteria of efficiency and equity.

The Role and Responsibility of Academics and Administrators in the Context of Accountability

Academics

The problem of measuring the outputs of an educational institution has already been discussed. For example, there are few performance indicators which may be applied to ensure that staff members are providing relatively equal contributions to the academic process. While an academic's research may be judged by its level of acceptance among his peers in the public forum of presented papers and published works, no similar system applies against which teaching performance may be assessed. Just how can academics be made accountable for their teaching competence? While many institutions of higher education in Australia have established centres for research into teaching, their impact is still minimal on the total teaching program of the institutions. Too often, demonstrated success as a researcher rather than as a teacher provides the main criterion for promotion. Evaluation of staff, where it occurs at all, is by peer assessment through collegiate discussion or by student evaluation, where response is left to the discretion of the individual. Evaluation may encompass course content and the quality of student work, but only rarely does a staff member's ability as a teacher come under scrutiny. Any suggestion that evaluation techniques should be applied to the teaching process are considered as an intrusion on the professional autonomy of the teacher:

> *Faculty members regard themselves as the defenders of academic values and ideals, besieged by lay persons whose insistence on the application of the business standards and measures will, whether intended or not, destroy the fragile character of higher education. Only they, educational professionals,*

can properly judge whether the educational process is working well on their campus; and only they can prescribe and implement proper remedies.

(Burke, 1977: 396)

Yet the defence of academic freedom does not exempt staff from being accountable for the quality and nature of the education they provide. The level of scholarship of academic staff is not in question; rather it is the staff member's level of commitment to his students (compared with his commitment to research) and the quality of the instruction provided.

The most recent Academic Salaries Tribunal Report, with its emphasis on quality of teaching as providing necessary evidence for progress within a particular academic scale or promotion between scales, has brought about a more conscious effort on the part of institutions to assess teaching performance as an important criterion.

Discrepancies between status and performance in teaching would be less disturbing if it could be shown that those not engaged in teaching were advancing the general stock of universal knowledge through indpenedent research. This remains to be proven, but what is clearly needed is a greater concern to measure overall productivity, a more searching instrument of internal management than the present cursory enquiries on class sizes and teaching commitments.

(Scott, 1978: 6)

The Tertiary Education Commission has maintained that "standards in the provision of tertiary education should be capable of improvement whether the system is static or expanding" (*op. cit.:* para. 4.85d) and has stated its commitment to "raise the general quality of tertiary education by promoting a climate of critical self-assessment within institutions and encouraging the development of evaluative skills" (*op. cit.:* para. 4.85). Critical self-assessment rests on a spirit of academic autonomy, yet it will be for each institution, through whatever structure it may adopt, to ensure that the combination of teaching and research functions are performed at a sufficient level for each academic staff member, and these will be considered particularly in the granting and maintaining of tenure. It is difficult at the moment for an institution to demonstrate to the public that the quality of its teaching, as well as its research, are at a sufficient level. In the face of growing public demands for accountability such demonstrations may well be required.

Administrators

To whom are administrators responsible? Line and function responsibilities are determined by the governing body of an educational institution, or, in the case of very senior administrators, are incorporated in the relevant Act and its attendant statutes. Yet such responsibilities are usually very broadly defined. More important to the question of accountability for administrators are the methods for measuring the effectiveness of those responsible for coordinating and implementing institutional activities.

Hawkins (1975) discusses the problem at length and notes that (as in the case of academic staff) the task requires a different approach from that of private business management with its clear efficiency determinants (such as profit yardsticks with respect to assets and sales). He suggests that indirect measurement of the performance of educational administrators could consider the efficient running of the organisation, the attitudes of students and staff to the performance of administrators, the non-functional requirements imposed on students and staff by administration, and the concern of administration for quality in teaching and in degree programs offered. In particular, he raises a number of questions which are highly relevant to the efficient functioning of administrators: Does the administrator learn from errors, or do the same ones continually occur? How well does the administration anticipate and plan for problems that can be reasonably predicted? How much red-tape and paperwork does the administration require of staff and students? To these might be added: Does the administration believe in self-assessment? Is it prepared to initiate review of existing organisational practices and structures with the object of improving quality and efficiency? For, as administrators are often at the peak of the power structure, a review of their effectiveness must in general be self-initiated. While administrators are accountable to the governing body of an institution the question of review of efficiency and quality is seldom raised (except in serious matters relating to internal crises or a threatened termination of appointment). Moreover, as external review procedures are more likely to present a realistic assessment of institutional performance, perhaps the notion of an "institutional ombudsman" as promoted by the University of Melbourne Working Group (Skertchley, 1974a) or a similar permanent consultative body capable of ongoing appraisal of the institution (and of itself) could be appropriate. Alternatively, research units within educational institutions could undertake impartial review of various aspects of institutional functioning. Perhaps, as Hawkins (1975: 31) states:

> *Administration can in the final analysis do no more than try to foster faculty to teach and interact with students and grow in their disciplines. It can attempt to efficiently utilise resources, see that details of operating the instituion (are) as smooth and functionally positive as possible, and create the climate for the most meaningful educational experience possible. In the long run these represent the real test of how well the administration has performed.*

While such sentiments are valid and desirable the problem of measuring efficiency and evaluating progress remains. It is the responsibility of administration to concern itself with more than "tidy academic book-keeping and the political justice of fund allocations between departments" (Harrold, 1974: 79). It is easy for administrators (as for academics) to be tempted to use arguments about intangibles to avoid efforts to come to terms with the problems of qualitative accountability; yet the need for them to explore possibilities openly is as important as it is for academics to accept some accountability for the consequences of their performance.

Constitution of Institutional Structures

The governing body of an institution is accountable to government for the management and administration of the institution. Subject to Parliamentary approval, a governing body may make, alter or repeal statutes and by-laws. The powers and functions of the governing body, as well as its composition, are prescribed in legislation establishing the institution. The level of autonomy granted to an institution by virtue of its Act indicates the extent of self-determination that may be achieved. The higher the level of autonomy granted, the lower the formal accountability processes imposed from outside and the greater is the assumption by the governing body of responsibility for institutional activities. In such cases, where Parliament makes the institution largely accountable to itself for its activities, it is the composition of the governing body which is relied on to act *pro bono publico*. Generally this is achieved by appointing to a governing body a greater number of outsiders than employees of the institution. For example, the Council of Torrens College of Advanced Education comprises fifteen government appointees and ten employees of the College.

Governing bodies are generally considered to include "responsible" members of the general community. As they are not paid for their services and are not shareholders it is reasonable to ask to whom they are responsible. One might simply answer to no-one but themselves, at least for their term of office. Harman and Selby Smith (1976) discuss the issues regarding the composition of college councils, particularly in relation to the question of what characteristics determine those who have a legitimate interest in advanced education and a case for representation on such councils:

> *What kind of balance of interests is desirable? Should this vary substantially between colleges? What is the real function of a college council: is it, for example, a means to channel the opinions of interest groups, a link between government and tertiary teaching, a governing board, or a board of review?*
>
> (138)

They cite data which, as might be anticipated, shows that college council members "are by no means a typical cross-section of the community" (*ibid*) as they have a male-dominated, generally highly educated and highly paid membership; that is, members are most often in positions of high occupational status. While their composition is partly intended to ensure the desired balance of expertise, opinion, contacts and community acceptance:

> *Some critics have seen the heavy concentration of representation from industry and government as part of a neo-capitalist conspiracy to immobilise 'human and natural resources ... in direct pursuit of corporate ends'. Others, perhaps less radical in outlook, have been more concerned about balance between the interests and occupational groups represented in College Councils and State advanced education boards."*
>
> (133)

There are generally some academic staff elected to a council. What are their responsibilities to their electorate? To whom is the "nominee of the [State] Director-General of Education" responsible? What relevance have such clauses as "A member of the Council should not, in the exercise of his powers or functions as such, be subject to the direction of any person or body of persons"? (Torrens College of Advanced Education Act, 1972, Clause 8.7). While the integrity of members of governing bodies is not being questioned here it is clear that the powers, functions, duties and obligations of such bodies have not been analysed adequately. The governing body of an institution of higher education, as the ultimate decision making body, must act at times as a Board of Review and as such provides a focus for institutional accountability. In many ways it should represent its publics—staff, students, employers and so on, in microcosm. Yet how do the individual members remain responsive to the sectors from which they are drawn and so be in a position to ensure not only appropriate internal structures for accountability, but in some measure to protect the institution from unfair external demands for accountability?

There is rarely debate whether a governing body's meetings should be held in open session. They generally are, and this provides a measure of accountability both to internal and external publics. Even if a large number of staff or others do not attend, the availability of agenda papers and minutes ensures that decision making in the institution is subject to the widest possible scrutiny.

Committees are formal mechanisms established to aid the decision making function of the governing body. A committee may only act with the power delegated to it by the governing body. Committees ensure that democratic participation in decision making can occur; they provide a system of internal checks, enable a devolution of authority which is important to the coordination and efficient functioning of the institution, and by delegation have a certain measure of autonomy which allows some sense of participation and self-determination for an institution's members. Whether committees are "open" or "closed" varies from institution to institution. An increasing number of institutions conduct virtually all such meetings in open session except where matters pertaining to individuals are being discussed. Also, many institutions make their chief executive officer and their titular head *ex officio* members to reinforce the fact that such committees are always answerable to the governing body. The composition of council committees varies. Generally governing bodies allow the academic business of the college, conducted through an academic committee, to be the responsibility of the academics and students of the institution. On the other hand a finance committee may have a preponderance of persons from outside the college as members. Generally, any committee of a council would have student, academic and general staff members, again ensuring a measure of internal accountability.

Appointment and promotions committee meetings are generally held in closed session because individuals are always involved. There is considerable debate on whether students should be appointed to such committees, on what the actual committee composition should be, and on the extent to which information from the deliberations of these committees should be released. There is no doubt that the policies and procedures of such committees, if not the meetings themselves, should be open to scrutiny.

The recording of the business of any committee is an important part of the accountability function. Agendas and minutes should be available for scrutiny and should be to inform rather than confuse.

The committee system provides a useful paradigm for the operation of accountability within an institution. However, as Topley and Willett (1976: 57) note, "there tend to be pyramids of committees and, often, the traditional (institution) has replaced hierarchy of position by a hierarchy of committees". Moreover there is an informal power structure which operates—perhaps inevitably—within the committee system. Whether the internal power politics interfere with the formal processes of accountability is difficult to determine. Certainly it is possible for dominant and powerful members of an institution to manipulate the system to personally-designed ends; hence, while members are accountable to those whom they represent, it is not always the case that their interests are properly served. It is unlikely, however, that an institution can formally legislate to preserve ideal democratisation.

One effect of the changed environment in tertiary education where increasingly rapid decisions need to be made is the establishment of small *ad hoc* committees to undertake specific tasks. Sometimes these committees have delegated power to act, sometimes they must report their findings back to a superior committee. Generally a council looks to its main standing committees and to its chief executive officer for advice. Major areas for which a governing body is accountable usually have their own committees. For example legal matters, recurrent finance, capital, academic matters and staffing are usually the responsibility of separate committees and policies in such areas. A chief executive officer is likely to establish his own series of committees to advise on matters not covered in the major committees. These often relate to matters of implementation, such as publicity and publications, timetable, leave and so on.

The participative process functions adequately where deliberation and discussion are essential and where time is available for the often lengthy involvement required for policies to be determined. However committees can often provide an impediment to action; the diffusion of responsibility means that implementation of committee initiatives may be delayed. Nevertheless, as external restraints on institutional initiative can be beneficial, particularly in ensuring that inappropriate actions are not taken, so the committee system within an institution is an important means for ensuring responsible action.

Responsiveness to Change

The obligations of an institution to act on evidence presented through internal self-examination imply that the institution should be responsive to and undertake change. Changes may occur either because of external forces (for example, changes in funding levels or the fundings of a duly constituted State or national enquiry) or because of internal forces (for example, students pressing for greater representation on decision making bodies). The higher the level of autonomy of an institution the more important it is that the impetus for change must come from within the institution. Generally, universities are less affected by external forces than are colleges of advanced education, and the possibilities for institutionally derived change are therefore greater.

The enabling Acts for the college of advanced education sector are clear. The institution generally has authority over its internal organisation whereas external forces operate in relation to the establishment and standards of courses. Universities have complete internal control over their courses and hence one might expect considerable innovation and change in this area. This is to some extent true, but the external academic press has a significant effect on the courses offered. Skertchley (1976) has noted that "the established Australian university scene is characterised by conformity" (15), that "in essence we have numerous well-established educational institutions formulated to meet the past"

(16), and that "existing learning institutions are not constituted and operated so as to effectively meet continuing change" (14). He considers that innate conservatism and a high degree of bureaucratisation have provided two major constraints on institutional "self-renewal", and notes the temptation for new institutions to replicate traditional models, which merely perpetuates the dominant change-inhibiting factors of rigidity and conformity. Hence the traditional university model is seen as counter-productive in relation to adaptability and responsiveness to change, which are becoming increasingly important in the politics of survival. Such a view highlights the shift in the role of the university from an active initiator of social change to the more "passive"   respondent to external change, which characterises the higher education institutions today. The complexity and bureaucratic coordinating structures of modern institutions are seen by Skertchley and other writers as formidable obstacles to internal (and cohesive) commitment to change. One suggested mechanism for enabling the massive bureaucratisation of institutions to co-exist with the dynamic initiative necessary to implement change has been the formulation of an 'opposition' or 'shadow administration' within an institution. Skertchley (*ibid.:* 17) cites the establishment of an 'agent for change' in the form of "an all-campus consultative University Assembly ... (which) has as one of its functions the initiation of change outside the formal executive bureaucracy" and whose members are drawn from the whole institution. The aim of such a body is to "maintain a constructively critical dialogue" about the institution. Such a body could well provide a useful ongoing review of institutional directions while facilitating change.

While colleges of advanced education are already prevented from easily implementing socially-related change in terms of course development, there are numerous areas where organisational change is possible; indeed, the potential for self-determination in relation to course development exists in that all colleges of advanced education have a capacity for imaginative resource allocation and an opportunity to discuss and develop course initiatives to be presented to coordinating authorities for approval.

With the fall in numbers of students entering pre-service courses, particularly in education and some sciences and technologies, both colleges and universities are proposing new courses to attract students. In colleges such courses are often proposed at the Graduate Diploma level in a whole range of highly specific areas never before offered in this country and which tend to leave the coordinating authorities gasping. The conservatism of coordinating bodies generally manages to restrain the wilder flights of college fancy. Universities are not blameless in this regard but their natural conservatism tends to constrain any tendency toward academic excess. Nonetheless, change is needed and the trial of innovative new courses should be encouraged in both sectors.

For both types of institution, the demands of bureaucratisation and the tendency to retain familiar and proven structures are perhaps the greatest factors in change inhibition. There is an institutional need to "maintain stability within a context of change" (Australian Conference of Principals of Colleges of Advanced Education, 1977: 2).

Moreover, should an institution decide to review structures and policies which could include the offering of innovative new courses, evaluation of alternative futures is a diffucult procedure. Such a process requires some clarity of institutional goals translated into short term objectives. As goal ambiguity is one of the main characteristics of academic organisations the process of change is further complicated:

> *The traditional, departmentally organised (university) has typically, little development of positive, purposive institutional goals ... the very diversity and number of goal sub-sets cannot, in any operational sense, be summed into an institutional goal-complex.*
>
> (Topley and Willett, 1976: 57)

Even where an institution has a fairly clear idea of the objectives to be attained, cost considerations and qualitative assessments of outcomes are not easily taken into account. In fact, from the time a decision is made to investigate the possibility of introducing a new four-year course to the time the first graduates emerge can take up to ten years.

Institutions are in the midst of change, but unlike the changes of the past decade the changes in the next will be brought about in a context of constraint. Present pressures for institutional change are directly related to the accountability of the university and advanced education sectors for the type, quality and relevance of the education they provide. Acceptance of responsibility at the institutional level requires a thorough review of internal structures and methodologies in relation to perceived functions and goals. The two sectors are experiencing restraint, yet there is considerable room for improvement. A major challenge for the future involves a real need "to maintain a spirit of change and community responsiveness within a context of stability" (*ibid*). It is one thing to implement change in the context of growth, quite another in a climate of static funding. For an institution to retain the freedom to direct its own development requires a willingness to examine present realities and future possibilities and to implement change within constraint. If the institutions do not change themselves using their own internal structures, then it will be their own fault if institutional change is imposed from without. The dynamic tension between external and internal demands will require the refinement of institutional structures to make the public face of our higher education institutions more acceptable, and will become a major issue in higher education to be resolved in the next decade.

Chapter Six

Academic Accountability—Resources

G. Burke and P. A. McKenzie

Introduction

Calls for accountability in education are most often heard when resources are in short supply and when attention is drawn to supposed waste of resources. This chapter looks briefly in the first section at the notion of accountability and its relation to the concept of efficiency of resource use. A number of factors impinging on the availability and use of resources in higher education are discussed in the next section: fluctuations in student demand, graduate manpower problems, restriction on government expenditure, age of staff and tenure, and federal oversight of higher education.

In the light of these conceptual and empirical discussions the final section reviews the alternative procedures that are being urged, mainly from outside of higher education, to promote accountability, namely, an increase in market pressures through the reintroduction of fees or an increasing degree of bureaucratic control through State and Commonwealth Commissions.

Accountability and Objectives and Efficiency

The notion of accountability is based upon liability for responsibility, or in its simplest terms, "... making sure someone does what they are supposed to" (Wynne, 1976: 30). In the case of "someone" being the higher education sector, just what is it "supposed to do"?

Among the many objectives put forward for higher education are the following:
1. the advance of scholarship and knowledge,
2. the development of highly skilled manpower,
3. the promotion of a more equal, just society,
and
4. the full development of the individual.

The meaning of these objectives and the relative weight attached to them varies considerably between interest groups concerned with policy making for higher education: students, political parties of conservative or reformist outlook, taxpayers in general, employers, and, far from least, the staff of tertiary institutions. Hence, when we discuss alternative ways of promoting accountability, the discussion will necessarily be related to the power of different groups to emphasise particular objectives not only at the level of declared government policy, but also at the level of implementation of policy. For example, a commitment of governments toward greater equality of opportunity may be largely frustrated if tertiary institutions and their staff are able to apply strictly elitist entry criteria or to orient their teaching only to the more able.

The notion of *efficiency* logically should be subsumed by that of accountability: we should wish to be sure not only that resources are directed at the "agreed" objectives but also of the maximum achievement of those objectives for a given input. It is relatively easy to devise a system of accountability for control of government funds to ensure that they are not devoted to personal expense accounts or ski lodges. It is more difficult to ensure that resources are used efficiently. Some examples of inefficiency appear easy to define if not always easy to eliminate: for example, arbitrary or accidental differences in resources per student in similar courses (perhaps arising from declining enrolments, from historical differences in funding patterns or even from incorrect statistics).

A danger, however, even in such simple cases is that we will identify efficiency with inputs alone and presume that outputs are similar. There is a difficult—perhaps insuperable—task of finding appropriate indicators of outputs. Measures of student progression/graduation ratios (by social class), unemployment rates or earnings of graduates, and research articles published may be seen as relevant indicators but are inadequate and incomplete. A variety of outputs would be seen as non-measurable, particularly the external or "spillover" effects of more educated persons in society and of research. Even if we could find an acceptable set of indicators of output the problem of attaching appropriate weights to indicators of gains in knowledge relative to indicators of, say, manpower or equality remain.

Finally, we have little knowledge of the form of the production function in education, of the nature of the relationship between various combinations of resource inputs on the one hand and various outputs on the other. One of the major problems in any attempts to estimate production functions is to control for the effect of student characteristics such as social class or natural ability in educational achievement. It has proved very difficult in educational research to show that any particular combination of resources, or even an increasing quantity of resources, substantially affects student achievement.

In reviewing approaches to fostering accountability, we attempt in the last part of this chapter to indicate their likely influence on the efficiency with which various objectives are pursued. What we have shown in this section is that we should not be optimistic of firm conclusions because it is very difficult to say conclusively that one use of resources is more or less efficient than another. However, resources are limited and decisions must be made about their use, and these decisions will assume greater importance as the resources available for higher education come under even greater pressure; we now want to outline some of the major recent factors affecting inputs, the production process, and outputs in higher education in Australia.

Recent Trends

Before considering the prospect for improving the effectiveness of resource use in higher education it is necessary to consider a number of recently emerging

features of the Australian scene that have highlighted the need for efficiency but made its achievement more difficult. Among the most important factors are:
1. the possibility of declining student numbers from the early 1980s;
2. emerging graduate manpower problems;
3. the increasing pressure to contain all government expenditure and the declining priority given to education;
4. the increasing age of staff and reduced opportunities for new appointments;
5. the complexity and flux in Commonwealth-State arrangements for funding of tertiary education.

Student Numbers

Table 1 shows the projected numbers of students in the final year of secondary school (year 12). The projections are made on the assumption of a very slight rise in the retention of pupils to year 12 to about 1982 with an almost constant rate of retention thereafter. On these estimates final year enrolments will rise in 1978 and 1979, decline slightly in the early eighties, and then experience a sharp, short revival in the late eighties. We can expect a continued decline in the nineties as a result of the fall in births since 1971.

Students in the final year of secondary school are still the major single source of entrants to tertiary education in both colleges of advanced education (CAEs) and universities. On the estimates in Table 1 we might be hopeful of an increase in tertiary enrolments in the next few years at least, with fluctuations during the eighties.

We need to ask, however, whether
1. the projected final year enrolments will be achieved;

Table 1

Actual and Projected numbers of final year secondary students

Australia, 1977-87
(000's)

1975 (actual)	82
1976 (actual)	86
1977 (actual)	88
1978	91
1979	94
1980	93
1981	92
1982	90
1983	89
1984	90
1985	92
1986	96
1987	97

Source: Prepared by applying 1976-77 grade progression ratios progressively to enrolments in "years" 2 to 11 in 1977.

2. the proportion of final year secondary students proceeding to tertiary education will be maintained; and

3. entry to tertiary education by students other than those coming directly from secondary school will continue to rise as in recent years.

At least in the medium term (say, 3 to 5 years) it is doubtful that retention to year 12 will be as high as projected, or that the proportion of these students seeking tertiary enrolment will be maintained. On the one hand the emergence since 1974 of a high level of youth unemployment has encouraged school retention and tertiary participation. On the other, the decline in the expected financial benefits of tertiary education may be a stronger opposing factor, as English and American experience discussed by Gordon and Williams (1976) and Freeman (1976) would indicate.

The decline in relative earnings of tertiary graduates and their increasing difficulties in finding employment in specific major occupations, especially in teaching and engineering, could possibly more than offset the stimulus for obtaining better qualifications that could come from youth unemployment. This means that some of those who in the past would have proceeded to tertiary education might now compete for the insufficient number of jobs with early school leavers, concentrating unemployment even more solidly among the latter. This view of concentration of unemployment among the least skilled and experienced is shared by the Tertiary Education Commission in its report for the 1979-81 Triennium, but *not* the view that school retention or tertiary aspiration might fall. The Commission (p. 34) argues that the tendency for employers to increase their educational requirements in a tight labour market will continue to maintain educational participation.

While the problems of 'credentialism' are undoubtedly considerable its mere existence does not offer any guide to changes in educational participation: what is relevant is how it affects expected earnings and employment for various levels of education. Evidence on earnings suggests that the relative position of male graduates has been declining, perhaps since the late sixties. The relative earnings of female graduates improved in the five-year period to 1973-74 and has possibly improved further since then (as the 1976 Census data may show later this year). The dismal outlook in teaching, where over 50 per cent of female graduates and tertiary diplomates in the labour force have been employed, suggests a future sharp decline in earning prospects. Table 3 shows nursing to be the only other professional, technical occupation to provide substantial employment to females, and prospects there are contracting too. How marked the effect on educational participation will be is hard to assess given that the alternative employment available to female school leavers is heavily concentrated on clerical and sales occupations, and given that the rate of unemployment among female teenagers is slightly higher than among males.

The changing pattern in retention rates in Table 2 is compatible with the earning patterns just discussed. The male retention rate has remained below its 1972 peak *despite* youth unemployment. The female rate has continued to rise rapidly, from 25.5 to 36.6 per cent in seven years to 1977. Both may decline in the next few years.

Some indication of the advent of a downturn in school retention rates and in progress from school to tertiary education is provided by recent data. *Grade progression* ratios (e.g. the proportion of those in year 11 at time *t* moving to

Table 2

Apparent Secondary School Retention Rates[1]
First Secondary Year to Final Year
Australia, 1967-77

	Males	Females	total
1967	26.5	18.7	22.7
1968	28.5	21.2	25.0
1969	31.1	23.7	27.5
1970	33.0	25.5	29.3
1971	*34.1*	*26.9*	*30.6*
1972	35.7	28.9	32.4
1973	35.2	30.8	33.1
1974	34.1	31.6	32.9
1975	34.6	33.6	34.1
1976	*34.6*	*35.3*	*34.9*
1977	34.0	36.6	35.3

Source: Department of Education, Canberra.

Note: 1.   Apparent retention rate in year t is the number enrolled in year 12 at
1 August expressed as a percentage of the number enrolled in the
first year of secondary school the appropriate number of years before
(year t-5 in New South Wales, Victoria and Tasmania, year t-4 in
Queensland, South Australia and Western Australia).

year 12 at time $t + 1$) have declined in a number of States for the year 11 to year
12 transition in 1976 and 1977: the overall *retention* ratio to year 12 is still
shown to rise for Australia as a whole owing to the cumulative effects of higher
grade progression ratios for the lower secondary forms in the years since 1972.

Victoria is one State where school retention to year 12 has actually declined
recently, with the effect being an almost constant number of school students
qualifying for the Higher School Certificate (Partridge, 1978: 3, 5-6; the method
of analysis of qualifiers in the Partridge Report is open to question but the
general thrust is acceptable here). In addition, there was some evidence of a
decline in the proportion of those in HSC in 1977 intending to proceed to
tertiary education in 1978. Early information for 1978 suggests a further decline
in the HSC score needed for tertiary entry. Decline in entry standards for earlier
years is indicated in the Partridge Report: "This continued rise in tertiary
enrolments was sustained increasingly by drawing upon the less able sixth form
students and on mature age students meeting minimum educational standards"
(1978: 3, 7).

The Tertiary Education Commission notes a recent decline in the ratio of
students aged 19 years and under commencing courses to final year secondary
students in the previous year, though it hedges with the comment that "It is not

clear to what extent this is due to the policy of stabilising intakes or to changing community expectations of the value of a university or advanced education qualification" (1978: 36).

The maintenance of tertiary enrolments may thus depend on a continuation or increase in the recent high levels of entrants other than those from secondary school, including persons seeking to add to existing tertiary qualifications. Only about half the students commencing CAE courses and university undergraduate courses do so on the basis of final school examinations in the previous two years (and some of these may be mature age persons) (Australian Bureau of Statistics, 1977a: 29; 1977b: 25).

It is difficult to predict developments in such enrolments. The introduction of conversion courses, graduate diplomas and degree courses for teachers qualified at lower levels and the introduction of a variety of new Masters courses seem likely to partly sustain the apparent student load in tertiary institutions in the near future, but the outlook in the eighties must be more doubtful and may be affected by the willingness of institutions to provide bridging courses for mature age candidates.

On balance then, on the basis of student demand for places with the existing system of student assistance, it seems possible that enrolments in higher education will suffer a slight decline over the next decade. There is some possibility of a more substantial decline if employment prospects for graduates remain as dismal as currently projected in teaching and engineering, and other government employment remains under tight rein. Of course, action by government to cut the number of students commencing particular courses could also affect total enrolments. If the recommendations of the recent Partridge Report (1978) in Victoria are adopted, a cut in enrolments in initial teacher education and engineering will lead to an overall decline in tertiary enrolments unless there is a compensating increase in other course enrolments. In fact, we anticipate that the fall in student demand for places in teacher education at least, and possibly in engineering, will be greater than recommended by Partridge. And we suspect that compensating enrolments will be insufficient to maintain total tertiary enrolments. To take an explicit example, the situation of the institutions currently in the State College of Victoria must be under threat: in 1977 the State College was funded on the basis of 14300 equivalent full-time students (EFTS), but virtually all the available places in teacher education in 1982 may be at least 2000 students short of this figure. And there is little likelihood of a compensating massive expansion of, say, business studies or humanities courses.

The effects of declining enrolments (given funding based on student numbers), on staffing, on maintenance of such facilities as libraries and on the quality of courses (given the loss of 'economies' of scale), will require careful analysis. It is not unfair to say that this has barely been started in the Partridge Report. The preliminary chapters of the Anderson Report (1978) at least show more awareness of the problems.

Emerging Graduate Manpower Problems

Throughout the post-war period to the beginning of the seventies unemployment among graduates was virtually non-existent. Delays in obtaining employment, particularly that related to the field of undergraduate study, became more noticeable in the recession of the early seventies. The position has deteriorated in the current recession that began late in 1974. So far, the effect has been most marked on would-be engineers, architects and veterinarians and now with increasing severity on teachers, by far the largest group of all in professional employment, as shown in Table 3. The unemployment rate of graduates appears to be lower than the unemployment rate in the labour force as a whole, in May 1977, 2.5% compared with 3.7% (TEC. 1978: 28) although the rate of unemployment among engineers appears to be in excess of the rate of unemployment for all males aged 20 and over (Partridge, 1978: 5, 5-6; A.B.S., 1977d). Credentialism on the one hand, or actual acquisition of skills and attitudes on the other, suggest that unemployment among graduates will remain relatively low with graduates being substituted in employment at the expense of non-graduates.

Table 3

Employed Persons[1], By Occupation[2], May 1977
(000s)

	Males	Persons
Professional and Technical		
Architects, Engineers and Surveyors, Professional[3]	59.9	61.1
Chemists, Physicists, Geologists and Other Physical Scientists	12.1	12.6
Biologists, Veterinarians, Agronomists and Related Scientists	6.4	8.0
Medical Practitioners and Dentists	22.7	27.2
Nurses, including Probationers or Trainees	8.7	136.0
Professional Medical Workers	11.2	23.0
Teachers	99.5	244.8
Clergy and Related Members of Religious Orders	10.9	12.4
Law Professionals	14.3	16.2
Artists, Entertainers, Writers and Related Workers	29.2	44.7
Draftsmen and Technicians[3]	85.7	105.7
Other Professional, Technical and Related Workers	74.3	96.1
Total:	434.8	787.9
Total Employed Persons	3824.6	5885.7

Source: Australian Bureau of Statistics, *The Labour Force,* May 1977, Ref. 6.20

Notes: 1 Civilians aged 15 years and over.
2 Occupation has been classified according to the Classification and Classified List of Occupations, Revised June 1971.
3 Coding used for these occupations is different from census coding.

The TEC (1978: 24) has noted that there are presently about 250,000 degree holders in the workforce. If the present number of annual awards of some 30,000 bachelor degrees continues the number of degree holders will inevitably rise in the long term to about 1 million. The TEC estimate may be excessive: in 22 years at the end of the century the total in the labour force on the basis of 30,000 annual graduations might be nearer 700,000 than 1 million.

Some of the possible implications of this for student demand for places have been mentioned above. The problem for any government which sets considerable store on a manpower objective is what sensible intervention it might make in addition to the inevitable student reaction. In the sixties the Martin Committee (1964-6) and the Universities Commission (1966, 1969) could confidently reserve their attention to the very expensive courses such as Medicine, and assert that in other courses places should be available to those qualified to profit from the experience.

The Advisory Committee on Advanced Education and the subsequent Commission on Advanced Education had the explicit task of ensuring the vocational relevance of the CAE courses but were never really faced with clarifying their approach in a situation of graduate unemployment.

The Tertiary Education Commission still retains a position of relying largely on market forces. There is much to be said for this in the light of the extreme inaccuracies of manpower forecasting and the view that higher education is above all for individual development. In its latest Report (TEC, 1978) it does review the position for teachers and for skilled trades, and again assesses the position for medical practitioners; and in the case of teachers recommends a cautious further reduction in places.

What seems a less admirable aspect of the TEC Report, if it were to influence students,is an apparent tendency to downplay the problems of teacher employment in the next few years. The TEC shows that the overall teacher surplus will be reduced substantially by persons trained as teachers withdrawing from the teacher market on failing to obtain employment as teachers. This is an obvious labour market reaction to a potential or actual surplus situation. What the TEC does not consider is whether this withdrawal involves hardship and disappointment of legitimate expectations (such as women remaining at home as 'discouraged' workers or in employment well below what had currently been considered relevant employment for tertiary graduates). There is also a danger that the TEC discussion could be taken to imply an easier market by the mid-eighties. Even allowing for 'adjusted' surplus and their revised output from teacher education, actual numbers seeking employment are likely to remain considerably in excess of jobs available each year.

It is likely that the TEC discussion will be used to downplay Partridge's suggestion on cuts in intakes to initial teacher education in Victoria in 1979. The TEC might have concerned itself with estimates of the numbers likely to seek places in teacher education in the face of emerging surpluses—the other main form of adjustment to a surplus. It could be that the effect of the TEC Report is to maintain the provision of places that will not be filled. (1978: 41-53).

In the case of trades the TEC throws doubt on the size and nature of the supposed shortage, and the recent survey on Apprentices and Tradesmen carried out for the Williams Committee by the Australian Bureau of Statistics (1977d) appears to confirm this.

The TEC (1978: 29-31) has clearly summarised the factors (including changing relative salaries and substitution possibilities) giving rise to an increasing margin of error over time in any manpower forecast. And in Australia, more than elsewhere, we have very poor data on the skill requirements of different jobs and the various educational backgrounds that might be associated with those skills. This is not to say that manpower forecasts should not be undertaken; rather they should be regarded as only *one* of the pieces of information to be considered in planning. Account should also be taken of the extreme uncertainty of the forecasts, and the forecasts should be continually recalculated in the light of recent data and policy decisions taken or under consideration.

The growing manpower problems in Australia have been the major reason for the establishment of the Williams Committee and the various State inquiries into higher education. They appear to be a main reason for the perceived need for coordinating authorities such as post-secondary commissions in virtually all States, for an extension of TEC involvement in the approval of courses in universities, and hence some further loss of autonomy to universities at least.

One should not be too hopeful that the State authorities will be particularly successful in any manpower planning they undertake. Their expertise is unlikely to be greater than that of the recent committees. Although the recent reports show an awareness of the uncertainties of manpower forecasting they reveal little understanding of the techniques used. The Partridge Report uses without comment a quite different method of analysis for pre-school teachers from that for primary and secondary teachers, and another technique again for engineers—the dubious engineers per million of population ratio. The Anderson Report (1978: 122) sees the method of calculating teacher surplus in the Australian Education Council Report as unrealistic, but then (with a footnote disclaimer that is likely to be ignored by most readers), calculates and refers to a surplus that is still more unrealistic in their own terms. The AEC Report on the other hand should have asserted even more emphatically that the emerging large gap between *potential* supply and demand would *not* eventuate in the longer term: the estimated potential surplus represented a signal for adjustment in supply (or demand) most probably by market forces (especially student demand), but also by bureaucratic decisions on employment and provision of places. That its message was not understood is evidenced by the Anderson Report's comments and even in the TEC's discussion which did not emphasise the major implication for higher education: falling student demand for places in teacher education. Early reports for 1978 suggest that even the reduced number of places available in teacher education have not been filled.

Freeman (1976: 40) shows the very sharp downswing in student choice of a teaching career in the United States of America. In the United Kingdom, despite the reduction of intakes to about a third of the 1971 level, the quality of the applicants may not have risen (*Times Higher Education Supplement,* 6.8.76 and 25.11.77).

Constraints on Government Expenditure

Several factors are likely to restrict educational spending: the overall commitment by governments to restrict expenditure as a means of controlling inflation in a period of very slow economic growth, the diminishing priority given to education within government expenditure, and the diminishing priority given to tertiary education within the education budget.

Calculations of expenditure per student (Equivalent Full-Time Students or Weighted Student Units) in real terms are a little hazardous. Indicators such as student/academic staff ratios were fairly stable at about 12.0 in the period 1970 to 1975 compared with 11.7 in 1966 and 11.5 in 1961. However, as the Universities Commission noted in their Sixth Report (p. 172), the apparent deterioration from the position in the early sixties was more than accounted for by changes in faculty mix (away from science-based areas) and by relative increases in library facilities and support staff. Analysis by Professor Williams (1976: 14) suggests that real recurrent expenditure per student rose some 30 per cent in the sixties and with some fluctuations remained near this figure to the mid-seventies. Changes in the CAE sector are less well documented. Apparent academic staff/student ratios in 1975 were a little over 11 although support staff and expenditure per student were less than in universities.

Since late 1974 economic growth has been minimal. Using 1975 as a base, operating funds in real terms have not quite kept pace with the increase in enrolments (TEC, 1976: 70). In addition, cost increases such as 'incremental creep' discussed below reduce the purchasing power of the available funds. So far the most noticeable effects have been a rising student/staff ratio in CAEs and a declining relative number of support staff in universities.

The Commonwealth Government has restricted its expenditure more stringently than the States. Despite giving a few crumbs to the Technical and Further Education (TAFE) sector it has not noticeably altered the balance of its expenditure between schools and the various sectors of tertiary education. During the period since 1973, mainly as a result of the Karmel Report of 1973, but also because of expanding State efforts, real expenditure per pupil in primary and secondary schools expanded in relation to expenditure on tertiary students. In part this was in line with the pursuit of equality of outcomes espoused by the Schools Commission; Karmel himself had drawn attention to the inequality in public expenditures on an early school leaver compared with those on a Ph.D. graduate.

Opinion now seems to be turning against the schools as well, and State governments are imposing quite severe restrictions on staffing in 1978. The massive improvements in resources in government schools since 1972 as measured by the Schools Commission (and the achievement of Karmel targets ahead of time), together with the growing concern about literacy and numeracy, appears to be undermining the case for expansion of school funding. TAFE appears to have remained in favour even to the extent of an extra $50 million for capital expenditure (over 3 years) as an election promise. For the Commonwealth, which funds only a small proportion of TAFE, large apparent percentage increases in funds can be made for a fraction of their funding of higher education. It will be interesting to see what happens to the case for TAFE now that the TEC is expressing doubts and now that some of the assertions of a skill shortage and an ageing labour force in the skilled trades appear to have been undermined by the recent Bureau of Statistics survey undertaken for the Williams Committee (Australian Bureau of Statistics, 1977).

Age, Tenure and Opportunity

The problem of 'incremental creep', the cost increase associated with the movement of staff up salary scales in a period when few new appointments are made, was estimated by the Universities Commission in 1976 (1976: 41) to be adding 0.75 per cent to annual recurrent costs (a movement in average academic salary of one step up the lecturer scale in 1978 would add about 3.5 per cent to the salary bill). Such additions to cost would cease when all staff reached the top step in their class (presuming the balance between lecturer/senior lecturer, etc. remains constant), leaving salary cost at a considerably higher level than at present for a given student/staff ratio. Such incremental costs are estimated to continue at least until the early eighties. As staff get older, their eligibility increases for long service leave and eventually for superannuation. As a result of the recent period of inflation it will be necessary to supplement past contributed funds from recurrent funds. The adoption of supplementation schemes based on the Commonwealth Public Service scheme could lead to very substantial proportions of recurrent budget being diverted to paying retired staff in the coming years.

Hence, even if real recurrent expenditure per student is maintained there is likely to be a decline, perhaps a sizeable one, in staff resources available per student. It could be argued that this is offset in part by the increasing age and experience of staff, but the weight of opinion—not evidence—would be to the contrary. It is possible that the quality of staff will decline as opportunity for mobility declines. The quality will be less than if talented aspirants for tertiary employment could obtain employment in place of those relatively poorly qualified staff who obtained their positions in the easy job market of the sixties. An additional issue is the justice of denying the young and talented the opportunity of such employment.

The TEC (1978: 71) has recommended that no funds be provided for such cost increases and has suggested that institutions rearrange their expenditures and modify their procedures to obtain improved efficiency. In a recent article in the *National Times* (13 March, 1978) Professor Karmel was reported as suggesting a reduction in tenured positions to about 50 per cent of all appointments. Such a suggestion has some advantages as indicated in the previous paragraph. However, as Campbell (1978: 5) notes, "We perhaps need to be reminded that the protection of academic freedom, and not any industrial matter, is the prime purpose of the now vexed question of tenure". In more concrete terms the employment of short term staff has considerable implications for long term research and for continuity in supervision of post-graduate students.

Commonwealth-State Relations

The Commonwealth has had an involvement in the funding of university students and universities since the thirties. A formal continuing basis of finance for students was established in 1950 and for universities by the end of the fifties. From the mid-sixties the newly established college sector was funded on the same basis as universities. The teachers colleges received capital grants and then joined the CAE sector in 1973. In 1974 the Commonwealth assumed responsibility for virtually the whole funding of the tertiary system, that is, it replaced the long established system of a Commonwealth $1 for $1.85 of State recurrent funds and $1 for $1 State capital funds; the competitive element was removed from the means-tested student assistance scheme, making it available to virtually all undergraduate students who met the means test,and tuition fees were abolished.

Only minor changes have been made to the pattern of Commonwealth/State finance since 1974 (although the States have progressively reduced or eliminated their own major contribution to student assistance, the teachers' scholarships and studentships). The Fraser government, in office since December 1975, has had under consideration an alternative "cost-sharing" arrangement whereby the States re-assume responsibility for part of the expenditure on tertiary education and the Commonwealth increases the proportion it contributes to TAFE and schools. Like some other aspects of the "New Federalism" these suggestions have not been meeting with enthusiastic State response.

In retrospect the abolition of fees and the removal of State funding may have made higher education too dependent on a single source of funds for independent research and teaching. Additionally, the removal of fees may have been inequitable by some criteria as discussed in the next section. Moreover the Commonwealth's assumption of responsibility for funding the CAEs thrust on them a bureaucratic role that they were not able to cope with and which can be seen as responsible for some of the present supposed or real problems. The blame does not lie on the former Labor Government alone in assuming full funding in 1974. For example, the Cohen Committee appointed in 1972 during Fraser's time as the Minister of Education provided detailed recommendations on the absorption and funding of the large teacher education sector with little knowledge of the situation in individual States: Victoria's request for funding for a 44 per cent increase in enrolments was supported, as was Queensland's bid for only 22 per cent (see Cohen Report, p. 42). The TEC implicitly admitted in 1977 its incapacity to deal with detailed State matters in the deference it gave to the forthcoming Partridge Report. The latter is explicit:

> ... we doubt whether a Commonwealth Commission even with three Councils which must deal with the development and funding of a large number of institutions throughout the nation, can obtain that detailed knowledge of the circumstances of each State and of its institutions which is essential for decisions about the distribution of funds amongst sectors and institutions of post-secondary education.
>
> (1978: 9.9)

The Anderson Report's (1978: 70) suggestion that in the absence of State funding some State bodies may take the role of advocate rather than planning agent is relevant here. An advocate who controls the supply of essential data to an understaffed judge is in a strong position, and subject to inadequate pressures for accountability.

Fostering Accountability

In Australia the groups external to the staff of higher education institutions who have the most potential power over resources are students and government.

Students as a group exercise considerable influence on matters such as assessment, but more important than this is the collective effect of individual decisions to seek enrolment in tertiary education and in particular courses. The collective power of students depends on their capacity to exercise choice. Now that places in tertiary education are relatively plentiful their power to determine resource allocation is strengthened—on the assumption that the Commonwealth government in funding higher education continues to allocate funds largely in proportion to enrolments. It is further argued by some that the power of students should be increased by making them responsible for most funds for tertiary education through the re-introduction of fees and an increased emphasis on market forces to determine the pattern and efficiency of tertiary education. This point is taken up below.

Governments through their power to approve and fund institutions or courses and to assist students have considerable power to influence, if not fully to determine, the pattern of resource allocation. This is not to say that it is easy for a government to determine the pattern of resource allocation that would help achieve desired objectives. It is arguable that research workers know better than government the ways in which knowledge might be advanced, that individual development is best promoted when students take courses of their choice rather than enrol in a pattern determined by government. It is not outlandish to suggest that even the distribution of qualifications in relation to industries' manpower needs may well be superior if decided by student choice rather than determined by government.

Given, however, that the government continues to affect the size and pattern of tertiary education and attempts to promote the efficient use of resources, it is easy to argue that they should continually review the means by which they monitor the achievement of objectives. As already suggested governments have not been notable for effective oversight. We later examine the question of improving bureaucratic procedures.

Market

There is no unique system for ensuring the direction of resources toward particular objectives and the efficient use of those resources. There is at the moment a revival of belief in the power of a market system to promote efficiency in education, hence the emphasis on the establishment of fees related to course costs and loans for students in addition to, if not in place of, means tested grants. However, despite the stated policy of the Liberal and National Country Parties on loans and the committee of inquiry into some aspects of the matter in 1977, the introduction of a scheme even to supplement the present Tertiary Education allowances Scheme for students does not seem likely in the near future.

A market system is seen as emphasising the "right" objectives as well as promoting efficiency in the pursuit of them: relative freedom from government control in research, as funds are provided by students; expansion or contraction of courses in relation to student perception of individual needs; a fairer distribution of the burden of costs of higher education between those who profit most by it (the students) and the rest of society. Even in the manpower field such a system, through discouraging enrolment in expensive courses, could lead to a distribution of private investment in education more in line with social benefits.

On the other hand there is concern that inequality between students attaining entry to higher education would be increased: wealthy students could enter the expensive courses without a consequent burden of debt. There is also concern at the ability of students to choose sensibly for their own personal development or for manpower reasons. This, however, seems mainly to be an argument for improved counselling and information on likely manpower trends. One problem that counselling may not be able to offset is the development of a pecking order of credentials (based on a perception of employers' judgement of institutions) that might not be at all related to the quality of the courses. It may be in a student's economic interest to choose a second rate course (if one existed) at a university rather than a first rate one at a college of advanced education.

Even without the introduction of fees and loans, market forces will determine the pattern of reduction in places in teacher education in Victoria if the proposed (bureaucratic) cuts in intake recommended by the Partridge Committee are postponed. For example, Coburg State College in the north of Melbourne may lose badly in competing for teacher education students with Melbourne State College. There is no reason to suppose this would mean a decline in the better institution, but one result of a closure of courses at Coburg could be a reduction in access to and aspirations for tertiary education for those living in the northern suburbs.

Whether increased market pressure would affect performance markedly within institutions is hard to determine. The impact will in any case be cushioned while government bodies retain the power to establish institutions, while senior staff have tenure, and as already mentioned, credentialism determines a pecking order.

The introduction of fees and loans would seem likely to reduce government expenditure, an important espoused government objective, but only or mainly through a consequent reduction in enrolments. In the short term, outlays on loans and associated administrative costs could well outweigh any savings recouped through fees (unless of course the loans are financed by the private sector). Even in the distant future the repayment of loans, unless indexed for inflation and insured against default (reported as fairly common in USA), may make only a small offset against other government outlays.

The main drawback of a return to the market would seem to be that in 'freeing' research it might deprive it of funds. In so far as universities in particular have a role it would seem unlikely that they could finance it from funds collected largely from students for tuition. Universities still obtain a considerable proportion of their funds (about 6 per cent) independently of Commonwealth Government grants recommended by the Tertiary Education Commission. A large part of these other funds represent government grants for research purposes, in some cases for specific contract research. The continuing worry about these sources of income is that they may become smaller in financially hard times and they may become increasingly directed to specific research projects. In this regard a return to the market does not seem to offer any solution.

Bureaucracy

It is without question that government will provide most of the funds for tertiary institutions in Australia even if some move toward increasing private finance eventuated. Largely because of the events discussed in the section above on recent trends there has been an increasing pressure to improve the method of government oversight, and in some cases this has been interpreted as reducing the autonomy of individual institutions. The key words have been "rationalisation", which appears to mean the elimination of supposedly unnecessary duplication of courses and the adjustment of output of graduates a little closer to manpower needs, and "coordination" which means the establishment of tertiary commissions or boards in most States (Anderson (1978: 67-70) reviews State coordinating procedures).

The case for autonomy in universities at least was reaffirmed by the Universities Commission in its Sixth Report where it commented:

> *The purposes for which universities were founded and for which society continues to maintain them include the preservation, transmission and extension of knowledge, the training of highly skilled manpower and the critical evaluation of society in which we live ... society is better served if the Universities are allowed a wide freedom to determine the manner in which they should develop their activities and carry out their tasks.*
>
> (1975: 58-59)

However the Commission also noted that "universities would not make their full contribution to social life if they were unresponsive to social needs" with particular reference to highly skilled manpower. As already noted manpower problems have since worsened and the TEC Report in 1978 is less explicit on the autonomy of universities. The pressures exerted through refusal to supplement for incremental creep (1978: 70-72) and hence on fixed term appointments, the recent recommendations on study leave, and the new guidelines on course approvals (1978: 17-21) appear to be reducing autonomy.

Even if we considered that considerable restriction in autonomy were justified in order to constrain expenditure, promote quality and improve the balance of manpower supply there is a very real question of the ability of the bureaucracy to devise and implement policies to achieve their objectives. As already discussed above, it is now publicly acknowledged that a Commonwealth Commission cannot either obtain or analyse the detailed data on costs, enrolments, progression ratios, and employment trends relevant to decision making on individual institutions, at least in the CAE sector. The size of the current teacher surplus in Victoria compared with that in Queensland owes something to bureaucracy: to the Cohen Committee's inability to get to grips with State data (Cohen, 1972: 42) and to the Victorian Education Department's claims of a continuing shortage.

The establishment of institutions to oversee the whole of post-secondary education in each State is a necessary but not sufficient condition for improving the use of resources in the direction that governments think fit. What is more important is the way in which these commissions formulate policy and their power to implement their decisions.

The power of commissions or committees or boards to implement decisions depends very much on support from the relevant Government: even the commissions are only advisory bodies. The Victoria Institute of Colleges advised against the establishment of a CAE in the electorate of Wannon yet it exists today, under attack from the Partridge Committee but receiving stout defence from the Prime Minister in whose electorate it is located. The State College of Victoria and the Commission on Advanced Education in the face of a teacher surplus advised against the introduction of a Diploma of Education course in the Institute of Catholic Education in 1976, yet the course was established. Even at this early stage it seems likely that political pressure groups will be effective in overthrowing or substantially delaying most of the Partridge Committee's recommendations on course closures.

There remains the question of how soundly based are, or will be, the recommendations of State bodies. The picture at State level is not substantially more reassuring than at Commonwealth level. The Partridge Report in dealing with manpower questions in teaching and engineering used questionable techniques virtually without discussion. For debatable reasons, when considering teaching, it virtually excluded from consideration the non-government school sector and the secondary technical schools (approaching a third of all pupils), and the relevant institutions of teacher education. It stated that small tertiary institutions can be viable but presented no cost or qualitative data. Again, as noted above, the use of different methodologies of manpower analysis by various reports makes one doubtful that the pattern of manpower resulting from any consequent decisions will improve on the outcome of market forces which at least have the virtue of allowing students their choice. In addition, there does not appear to be anything in the recommendations of these bodies to stimulate the efficient use of whatever resources are allocated. Indeed, by protecting particular institutions from competiton for student numbers the reverse might be the case.

There seems to be a case for considerably more attention to be given by commissions and committees bent on detailed oversight to the investigation of procedures such as Planning Programming Budgeting (PPB) Systems which attempt to provide coherence to the planning of a set of decisions.

Traditional budgeting procedures tend to classify activities by means (such as wages and salaries or capital expenditure) rather than by objectives. Scott (1978) distinguishes fiscal accountability for simple control of funds, program accountability related to objectives, and process accountability relating to procedures and time and effort in an activity. Under program budgeting the budget would be drawn up to show the expenditure on programs related to particular objectives and cover the time span of those programs. The purpose in finding what is spent on a particular program is to investigate ways of doing it more effectively at the same cost or, alternatively, achieving the same results for a lesser cost. For example, it might be possible to show the expenditures directed toward part-time as distinct from full-time students; or toward students in classes with high enrolment compared with those having low enrolment. It is possible, of course, for researchers to piece together such data from existing budget data. What is argued for is a system where much of the data for cost analysis is readily available from the ongoing records of institutions.

There has not so far been any real attempt to pursue a PPB analysis of expenditure, even in universities where better data is available, although there is a strongly argued case for a minimum period of three years for the planning of budgets. One constraint is the lack of expertise to undertake the task of PPB. More important are

1. the problem of objectives and their weighting, already discussed;
2. the problem of joint costs, for example of research and teaching, and the allocation of administrative overheads. There are various means of tackling such problems but each tends to involve some subjectivity;
3. the estimation of costs as distinct from expenditure. For decision-making it is sensible to regard the cost of any activity as the alternatives forgone by undertaking that activity. That this is not always easy is illustrated by the problems of estimating the cost of the use of capital (as distinct from capital expenditure) and the costing of students' time;
4. the measurement of output, as discussed in the section above on objectives and efficiency. At best we can get indicators of various dimensions of performance but we should not be too hopeful of their acceptance;
5. the problem of implementation: any planning system introduced to engender greater accountability is not costless. In particular, a heavy outlay in establishing the analytical structure and information-collecting process is to be expected. Furthermore, substantial recurrent costs in monitoring current programs and evaluating alternatives will have to be borne. And any attempt to impose a system that is unwelcome to administrators and staff in tertiary institutions is likely to be unsuccessful: either the appropriate data will not be forthcoming or, if it is, the effect may be great in loss of morale and in qualitative aspects of research and teaching.

Various data systems are being developed in Australian tertiary institutions to permit the easy assembly of data even if commitment to a PPB system is not forthcoming. The development of an agreed Data Element Dictionary for use by all institutions has proceeded in the university sector but is still in the early stages in the CAE and TAFE areas. In Victoria some of the State Colleges have been investigating the operation of Costing and Data Management Systems. Such systems may permit an increase in what Scott (1978) calls process accountability —seeing what activities occur with particular expenditures. Until such systems are in operation it is difficult to see how any controlling body such as the State level Commission or the TEC can have a good idea of what is going on in the CAEs or TAFE.

Concluding Comment

Groups and individuals affected by higher education, either as consumers of its output or suppliers of its finance, are paying far greater attention to the processes and outcomes of the sector. Much of the increased interest in the higher education sector stems from two sources:

1. its large consumption of resources (nearly 2 per cent of the Gross Domestic Product) both absolutely and in relation to other sectors; and
2. the apparent decline in economic usefulness of tertiary education to many individual graduates and the wider society.

In the short term the tertiary education sector is likely to be faced with a diminishing supply of resources. Factors involved here include an expected slow-down in the growth rate in student numbers or even an absolute decline (for both demographic and manpower reasons), limitations on overall government expenditure and internal pressures upon higher education institutions' budgets, including that of incremental creep.

One common thread among all the pressures for accountability will be a demand that the higher education sector be "efficient" in the use of scarce resources. However in the context of higher education the notion of efficiency is difficult to apply and its unqualified use could be misleading. This is not to say that the higher education sector should not attempt to eliminate obvious areas of waste, duplication and ineffective use of resources. Rather it is to note that tertiary institutions are not production lines producing homeogenous, saleable outputs and that efficiency analysis needs to be modified accordingly.

The position is complicated by the differing positions of CAEs and universities. Both are heavily dependent upon federal government funding, but it would appear that CAEs face far greater restraint upon the development of new courses than do universities. The universities possess greater internal freedom to adopt policies and programs which of themselves can serve to improve their internal efficiency and accountability processes.

The greater degree of autonomy possessed by universities is partly historical in origin. Paradoxically, however, the traditional view of a university and its functions tends to militate against the very notion of accountability in its narrower sense. The traditional emphasis upon research and the criticism of established works as the basis for a community of scholars leads away from the concepts of short-term objectives and measurable achievement-oriented performance which are gaining so much favour in the accountability literature.

Many argue of course that the traditional view of the university is no longer valid and that CAEs and universities are for practical purposes indistinguishable. To the extent that these observations are true, their primary cause would appear to be the fact that for the last two decades the major client group of the whole tertiary education sector has been trainee teachers. When institutions are mainly dealing with the same type of student it is inevitable that initial differences between the institutions will become blurred. The declining career prospects in teaching could mean that the common element between individual tertiary institutions will disappear. The result of this would be a greater differentiation of tertiary institutions and this differentiation may itself facilitate accountability.

As tertiary institutions are forced to distinguish themselves from their fellows and adopt more specialised functions it will be far easier to determine the degree to which they are achieving their objectives. One of the great problems so far in the accountability debate has been that the basic similarity of tertiary institutions has made it difficult to discuss rationally the objectives of each institution. What has tended to happen is that each institution has been seen as attempting to achieve *all* of the objectives of tertiary education, thus making any assessment of its performance virtually impossible. What is argued here is that because the number of trainee teachers entering tertiary education is likely to decline significantly, the removal of this common element may force tertiary institutions to become more differentiated thereby facilitating the process of accountability.

In the recent debate on the future of tertiary education in general, and on issues such as study leave for academics in particular, one group which has been strangely quiet in the defence of tertiary education has been the graduates. Their reticence could have two main causes. Firstly, having acquired the benefits of tertiary education they may wish to preserve their privileged position by not encouraging any further expansion of the tertiary sector. Secondly, they may in fact see the process of tertiary education (as distinct from the certification gained at its completion) as being of little value and thus not worthy of any defence. In regard to the latter reason, the disillusionment of the largest single group of graduates, namely teachers, with their training has often been noted.

Graduates often play an important opinion-forming role in the community, and if the graduates themselves are disappointed by the education they have received it is not surprising that the community generally is looking upon tertiary education with displeasure. The message is clear: unless the tertiary students themselves see their work as being interesting, relevant, meaningful and well taught, public dissatisfaction with tertiary education may be expected to grow.

To the extent that student dissatisfaction exists, tertiary institutions could well need to develop measures which seek to improve the teaching and learning process. However this is far easier to state than to implement. Policies which improve the coordination and presentation of learning resources, which offer staff the opportunity to improve their communication skills and then reward those who do so, could well be examined. In particular the empirical status of the popular assertion that researching the frontiers of knowledge makes for better teaching needs serious testing.

The pressure for improved teaching is likely to come increasingly from students themselves. If graduate unemployment worsens, students are going to be less inclined to accept whatever is presented by the academic staff than were their counterparts of earlier years, who at least were certain that their degree or diploma could itself gain them satisfactory employment. Furthermore, the increasing number of mature age students who tend both to have more confidence than their younger fellows and to have made greater sacrifices to attend tertiary studies, are likely to put greater pressure on poor, inefficient teaching.

Some groups believe that through a change in financing methods tertiary institutions would gain by becoming more accountable directly to students rather than to governments. This view is understandable given the recent unhappy effects of bureaucratic controls upon the pattern and direction of higher education. But it is not clear in the Australian context that increased market pressures will necessarily lead to better decisions being made either by students or by institutions. Moreover, some disadvantaged groups with only limited current access to higher education might suffer under such a system.

On the other hand we cannot be optimistic in the short term that State or Commonwealth bureaucratic procedures will lead to improved manpower decisions; or that simply by controlling course approvals and study leave, efficiency in teaching will increase. But it does seem that higher education will only avoid such increasing bureaucratic control if it can find ways to demonstrate its responsiveness to community needs and its effective use of available resources. The increased involvement of lay persons on governing boards in higher education may be one means of doing this. The involvement of staff at other instituions (even as external examiners) in assessment of courses might be another. Individual CAEs and universities might find it worthwhile to develop their own process or program accounting systems to draw continual attention to objectives. Universities in particular have been able to point to reports of research published in international journals, but they may need to increase still further the effectiveness with which they bring this to public attention.

One of the great dilemmas for tertiary education is the conflict between, on the one hand, the need to inform the public of their activities, and on the other, public resentment or suspicion of the same activities. Anti-intellectualism has always been a strong undercurrent in Australian life and this, combined with a dislike of "tall poppies", could mean that the earnest professor publicly listing the number of research articles he has published as part of his duty toward "accountability" may in fact be doing tertiary education a disservice in the short term. This could be particularly the case where the work is perceived as a threat to existing values or institutions. In this climate, the work of the more socially neutral physical sciences may prosper unduly at the expense of the (necessarily) more controversial social sciences. The problem of the public being aware of the activities of tertiary institutions and their possible opposition to some of these activities could be very real in future years.

Chapter Seven

Academic Accountability—Courses and Programs

G. S. Harman,
R. St C. Johnson

Accountability in higher education has many dimensions and may take different forms. In this chapter our concern is with only one such dimension—what we define as academic accountability—and with this particularly in relation to courses and programs. We first discuss the meaning of the concept of academic accountability in the context of higher education, and then attempt to explore three specific questions:

(i) To whom are universities and colleges accountable with respect to courses and programs?

(ii) What mechanisms of accountability are used by universities and colleges with respect to courses and programs, and how adequate are these?

(iii) Are there any particular policy or administrative changes which appear both desirable and feasible?

Academic Accountability in Higher Education

Accountability is by no means a new concept in scholarly literature. For instance it has been used for many years in the study of public administration, political science and management. In public administration accountability means essentially responsibility—responsibility of one public servant to a senior officer, of a senior public servant to a Minister, of a Minister to the Parliament, and of a senior public servant, a Minister and a government to society. But even in public administration the terms accountability and responsibility have their problems. An officer may be said to be responsible for particular functions, but seldom is it possible to spell out all these functions in detail and to say what is the relative importance of each. In many cases an officer's responsibility may have to be seen more in terms of progress toward certain goals—it is, as Spann (1973: 67) says, "responsibility for getting things done by others, and often very unclear about the edges". Then there are problems about the sense in which a person can be said to be responsible. A simple meaning might be that one is accountable to and blamed by a superior if some result is not achieved or some rule is not followed. But though this does happen, its incidence is uncertain. Spann (1973: 67) writes:

Some activities which have very low priority in the total spectrum of responsibilities may be much more visible to superiors than others, and their non-performance is far more likely to attract unfavourable attention. For example, if certain returns are wrong or late, this may attract blame, though more important forms of misbehaviour will remain unnoticed.

Responsibility or accountability are also used in public administration in a more subjective way, to indicate those persons, institutions and norms to which a public servant feels responsible.

Notions about accountability go back a long way in education and in the study of education. In early New South Wales, for instance, the colonial governors took pains to ensure that the colony's money for schools was being spent as efficiently and economically as possible, and saw themselves as accountable for the schools, not only to the colonial office, but also to the church and to children (Walker, 1972). But over the last few years, within education accountability as a term has come to great prominence, and today it is bandied about by educators and non-educators alike. Largely from the United States of America there has come a rapidly burgeoning literature on accountability, and in this literature accountability is used in a variety of ways (Levin, 1974). Some authors assert that the provision of information on the performance of schools constitutes accountability—and sometimes they would hold teachers directly responsible for such functions as improving mathematics and reading scores of children in their classes. Others see accountability as a matter of redesigning the structures by which education is governed. In some cases accountability is ˙defined as a specific approach to education such as performance contracting or educational vouchers, while in others accountability is referred to as part of all educational systems. In the U.S.A. it is common to hear of statewide testing programmes as well as recent legislation which would enable schools to terminate the appointments of 'poor' teachers being explained as responses to the need for accountability.

This recent educational literature on accountability gives little real help to a discussion about the accountability of universities and colleges of advanced education. This is partly because it refers mainly to schools and the performance of teachers and administrators, partly because it relates to American phenomena, and partly because it demands the scientific measurement of many human outcomes that are not readily quantifiable. In our view, when discussing higher education in Australia it is more sensible to rely on a more traditional view of accountability. Thus for this chapter we will define accountability simply as the condition of being accountable, liable or responsible. A university or college council is delegated considerable powers and resources, both human and financial. But in return it is responsible and answerable for its use of these both in a legal sense and, in some respects, a moral sense. Such councils are accountable in much the same way as the board of any public authority or statutory corporation is accountable, except that by tradition tertiary institutions are supposed to enjoy a greater measure of independence and autonomy. But in addition, accountability is shared by others as well within any higher education institution. Clearly various boards and committees can be held to be accountable, and so can the vice-chancellor or principal and other senior administrative staff. Then too, so can the academic staff: in some senses they can be accountable in a financial or management sense, but also they can be accountable in a moral sense and as professionals. To our list we should probably add support staff and students. Some may want to question whether students should be thought of in any meaningful sense as being accountable. While we would not want to say that students are, or should be held, accountable in the same senses in which a university or college council or their academic staff may be held accountable, we would point out that students in higher education benefit enormously from their college and university experiences (particularly in the sense that they acquire qualifications which enable them to enter professional careers or highly paid and high status occupations) and that they do so largley at public expense. Thus in some respects it would seem reasonable that the community should expect graduating students to accept some sense of responsibility to society, especially to use the skills acquired in the public good and not just to achieve personal goals.

At this point there is one further question that needs to be raised: for what activities or functions can a university or college and its members be held accountable? Perhaps the simplest method is to attempt firstly to answer this with respect to a university or college council. In essence, a council is accountable for the good governance and functioning of the institution, though the sense in which it is accountable varies between different functions and activities. This accountability can be broken down into a number of components.

First, there is *legal* accountability; a council is responsible to a minister and government to ensure that the institution operates within the formal legal framework provided by legislation, government regulations and government instructions. For example, as a result of provisions included in the Education Act, 1964-1973, the various councils of Queensland colleges of advanced education are required, among other things, to cooperate with State authorities to provide courses and programmes to meet local and State needs, to make financial submissions as required to the Advanced Education Board and approve expenditure within funds allocated by the Board, to delegate powers to the college principal, to submit all by-laws for State approval, and to have the Advanced Education Board approve annual budgets.

Second, there is *financial* accountability—simple accountability for the actual expenditure of funds and the procedures by which that expenditure is accounted for. This includes responsibility for the detail on such items as vouchers, time sheets and purchase orders, and responsibility in terms of the accounting conventions and reporting procedures which demonstrate the propriety and legitimacy of expenditures within the institution.

Third, there is *academic* accountability—a council is accountable in broad terms for the goals set by the institution, for the academic policies followed, for students admitted, for the courses and programmes offered, for assessment practices and for the results achieved. This can be explained in another way as accountability in terms of effectiveness (defined as the degree of success an organisation enjoys in doing whatever it is trying to do) (Cutt, 1976). It is a combination of our second and third kinds of accountability that governments often appear to have in mind. In 1961, in announcing the appointment of the Martin Committee, Sir Robert Menzies stressed the increasing demands on tertiary education and went on:

... the rapidly increasing number of students who may wish to take advantage of tertiary education, and other factors such as student wastage, staff shortage and the pressure of universities generally, make it imperative that we investigate the best way of making the most efficient use of available potential resources.

(Martin, 1965: 225)

We have noted that the sense in which a council is accountable, or can be called on to give explanation, varies somewhat between its different areas of responsibility. For instance, a council is responsible for financial management in a somewhat different sense from that in which it.is responsible for the institution's academic goals. On the first it is generally clear whether rules have been followed, but on the second it is much more a matter of judgement, of taste, and of whether key constituencies are happy with the institution or not.

There is not space here to explore in similar detail the areas of accountability for other groups in higher education institutions. However in passing we should note that, while academics have some responsibility with regard to matters of good governance, financial management, the proper use of resources, and institutional goals, their main areas of accountability relate to academic functions—to the appropriateness and quality of courses, to teaching effectiveness, to evaluation and assessment of student performance, to the granting of diplomas and degrees, and to the quality, direction and value of research.

Accountable to Whom?

To whom the universities and colleges of advanced education are accountable with regard to courses and programs is an issue that is seldom raised directly. Further, it is an issue that is seldom discussed at length by university or college spokesmen, or by prominent members of the public. Yet it is clear that in higher education institutions and in society there are deep-rooted assumptions concerning where responsibility lies or should be for these matters. It is on these various and often conflicting assumptions that universities and colleges are frequently criticised, and that academic spokesmen from time to time defend themselves. These assumptions have also had a considerable influence on the development of administrative arrangements within higher education institutions, and on the structuring of systems of administrative coordination at both federal and State levels.

Perhaps the most common and widely held assumption is that universities and colleges are academically accountable to society and the community. This assumption is widely, though not universally, accepted in higher education institutions; especially in CAEs, administrators and academics often speak with regard to courses and programs of 'being responsive to community needs' or of 'serving society'. Then too, it is significant to note that both university and CAE governing bodies and State and federal coordinating agencies allow for substantial lay representation. Yet because the terms 'society' and 'community' mean different things to different people, to say that higher education institutions are or should be accountable to society or the community does not tell us very much at all. Indeed, it seems certain that this statement probably means very different things to different groups. In the context of this discussion the words 'society' or 'community' probably mean one or a combination of the following:

1. society at large or the public interest;
2. the 'local' community surrounding the institution, i.e. community in a geographic sense;
3. industry, commerce and employers;
4. the professions and professional associations;
5. social, cultural, artistic and religious interests and organisations;
6. students in higher education;
7. prospective students, and their parents;
8. disadvantaged groups or minorities; and
9. government.

It is reasonable to hold the view that universities and colleges are and should be responsible to all these groups and interests. Admittedly, not all academics would agree. Some would dispute, for example, how far universities should try to serve directly commercial or industrial interests. Of these a number would probably argue that professional education should be conducted outside universities, and that universities should be the independent critics of society. Then too, some university academics find repugnant the idea of direct accountability to governments, especially if this means government interference or coordination. In the United States of America, according to one political scientist (Epstein, 1974: 19), some academics in public universities and colleges hold a 'leave it on the stump philosophy'. They reject

> ... *state authority altogether, proposing that the state's elected representatives simply deposit the taxpayers' money, preferably in the amount requested, for the university itself to allocate and spend according to self-generated preferences.*

Some people may question whether universities and colleges should be held accountable to students. We take the view that they should, and especially that academics should be held accountable in the same sense that doctors are held accountable to their patients, or lawyers to their clients. Of course, there are problems in practice with this notion and in devising appropriate mechanisms to ensure that the student voice is heard with regard to courses and programs. One problem is that even in the most liberal institutional contexts, consultation with students generally occurs at the beginning or in the early stages of a course, with little or no accountability with regard to results or of the whole course after completion.

Apart from the confusion we have mentioned in usage of the terms society and community, there are also problems with related assumptions. For example many people who talk of CAEs responding to community needs and demands, and of close interaction between a college and the local community, appear to hold a consensus view of society. Overall, it is assumed, everyone wants the same things from a college, and all a college really has to do is to find out what these things are. A different point of view is that in certain cases a conflict view of society is more realistic—that a college serves different constituencies, each with its own goals. These goals represent the expectations of particular groups for the college. With limited resources, a college cannot satisfy all expectations;

and apart from this it is possible that the goals of some groups may be diametrically opposed to the goals of others.

In addition to being academically accountable to all the various community components already mentioned, higher education institutions, and especially their academic staffs, should be thought of as being accountable to both national and international academic and scholarly communities. Both universities and CAEs share accountability to both these communities although the universities, because of their orientation to research and scholarship, generally feel a stronger sense of responsibility to and links with both national and international scholarly communities than do the CAEs. This has been recognised by various government committees. The Partridge Inquiry on Post-Secondary Education in Western Australia, for example, reported:

> *The universities cannot be considered to be merely components of a State system of post-secondary education. They belong also to an Australia-wide system, and indeed to an international community of universities. Within this system, there is very free communication and exchange of ideas and persons; their activities are deeply influenced by traditions maintained within that wide community; and, very importantly, their standards both in teaching and research are exposed to the scrutiny and judgement of sister universities elsewhere in Australia and throughout the world. While it is essential that they should be responsive to interests and needs of their own local community, it is equally important that they should be free to respond to the intellectual and educational movements flowing in from universities and other institutions all over the world ... We would fear that an attempt to place them under the close control of a local academic authority might impair their capacity to provide such a leadership.*
>
> (Partridge, 1976: 154)

It is sometimes asserted that universities have a national and international scholarly orientation, while CAEs have a State and local orientation. This, however, is something of an over-simplification. Rather, the difference between universities and CAEs on this dimension is one of emphasis and degree. Further, both individual universities and CAEs differ from one another in the extent to which their orientations are national and international.

The differences between universities and CAEs with regard to their national and international orientation have been used by university spokesmen in a number of States to argue against universities coming under the effective control of new or proposed State statutory coordinating agencies for higher education. Universities have also argued against such State coordination on the grounds of infringement of traditional institutional autonomy. In Victoria, both arguments were used in 1978 by university vice-chancellors in opposition to the State Government's proposal to introduce legislation to set up a post-secondary education commission on the lines suggested by the report of a recent committee of enquiry (Partridge, 1978). One vice-chancellor said the new body would mean the loss of university autonomy and would damage the national and international standing of Victorian universities. Another said

> *Universities are not only concerned with education and training to meet State needs, but also to react to national and international trends.*

The bill in its present form would partition the national system of university education along State lines ... (The Australian, 25 April, 1978).

In this section we have suggested that universities and colleges can be considered as being academically accountable to a large number of different community constituencies, and that higher education institutions and their academic staffs are accountable to both national and international scholarly communities. But in addition, a higher education institution, and its governing body and senior officers, can be thought of in some senses as being responsible to their academic and other staff. Staff have every right to expect their institution to be sensibly, efficiently and fairly governed. Academics, in particular, have a right to expect that the importance of academic and scholarly values will be recognised, and that every effort will be made to protect these values and traditional academic autonomy from undue government influence and interference.

In an earlier section we argued that many bodies and groups within a higher education institution can be held, in some senses, to be accountable. In this section we have noted the large number of different constituencies who may, quite fairly, demand accountability from others. This suggests that the accountability relationship with regard to courses and programs is by no means a simple one-way relationship from a higher education institution to some outside clearly defined community. Rather there are a myriad of relations— from many groups within the institution to others outside, and from one group or body in an institution to others in the same institution and in other institutions. Further, many groups such as academics have the right to demand accountability from others, but at the same time owe responsibility to various other groups. This complicated pattern of accountability relationships is one cause of the considerable confusion which surrounds discussions of academic accountability in higher education.

Mechanisms of Accountability and Their Effectiveness

In our attempts here to explore the mechanisms of accountability and their effectiveness with regard to courses and programs we will concentrate on the mechanisms used to ensure academic respectability and community acceptance. This, of course, is only one dimension of academic accountability. Five main groups of mechanisms will be discussed; and for each we will comment, at least briefly, on effectiveness. It is important to bear in mind not only whether a particular mechanism looks adequate, or would be adequate if it were properly functioning, but also whether in fact it is operating as designed or intended. It is possible, for example, that some well-designed and well-intentioned mechanisms are virtually useless because of the strong influence of traditions, or of notions and values about such things as 'academic freedom' or 'senatorial courtesy'.

1. Legal Status and Government Recognition

Perhaps one of the most powerful mechanisms is that provided by the legal status and recognition given to universities and colleges, under their charters or under the Acts by which they were founded and operate, and by the degree of autonomy given to them by governments. Of course, both give a more advantageous position to universities.

In the case of universities, the charters or Acts generally confer on the institution not only the right to design and offer courses but to examine and award qualifications. In a number of States even the name university is protected; in Victoria Ivan Madder's private 'university' was obliged to change its name. With CAEs the situation varies. In a few cases colleges have their own separate Acts of incorporation, but in most cases they operate under legislation empowering a minister or government to establish colleges. Some colleges have the legal right to award degrees or diplomas, while in other cases this right is held by a central coordinating body (Harman, 1978). Still, even in the case of CAEs, the recognition and legal powers and status given, and the large measure of effective academic autonomy allowed, help greatly to win community acceptance for courses and awards. They also operate to some extent to help these institutions win academic acceptance by universities. Generally universities have been reluctant to place a high value on work done in higher education institutions which do not have their own governing councils and which operate as a branch of a government department. This is probably because of a fear that non-academic values may put pressure on academic values; for example, a government controlled teachers college might well be instructed to produce a particular number of graduates irrespective of the calibre of the students entering the course.

Then too, in some cases charters or Acts of incorporation have stated that an institution or its awards would achieve some recognised standard. For example, by their charters from the Queen, the early Australian universities were guaranteed status with the universities of Great Britain—and thus with the world. Or again, the legislation setting up the State College of Victoria (State College of Victoria Act, 1972) required that no degree be awarded unless 'the student has successfully completed a course of study which is comparable in standard to that required for the awarding of a degree in the universities of Victoria. Of course, such guarantees in charters or requirements in legislation do not automatically mean that an institution or its courses will have a particular status or standard. But they have operated and continue to operate as mechanisms which assist the winning of status and acceptance.

2. Internal Procedures

Australian universities and colleges regularly use a number of well-established internal procedures in an effort to ensure that their courses and awards are of a suitably high standard, and are widely acceptable to both employers and the professions. These include peer review of course and student assessment proposals (these often take place at a number of levels, such as teaching group, department, faculty, academic board and even council), peer review of final assessment of student performance in a course or unit, outside representation (usually from the profession or industry) on advisory committees and faculties, staff recruitment procedures aimed to eliminate nepotism and to ensure that academically superior candidates are appointed, and various procedures aimed to achieve accountability of the individual teacher and department with regard to quality and standards. The last type of procedures may need further comment. A number of mechanisms are available to achieve a high degree of accountability from individual departments, and many are used regularly in Australian higher education institutions. These include the operation of departmental committees (with student and staff representation), student feedback during courses, follow-up surveys of graduates and periodic departmental reviews. The same mechanisms may also operate to achieve accountability with regard to the individual teacher. In addition, in the case of individual academics, departmental heads (and sometimes course coordinators) can do a great deal to ensure that the courses actually presented follow the agreed syllabus and that high standards are maintained. In some institutions a further mechanism used is publication of student opinion on the performance of individual lecturers.

On the whole, these procedures are clearly useful and do a substantial amount to protect standards and to ensure outside acceptability. At the same time we must acknowledge their limitations. For example the value of the various peer review and the counter-check mechanisms is sometimes diminished by the reluctance of a proportion of academics to criticise a colleague or a proposal from another department, unless something really serious is wrong. Hence often academic boards and committees merely 'rubber-stamp' what comes before them. There are also limitations with the safeguards built into appointment procedures; a selection committee can generally block an unsuitable appointment, but it can seldom force a head of department to accept against his wish the best applicant. Further, some heads of departments fail to take their supervisory duties as seriously as they should. Many of these weaknesses and limitations are unfortunate, since the large measure of autonomy given to universities and the lesser measure given to CAEs imposes on them a responsibility for self-scrutiny and tough evaluation of courses and procedures.

In some universities and colleges another procedure now being used quite extensively is the official review committee, appointed periodically to review programs, departments or faculties. For example this procedure is now being given considerable emphasis at the Australian National University. In the Institute of Advanced Studies it is policy to review thoroughly (by the use of outside and often largely overseas teams) each of the established research schools at least every ten years and to review individual departments whenever a chair becomes vacant. In the School of General Studies, the policy is to review individual departments whenever a new professor is to be appointed, or whenever there is to be a change in the headship; review committees include the Vice-Chancellor or his nominee, the Deputy-Chairman of the Board of the School, the appropriate dean, two members of the department, two student members, a senior academic from a kindred department, a senior academic from a non-related department, and at least two senior academics from outside the School of General Studies or outside the university. To take another example, the Darling Downs Institute of Advanced Education recently undertook a major self-assessment, validated by school validation teams (which included at least two outside experts) coordinated by an 'Expert Core' of three outsiders (two from outside Queensland) (Barker and McNulty, 1978). These review procedures are still relatively new in Australia, and it is probably too early to say how effective they will be in the long run. As mechanisms to assess quality and to evaluate current directions, emphasis and balance they appear to offer considerable promise. Moreover the self-evaluations and other preparations which these reviews require of departments or schools clearly bring many advantages—possibly such advantages may be even more valuable than the formal review procedure itself. At the same time we should recognise that the review procedure has its limitations. For example the reviews already conducted of the established research schools at the Australian National University have pointed to several difficulties. It is by no means easy to recruit a review team both with the necessary technical competence and high academic standing, and with a sense of good judgement and imagination and a willingness to provide an honest assessment of the work of colleagues. Then too, to conduct such reviews properly is a slow and time-consuming business. Further, there is the problem of whether the university council considers that the recommendations of a review committee should be mandatory on the research school, or whether the usual practices of academic self-government should be followed, allowing the school and its departments to decide whether to follow the advice given. Apart from all this there is a more general problem. The degree of change that can be achieved following any review is limited unless there is the possibility of some substantial changes in academic staff.

3. *Appeals to External Authorities or Standards*

Both universities and CAEs make frequent use of appeals to external authorities and standards. For instance, in all Australian universities external examiners are used to assess research theses. In the Australian National University, rules require that for the Ph.D. degree no fewer than three examiners must be appointed, and that two of these must be persons who are not members of the academic staff of the university. In many cases one or more overseas examiners are included. Sometimes there is a practical reason for this; because of the nature of the student's topic it may be difficult to appoint three Australian examiners, or appropriate Australian scholars may be unavailable at a particular time. However a more fundamental factor often operates; ANU staff consider it both appropriate and desirable to appeal to international authorities and standards.

Universities also appeal to external authorities and standards in other ways. Often enquiries are made of scholars in other Australian and overseas universities with regard to particular applicants for academic posts or research scholarships. Frequently outside experts are invited to be members of selection committees for appointments to senior academic posts. Courses are often modelled on what is done in leading overseas universities.

With CAEs, similar practices operate. In addition, colleges to a large extent use Australian universities as their yard-stick. This is the case whether it is to design the content of a particular course, to decide on the requirements of a particular award, or to judge academic standing of staff or prospective staff.

There are both advantages and problems in deriving course and assessment standards by comparison with other institutions, both nationally and internationally. The advantages are probably more obvious. Many academics can point to institutions where appeals to external authorities or practices have protected existing standards, or have led an institution to aim higher; many can also point to cases where weak institutions have existed in isolation from the mainstream of academic life, usually with unfortunate consequences. At the same time, there is a danger for any institution to be over-concerned with outside standards at the expense of proper concern with the particular needs of students and their careers. Too much emphasis on looking over one's shoulder can be harmful; it could lead to the aping of details from elsewhere, to a barrier to innovation, and to setting of course content and standards quite inappropriate to the particular context.

In another sense both universities and CAEs appeal to external standards in the use of symbols and ceremonies to identify themselves with the traditions of the academic world and scholarship. Consider a university graduation ceremony: the gowns, the academic procession, the formal conferring of degrees by the Chancellor, and other formalities can be powerful vehicles to link symbolically even a new and small institution with the long-standing academic traditions, especially of British and European universities. They also, presumably, are useful mechanisms to help assure graduands and their parents of the academic respectability of awards. Such mechanisms serve a useful purpose. There is a real danger, however, in too much emphasis on such appeals to tradition. For one thing, with frequent use such appeals lose their power; for another, they cannot take the place of other mechanisms designed to ensure that the work is in fact academically sound.

4. *Course Accreditation by Professional Associations*

Two kinds of course accreditation operate in Australian higher education. One is conducted by various professional associations and covers both university and CAE courses in particular fields, and the other is operated by government agencies and applies only to CAEs (Houston and Harman, forthcoming).

Accreditation in higher education is simply recognition afforded to an institution (such as a university or college), a faculty or division, or a course or program which meets some minimum standard or set of criteria demanded or defined by a competent and recognised outside agency or association. It is essentially a device of quality control and quality improvement. Its basic aim is to promote and ensure high quality in particular academic programs, and at times to improve quality. Generally its purpose is to afford protection to particular groups—to institutions (against other institutions offering poorer quality programs of the same kind), to students (against institutions and courses of poor quality), to employers (who wish to know that prospective professional and sub-professional employees have been competently trained and to know what various credentials mean), and to professional associations (who wish to ensure that only properly trained personnel enter particular professions). But at the same time accreditation can achieve, or help to achieve, other goals. For instance it is sometimes a valuable device to enable a small and new college to get expert advice on course proposals. Or again, institutions or faculties sometimes use the threat of loss of accreditation as a lever to press for additional resources. Still again, many accreditation systems operate in such a way as to standardise the usage of certain terms, such as degree or diploma, and the nomenclature used for particular kinds of qualifications.

In Australia a number of professional associations including the Institution of Engineers, the Australian Institute of Physics, the Royal Australian Institute of Chemistry and the Institute of Mining and Metallurgy run accreditation systems. Basically these are concerned with giving recognition to particular courses which, on the basis of their length, standards of entry, course content and quality of their teaching staff, are considered to provide a basic minimum standard for entry into a profession. In the case of well-established professions, such as engineering, if recognition is not given to a particular course or if recognition is withdrawn it has very serious consequences both for the college or university concerned and for students in the particular course (Graycar, 1975: 123). Most of these accreditation systems operate in a similar fashion. They involve a formal application by the college or university concerned, a visit to the campus by a panel of experts, the submission of a report, and a decision on whether accreditation should be given.

Course accreditation by Australian professional associations has received little outside scrutiny to date. The little evidence we have suggests that it performs useful functions, particularly ensuring that all courses recognised for entry to a particular profession come up to minimum standards. Visits by panels also have many useful effects, both for an institution and the academics in the field concerned, and also for the particular professional association; among other things such visits help promote better understanding and cooperation.

On the other hand it is possible that this form of accreditation may enable professional associations to have too dominant an influence on professional training in particular fields. Graycar's work certainly suggests that the Institution of Engineers is seen by engineering academics to have a major influence on university and CAE engineering schools. A considerable proportion of a sample of academics interviewed by Graycar said they considered that this influence was undesirable, and that it unnecessarily restricted the freedom of a university or college engineering school to innovate and make curricular decisions on educational grounds. Significantly, nearly all these people were members of the Institution of Engineers. One full professor told the interviewer:

> *There is a definite restriction on our autonomy ... Most members of the staff think the course is O.K. but the Institution of Engineers says it is too short, and because of the status that attaches to Institution of Engineers accreditation, there will be a course revision here ...*
>
> (Graycar, 1975: 124).

Apart from this it is well known that in 1967 the Institution of Engineers unilaterally decided that from 1980 only those students who followed an approved four-year course would be accepted into membership. This raises the crucial issue of whether a professional body alone should have the right to determine, admittedly indirectly, that a particular course in a university or college should be lengthened, or that its content should be sifnificantly modified.

In addition, this kind of accreditation raises other important questions. For example, how should effective power over the control of professional courses be shared between professional associations, higher education institutions, employers (where appropriate) and government. Are there some harmful consequences from too much influence by professional associations? Is there sometimes a problem with the dual system of accreditation (i.e. by government and professional associations) for particular professional fields in CAEs? We are not in a position at present to attempt to provide adequate answers to these questions, but on the basis of overseas studies and the little work done here there seems good reason for concern. Obviously the interests of professional associations do not always coincide with those of professional schools in universities and CAEs, nor with those of students wishing to enter particular professions and of the public. Above all most professional associations understandably seek to achieve high exclusive status for their members, to control entry to the profession, to foster professional ethos, and to secure higher incomes and other benefits for members.

5. Government Course Accreditation in Colleges of Advanced Education

This system was established in the late 1960s by the Federal Government in conjunction with the six State governments. With the rapid development after 1965 of CAEs there was considerable concern about variations between institutions with regard to the nomenclature of awards and course content, and about the academic standing and community acceptance of CAE awards. Sir Ian Wark (1978: 162), the first Chairman of the Commonwealth Advisory Committee on Advanced Education, has explained how the Commonwealth Government came to take action on this matter:

> *The forty-three different colleges of the day, left to their own devices, could have adopted widely differing standards for their awards. Some form of accreditation was needed, first, to protect the well-established colleges from currency depreciation in awards, and second, to confer authenticity on the awards of the lesser-knowns. On the recommendation of the CACAE, the Commonwealth Government, with the agreement of the States, in 1968, set up a Committee of Inquiry into Awards and Standards in Colleges of Advanced Education, headed by Mr. F. M. Wiltshire.*

The Wiltshire Committee was asked to make recommendations on the desirability of conformity in nomenclature for awards, on criteria which should be applied in the assessment of courses for awards at various levels, on the nomenclature to be used for awards, and on the possible structure for a national body to advise on comparability of standards in awards. It soon decided against any rigid conformity in courses, but in favour of a nationally recognised and consistent system of nomenclature of awards which it hoped would help establish the CAE system 'in the minds of employers, professional bodies and the community generally' (*Academic Awards in Colleges,* 1969: 24). On the basis of the amount of knowledge imparted, the depth of study, level of attainment and stage reached on completion of a course, it classified all existing CAE courses into four broad categories: three-year full-time (or part-time equivalent) courses to professional level; two or three-year less demanding courses; one-year post-graduate courses; one or two-year more demanding post-graduate courses. It recommended a uniform usage of the term 'diploma' and 'degree', and to help achieve national accreditation of awards it recommended that "a national body designated the Australian Council for Accreditation of Awards in Advanced Education be set up to accredit awards in advanced education" (*Academic*

Awards in Colleges, 1969: 43). Following publication of this report, protracted inter-governmental negotiations took place. After the Commonwealth Government agreed to bear the financial costs associated with a national body, agreement was reached and in December 1971 the Australian Council on Awards in Advanced Education (ACAAE) was set up jointly by the Commonwealth and States for a trial period of three years; in 1974 it was agreed to continue with this arrangement for a further three years until another review was held.

The ACAAE seeks to promote consistency in the nomenclature of CAE awards and to develop meaningful relationships between courses and their associated awards. Its main task is to maintain and publish a national register of awards in advanced education. Proposals for registration come from recognised State or territorial bodies and certify that a course has been properly assessed and accredited. Until recently the Council did not have the right to refuse registration, although it could refer back any proposal for further consideration by the State or territorial agency concerned. However under a new agreement approved by the Australian Education Council in February 1978 the ACAAE now has the power to refer back any proposal any number of times; this, in effect, means the right to refuse registration.

The main burden of the accreditation process is carried by State and territorial agencies and their various committees and boards. In each State except Victoria there is a single recognised statutory authority responsible for accreditation in CAEs; in Victoria there are two authorities, the Victoria Institute of Colleges Council, and the Senate of the State College of Victoria. For the Commonwealth colleges the Commonwealth Government has established the Australian Territories Accreditation Committee for Advanced Education. The internal structure of these agencies varies considerably. Most have a three-tier arrangement of a governing body, a standing committee (variously named, e.g. Courses Development Committee in N.S.W., Education Committee in Queensland), and assessment committees (variously named, e.g. Course Assessment Committees in Queensland and New South Wales). However in South Australia and for Commonwealth colleges the structure is two-tier and assessment committees report directly to the agency's governing body.

In each case course accreditation is a multi-stage process. Generally a college wishing to have a new course accredited applies formally in a prescribed manner. Often at this stage the submission is brief, including only the name of the proposed award, the objectives of the course, its proposed duration, and details on the composition of any special advisory committee involved in the course's development. This request is then considered and if supported in principle a detailed submission is requested. This submission is prepared by academic staff in the college, and can involve many hours of work. After the submission has been received by the agency, arrangements are made for the review and accreditation procedure to proceed. The actual procedures followed vary from agency to agency, but generally the essential pattern is as follows. After study of the submission and supporting documents an assessment committee visits the college, discussing the proposed course with academic staff and administrators and inspecting relevant facilities and equipment. A report is then prepared and submitted. Further advice may be sought from the college or some other authority, and in some cases the submission is referred back to the college for review and modification. Application for national registration may be made to the ACAAE once accreditation of a course and its award have been approved by the State or territorial agency.

This current system of official course accreditation for CAEs has many strengths. Clearly the establishment of a national register and the attempt to rationalise categories of awards are positive accomplishments. Accreditation has provided distinct payoffs to individual colleges and their staffs. Colleges which undergo the rigour of preparing an accreditation document, having it approved by the State coordinating authority and registered by ACAAE have the assurance that their program is nationally credible and creditworthy. The close and critical scrutiny from colleagues in other colleges and universities, as well as from employer groups, provides the necessary safeguards for the emergent advanced education sector still struggling to find its place in the sun. Accreditation can be particularly beneficial for the newer and smaller institutions; among other things, it often provides an effective means of securing expert assistance in the detailed planning of new courses and the review of course proposals.

On the other hand, there are some obvious weaknesses. At the national level the main weaknesses relate to the composition of the ACAAE, to its performance and to its staff resources. The ACAAE comprises two Federal Government nominees, two persons nominated by each State minister of education, and an independent non-educator chairman, acceptable to all ministers concerned. From the start, most members of the Council have been full-time chairmen or part-time members of State and territorial agencies responsible for accreditation in advanced education. Thus it is not surprising that the ACAAE has seldom taken an independent stance from that of the State agencies on various issues. It has also been argued that more could be done by the Council to promote public discussion and awareness of issues relating to accreditation, credentialling and the length and appropriateness of courses. But this would necessitate the ACAAE having a larger staff. At present it depends on very small staff resources indeed, provided by the Department of Education. We have already noted that one major weakness in the powers of the ACAAE has recently been corrected; until February 1978 it did not have the power to refuse registration of any course and award proposed by a recognised State accrediting agency.

Perhaps the main weakness at State level relates to the marked differences between States with regard to the structures responsible for accreditation, and to the procedures used. It has been argued by many informed individuals and organisations that one result of this particular variation is a lack of uniformity with regard to standards, and that consequently nationally registered courses of the same type and level may differ significantly in quality. We have already noted differences between State (and territorial) accrediting agencies with regard to their internal structures. But there are many other differences as well. First, there are differences with respect to whether or not the accrediting agencies have other responsibilities, and if so, what these responsibilities are. Most State accrediting agencies are statutory bodies, created primarily to take responsibilities for coordination. In some cases these responsibilities relate solely to advanced education, but in others they include all tertiary education or even in some cases all post-secondary education. This raises an important point: is it possible in particular situations that the interests of coordination may conflict with the interests of accreditation? Second, in some States assessment committees work from comprehensive guidelines prepared by the secretariat of the agency concerned (e.g. in Western Australia), while in other cases members of visiting parties are afforded less positive direction. Third, the composition and remuneration of assessment committees varies. In some instances only members from within the State are appointed. Fourth, the quality of documentation varies; in some cases an accreditation submission may be only available on the day of the panel's institutional visit; in others extensive documentation may precede a three-day accreditation exercise by some weeks. Fifth, there are significant differences in the quality of communication between accreditation panels and the State authorities or committees to which they recommend. In one State the Chairman of the coordinating body meets both before and after the technical consultations with the accreditation panel. In another, communication is encouraged only between the accreditation committee chairman and the authority; panel members, in this latter instance, are appraised of the outcome of their recommendations either by hearsay or only after their direct enquiry.

A second general area of weakness follows from this; there is reason for concern in some instances about the briefing, composition and tenure of assessment committees. In his 1975 report on the Australian accreditation system, prepared after a study tour of Australia, Dr. Edwin Kerr, Chief Officer of the Council for National Academic Awards in the U.K., expressed considerable concern about these matters. With regard to the briefing of assessment committees, for example, he commented:

> ... *members of the visiting party do not have a clear understanding of the purpose and principles by which they carry out their accreditation function or of the basis on which they are to judge courses. As a result there is often confusion within a visiting party and discontent within the college on the operations of the visiting party*
>
> (Kerr, 1975: 10).

At college level there are some problems too. The current accreditation procedures clearly take considerable time and effort and impose a significant burden on academic staff. But perhaps more important is the point frequently made that there is a possible conflict between the flexibility of an institution to adapt its programs to meet changing needs and the requirements to ensure programs respectability through cumbersome procedures for course accreditation.

Proposals

Our analysis in the previous section has demonstrated that both universities and colleges use a number of different mechanisms to achieve academic respectability and community acceptance for their courses. All of these mechanisms serve useful purposes, yet at the same time many of them have built-in limitations, or are not working as effectively as they might, or both.

Some might argue that despite these weaknesses the current situation is perfectly acceptable. We would like to put forward a different view. Because of the large measure of effective autonomy they enjoy, especially in academic matters, both universities and colleges have a responsibility to ensure that their programs reach appropriate academic standards and that they generally meet the community purposes for which they were designed. This means that mechanisms of quality control, of review, and of evaluation should not only be suitable for the task but should also operate as effectively as possible.

A number of the current mechanisms could possibly be modified or extended. For example the current official system of course accreditation for CAEs could be strengthened in a variety of ways. Among other things it appears that the national body needs a more independent membership, and that procedures at State and territorial levels could be reviewed and in a number of cases tightened. We understand that such changes are already in train. Possibly the system of external examiners for research theses could be extended in a modified form to the undergraduate level, along the lines of British or New Zealand practice. Another possible development would be for all higher education institutions to begin a regular schedule of internal reviews of faculties, departments and programs. Still again, all higher education institutions could well evaluate critically the effectiveness of their various current procedures of peer review regarding course proposals and course results, as well as their procedures for the appointment of academic staff.

There are other kinds of developments which also deserve to be given serious consideration. In a situation where public sympathy for higher education appears to be declining and where there are frequent demands for closer control over and scrutiny of universities and colleges, it seems essential that higher education institutions and their members attempt more seriously to face up to the issues of academic accountability. In the log run it could be a wise strategy for institutions to do much more in the way of quality control and review of their own programs. This could be preferable to having new mechanisms of evaluation and review or greater outside control imposed by governments. Universities should seriously consider the desirability of developing a voluntary accreditation system. Perhaps under such a system the accrediting agency could accredit whole schools or faculties rather than individual courses. On this point it should be remembered that in the United States the various regional accreditation systems often cover even the most prestigious universities. Perhaps there could be a national system of regular institutional reviews along the lines of the quinquennial reviews of English polytechnics in which the review covers the whole academic program and academic management. Of course, in the past in the university sector the triennial visits to institutions conducted by the Universities Commission were somewhat along these lines. Perhaps more could be done on a voluntary basis by individual university departments to use course assessors from other universities at undergraduate level. For a number of years in one arts discipline, departments in two adjacent New South Wales universities have operated a collaborative system of external assessors for final examinations; in each case, individual assessors for each course have been appointed from the adjacent department. This model, which involves little cost and sacrifice of substantive autonomy, would seem to be one worthy of wider application.

Strengthening of existing mechanisms and the development of appropriate new ones should produce significant gains toward protecting standards and helping all higher education institutions win academic respectability and community acceptance. But in the long run academic accountability depends primarily on the responsibility and integrity of academic staff. The various mechanisms that have been developed, or could be developed, will only work well if individual academics accept the notion of academic accountability for courses and programs, and recognise that the considerable freedoms they enjoy demand a high level of responsibility for their decisions and actions. It is on this, we believe, that academic accountability really depends. Thus, perhaps the most important strategy is for higher education institutions to work by various means to help individual academics recognise and appreciate more fully their great responsibilities to their students and to the community in its widest sense.

Chapter Eight

Academic Accountability—Staff

A. Patching

Introduction

Although the term "accountability" may be relatively new to educational literature there is no doubt that all staff in higher education in Australia are already aware of working under the constraints of an accountability era. The basis for this current vogue is a general public view that it is the prerogative of the taxpayer (consumer) to demand proof of effective performance or excellence of any product. Applied to education it refers to measuring effectiveness.

There are a number of factors that make the accountability movement so evident to staff at present, in particular the numerous inquiries both at State and Federal level involving higher education. In Western Australia Professor Partridge has reported recommending many changes to the organisation of post-secondary education, though leaving the universities least affected by the changes; in South Australia Professor Anderson has released his report with similar recommendations, particularly in merging colleges, and in proposing the establishment of a coordinating body for post-secondary education. In Victoria the long awaited other report by Professor Partridge was released provoking some rather acerbic debate over the subsequent government legislation to establish a Victorian Post-Secondary Education Commission. New South Wales has seen the appearance of the Butland Report and more recently the Hagan report. Tasmania has had a plethora of reports—Karmel, Cosgrove, Kearney, and more recently Connell. Even in Queensland, where there is yet to be a State enquiry into post-secondary education, a select parliamentary committee on education was recently established.

When one examines the terms of reference of each of these enquiries the same words appear again and again—the theme is to rationalise, to coordinate, etc. For example the terms of reference of the enquiry in Western Australia included:

> *The committee is to advise the Government of Western Australia on promotion, development and **co-ordination** of post secondary education in the State having regard to its future needs.*
>
> (emphasis added, Partridge, 1976:15)

It is interesting to recall the words of Professor Karmel, Chairman of the Tertiary Education Commission, in stating that

*Frequently the word co-ordination is used as a polite word for **control.*** (1978 6:3)

(emphasis added, Karmel, 1978b:3)

And with that theme of control we return to the central concept of accountability.

Overlying all these enquiries is the National Inquiry into Education and Training under the Chairmanship of Professor Bruce Williams. In announcing this Inquiry, Senator Carrrick, Federal Minister for Education, described it as "The most important inquiry into post secondary education since the Martin Committee was set up in 1964." (*Hansard,* 9/9/76: 876). It was the Martin Committee that gave birth to the College of Advanced Education sector as we know it today. The question remains open as to what will be the longer term effects of the Williams Inquiry, but the concern this has manifested in academic staff is evident.

In setting up the National Inquiry, Senator Carrick commented: "It is intended that the committee undertake a review of possible developments up to the year 2000." Included in the terms of reference for the National Inquiry are, under Section (a), dealing with the provision of educational facilities and services:

iii) The magnitude of the provision including the desirable balance between the sectors;
and
viii) The means of evaluating the quality and efficiency of the system.

Again Karmel, a man with a unique knowledge of higher education in Australia, has said of the Williams inquiry: "The establishment of the Williams inquiry is itself a symptom of the pressure towards increased coordination [control] and rationalisation." In a word, one of the main concerns is accountability.

A second source of pressure toward an "accountability era" was the introduction in 1976 of the rolling triennium, or annual funding. This was followed on June 3rd, 1977, and then June 9th, 1978 by funding guidelines from the Government. As a consequence of these, the Federal Government has effectively called a halt to expenditure increases in higher education in response to general concern over rising costs and the need for financial stringency. More generally, tertiary education is described as being in a 'steady state'. Allied with these changes has been evidence of a generally held view that academics waste money and that they have been given too much, too quickly in the past. In the words of Peter Samuel "the academic can get away with financial murder" and "plunder the public purse". (*Bulletin,* 12/3/77).

Another area of pressure for greater attention being paid to accountability has its source in the Federal Government decision to take over complete funding of Universities and Colleges of Advanced Education and to provide matching funds for Technical and Further Education together with the State governments. As a result, the doors have been opened for many people to obtain higher education. This change was associated with discussion of a "new" concept—the community college—a concept that received further support as a result of the report issued by Professor Dennison in looking at life-long learning (Dennison, 1976). This was seen by some as the ideal solution to many of the problems in Australian higher education. Conferences and educators all over the continent have examined this topic in recent years, again specifically related to its relevance for accountability. The community college movement has undoubtedly contributed to the current accountability era in further emphasising the importance of questions about the accessbility, relevance, and flexibility of higher education institutions and programmes.

Yet another incentive to consider accountability has come from other enquiries into specific aspects of higher education. In 1977 the Federal Government set up a national inquiry into study leave (staff development leave) in the tertiary sector. Study Leave is seen by many as an unnecessary privilege and a financial waste. The recommendations announced in the draft report, released in 1978, again emphasise this. Section 9.11 states:

> *The Working Party considered that there were inadequacies in the arrangements adopted by universities to monitor and control their study leave and has included in its recommendations proposals which it believes will achieve a higher level of accountability in special studies programs.*
> (T.E.C., 1978: 104)

In addition, Senator Carrick has announced more recently a National Inquiry into Teacher Education. It is clear that the context for this is the need to call teacher education, especially in a period of oversupply of teachers, into public account.

Features of the Accountability Era

There is no doubt that accountability is, and should be, a proper concern of educationists. However, the underlying context of the accountability era is important to recognise. In the United States, back in 1970, President Nixon in his education message stated: "All educators and administrators should be held accountable for their performance." (March 3, 1970). One may suspect, of course, that this emphasis on accountability was to some degree a reflection of the American desire to render every human activity—intellectual, physical, moral, social, and even sexual—accountable in terms of the dollar. This movement generated such activity that in the United States the disciples of accountability under Leon Lessinger have made accountability in higher education a dominant value, a dominance that is now becoming apparent here.

No doubt the cost cutting promises of various accountability schemes have been attractive to politicians seeking economies in Australian education. In fact, in a letter dated 6 October 1977 Prime Minister Malcolm Fraser wrote:

> *In considering the T.E.C. report the government's prime objective is to ensure as far as possible the significant **level of funds** provided for universities and colleges are most effectively directed towards the **benefit of students*** (emphasis added).

This shares in the view of Lessinger and a number of other accountability spokesmen who seem intent upon equating the functions and purposes of higher education with those of business and industry and of economics. Speaking from an organisational, managerial and technical point of view Lessinger compared higher education with a "cottage industry"—he claimed:

> *Costs accelerate, yet there is little improvement in productivity. The 'industry' is labor intensive. Over 85% of average budget is spent for salaries and for benefits related to salaries. Such a share of the education dollar, coupled with professional association militancy, collective bargaining and tenure, presents incredible community problems of runaway costs divorced from responsive improvement.*
>
> (1970: 12)

By such a means humanistic objectives are put forward while the success of higher education is judged in purely economic terms. Overall the exponents of accountability claim that:
* management and business practices introduced through accountability will increase the efficiency and effectiveness of the higher education system;
* all professionals are accountable—and thus the same should apply to educators. (The implication of this claim is that you are only a true professional when you are accountable: this raises interesting questions about doctors, lawyers, and the like);
* there are no existing procedures and practices of accountability;
* accountability and performance-contracting are modern phenomena in education.

However, many educators have objected to the accountability approach, and their views can be clearly contrasted with those above. They include the claims that:
* the accountability literature talks in general terms in a highly abstract manner that suggests a hidden purpose;
* when the advocates attempt to be specific they invariably identify the quantitative aspects of education—input—output—unit cost, and so on;
* the accountability literature abounds in statements of the kind "the public expects greater relevance in higher education", and yet avoids questioning who is the public, and whether or not it does have a common point of view;
* allied to the idea of accountability is a reference to a populist ethos to which politicians and educators appeal when they wish to win more supporters.

Obviously such objections are considerable but they have not had a major effect on the progress toward greater accountability. Why then has it continued? No doubt the current popularity of the accountability movement is related to both political and economic concerns. These views are voiced in Leon Lessinger's aptly titled "Every kid a winner", in which he invokes the right of students to learn and the right of taxpayers to know what results education produces in return for the money spent on it (Lessinger, 1970). The work of Lessinger and others judges educational success purely in economic terms.

> *The first [strategy] is to follow the lead of manufacturing industries—by substituting capital for labour (automation thus increasing the capital to labour ratio—educational 'hardware' is cheaper than lecturers).*
>
> *The second is to vary the labor mix, salary range still the same high to low but a larger number of employees are at the lower end—holding average wage down.*
>
> (Davis *et al.*, 1976: 5)

In his book on management Drucker (1974) declares that service institutions

(such as colleges and universities) must stop being parasites on the well-being of the market economy. He claims the major difference between higher education and business is that higher education must be based on effectiveness not efficiency. Effectiveness (that is, student achievement) can be measured easily and precisely using behavioural objectives. Lecturers are knowledge workers and should be managed like any other workers. What really matters, according to Drucker, is for colleges, universities, schools, and so on to be accountable— for example he believes that colleges need:
1. clear objectives and goals;
2. priorities of concentration;
3. measurement of performance;
4. feedback and to build self control from results;
5. organised audit of objectives and results;
6. identification of unsatisfactory performance and activities that are obsolete, unproductive or both;
7. abandonment of low performance activities;
8. competition between institutions to hold them to performance standards.
This is a view which fits in well with that of politicians. For example, President Nixon stated a few years ago:

> *From these considerations we derive another new concept: accountability. Administrators and educators alike are responsible for their performances and it is in their interest as it is in the interests of their students that they be held responsible ... We have as a nation, too long avoided thinking of the productivity in education.*
>
> (Nixon, 1970: 37)

The U.S. Commissioner on Education, Sidney Marland, himself a Nixon appointment, later proclaimed:

> *Accountability is implicit from day to day and from month to month as all echelons focus their energies on the objectives and perform the various tasks which lead to completion.*
>
> (1972: 4)

There are, of course, a number of other factors that characterise the current accountability era. The major professions of medicine, architecture, law, and education even act as a focus for accountability, and more recently such bodies as the teachers, registration boards and allied bodies have contributed to the need for professional accountability. Professional bodies have also become involved in another crucial area, that of course accreditation. The accrediting process certainly ensures that the CAEs in particular are both educationally accountable and accountable to the community and to other bodies (for example students and government). However to obtain course accreditation is an extremely time consuming task, and this results in a relatively slow response to community needs by comparison with that possible in the other two higher education sectors.

Effects on and Responses of Staff

Staff have felt the effect of the accountability movement encroach upon them in many different ways and with many changes to their academic life-style. These changes include, among other things, increased contact hours and increased responsibilities, both academic and administrative. At the same time, further demands have been placed upon staff, often of an administrative nature, due to the increasing demands stemming from new bureaucratic controls. Yet another effect has been a marked increase in the proportion of *contract* staff being appointed in higher education. Allied with this has been an increased feeling of job insecurity among staff, especially among contract staff. This feeling is being reinforced by the numerous post-secondary education enquiries and the open discussion of redundancy, especially in teacher education institutions. There is also an increase in the feeling of academic isolation, a feeling likely to be magnified greatly if the recent draft report on study leave of the Tertiary Education Commission becomes policy. Yet another area of response has been a tendency to increase the emphasis on differences rather than recognising similarities within the higher education sectors, complemented by an increase in emphasis placed upon all levels of accountability in relation to those differences.

Allied with these responses have been a number of effects on the conditions of service for academic staff. There has been a decrease in the possibility of obtaining study leave or a tenured position, and certainly a decrease in academic freedom for contract staff. And there has been a substantial decrease in resources made available for research.

Unfortunately it seems that many of the moves that have so far characterised the accountability era in Australia are a result of communication failures between the higher education system and the community it serves. The public does not appear to be regarding higher education as making any valuable contribution to society, with the consequence that government is unwilling to provide the resources that the academic community feels are necessary for their continued existence. This present crisis is described by Adams in the following way:

> *Higher education is not in crisis because the need for higher education has diminished, or simply because social attitudes towards the university have changed ... The needs for higher education are no less, now, than they were, if one approaches the question of needs normatively, i.e., if one considers what are the real and crying needs for the education of youth as the citizens and leaders of our nation. Unfortunately we have been hoodwinked into a purely passive and descriptive account of needs—i.e., we have fallen for a definition of needs derived from a reading of the facts of the market-place, as if social and educational needs were directly reflected in enrolment statistics, income available, birthrates, and federal funding. These don't express needs, but only the way in which resources are allocated to meet needs. That we don't allocate resources in conformity with our real needs is the present scandal of government and industry, and one of the main sources of our present national crisis ...*
>
> (Adams, 1974: 2)

It is crucial in responding to the demands for greater accountability that staff, and staff associations, should move toward a greater degree of self-management. Both staff groups and staff associations should be active in a number of areas to respond to the demands of accountability if they wish to preserve higher education in its present form. This will entail a number of strategies: an endeavour to illustrate by their actions the *value* of higher education; to draw public attention to the implications of the drain of funds away from public areas such as education, and to attack strongly any attempt to deny staff academic freedom and tenure. Tenure within tertiary institutions is fundamental to the preservation of academic freedom. It is designed to serve not only advanced scholarship and the scholars involved, but the public good.

> *To a large extent it exists and is recognized because of professional tradition and because it resides inherently in the functions of teaching, learning and research. Faculty members in colleges and universities are usually not employed to follow orders but to render instruction and to pursue inquiries in their fields of competence, largely free of supervision and direction ...*
> (Fuchs, 1963)

There are other issues that staff will need to keep in mind in the future. First, they will have to endeavour to arrest the trend of diminishing research opportunities. They will need to encourage innovation in education and respond to the changing needs of the community, and at the same time reinforce at all times university council and college council autonomy. Finally, staff associations should at all times try to improve conditions of service (a difficult task in an accountability era) and attempt to stop the move toward rationalisation, redundancy and retrenchment.

Chapter Nine

The Manpower Aspect of Accountability in Higher Education

J. Niland

The principles of institutional autonomy and freedom to pursue scholarly interests help place the academic in a special relationship to his work and employer. But this relationship is not so special that academics, even those in the university sector, are absolutely free of responsibility or accountability for their actions. Indeed, there may be no greater threat to academic freedom and university autonomy than society's (over)-reaction to a continued failure by academics to have regard for the labour market consequences of activity in the tertiary education sector. This is not to say that accountability exists only in a manpower dimension, but certainly as we approach the 1980s it is clear that the labour market problems of higher level manpower have become an issue of considerable concern to society.

Various methods for handling problems created by the changing relationship between education and work have been contemplated: job redesign, program restructuring, redistribution of funds between sectors, the introduction of retraining program, the implementation of quotas, early retirements, and so on. But more prominent than any of these approaches is the idea that many problems could be removed through effective manpower planning.

The aim in this chapter is to examine the proposition of accountability in the context of manpower planning. In the first section attention is paid to the credentials creep problem, which together with graduate unemployment usually gives rise to calls for accountability and greater manpower planning. The second section is devoted to a treatment of the various approaches to manpower planning, with an evaluation of the two main approaches—Manpower Requirements and Manpower Absorption—presented in the third section. A modified Manpower Requirements Approach is outlined and advocated in the fourth section. The role of the academic in manpower matters is examined in the final section (based on Niland, 1978).

The Credentials Creep Problem

Over the last 30 years governments in Australia have delivered what is viewed as the nation's birth-right: more and more education to larger and larger numbers. Many sets of statistics can demonstrate this, but one will suffice: in 1954 there were 1000 people in the labour force for every university graduate produced that year: in 1974 the relationship was 300 to one. The pool of "genuine" graduate level jobs has not increased at nearly the same rate, with the result that the relationship between education and work has changed. But this is only the tip of a pyramid that overall is undergoing widespread change. At the lower reaches of educational activity all new entrants to the labour force have spent significantly longer in the schooling process than was the case a generation ago. Today, about 55 per cent of all 16 year olds are still at school, which is double the proportion remaining during the early 1950s (Niland, 1977).

A similar pattern can be identified in most, if not all, western developed countries. The specific effects of such expansion-oriented education policies have varied from country to country according to "the political constellation, traditions in the relation between education and occupation, and the part the state plays in financing education". But overriding these differences in detail is one significant aspect the Australian experience shares with virtually all other western developed countries:

> *In time ... (the) ... optimistic view of educational reform gave way to scepticism. There now exists, for example, widespread doubt whether the expansion of higher education (at least at the tempo observable) noticeably spurs economic growth, and whether the general raising of the qualification* **niveau** *automatically promotes mere rational behaviour on the individual level. So far as the debate on equal education opportunity is concerned, there are growing doubts that equal education opportunity can be provided for all social classes. In addition, the question is being raised whether equality of educational opportunities—supposing this could be realised to begin with— could ever bring about a corresponding measure of equality in socio-economic status. There is, moreover, widespread doubt whether educational planning can be oriented toward equality of opportunity and at the same time satisfy the presumed qualification need of the occupation system.*
>
> (Teichler, 1976: 6)

Before the onset of mass higher education a much greater concordance between the education system and the world of work existed, at least in the sense that the type of job taken by the new graduate was seen to place some significant demands on the skill and perspective inherent to his education. On occasions this may have resulted in shortages in supply to particular occupations, but it seldom produced instances of imbalance through oversupply. Now, the position is rather the reverse as oversupply leads to graduate underemployment. Notwithstanding individual anecdotes to the contrary, educational attainment is used as a proxy for selecting the most suitable job applicant. This, in a sense, has always been the approach. But with the wave of mass higher education, the employer is facing more and more functionally qualified applicants. Other qualities are important, but where there are many applicants the employer comes back to those whose educational attainment is highest. As a result, individuals often have to go on and acquire higher and higher levels of education, not so they will have the ability to perform the *task* but so they will have the credentials to distinguish themselves from near rivals and get the *job*.

This process, with its growing emphasis on higher and higher qualifications, has been referred to in various ways: as credentialism; as the moving target phenomenon; as educational inflation; as the educational Brahmanisation of the workforce; and in this chapter as credentials creep. The key factor is the emergence of a dog-chasing-its-tail element in the nexus between education and work.

Credentials creep presents a number of important problems for manpower planning, not the least of which is the absence of an effective equilibrating or self-correcting mechanism. This means that manpower planners and forecasters must decide whether or not credentials creep is to be accepted or overcome. The issue, as difficult as it may be, cannot be escaped. Neither the employer, the individual nor the educational institutions necessarily find it in their own interests to provide what would amount to a circuit-breaker in this process.

The level of educational attainment provides a convenient label in the busy life of personnel officers, and the many employers who are too small to have such specialist units. This label is viewed largely as a free good by the employer, who makes use of it as a convenient way to separate out applicants. It is not suggested that employers blindly apply an educational attainment test in sorting out job applicants. But so long as educational attainment is used as a screening device, perhaps to determine the short list, those among the applicants who are better educated have a better chance of making that short list and therefore of success than those who are less well educated. The net effect, of course, is to generate even greater importance for educational qualifications, particularly where unemployment rates among youth are high. While there will be cases where particular employers are prepared to factor out the educational effect, in the main they have absolutely no incentive to do this: indeed, by their own standards they behave rationally in using the educational system as a filtering device. For example, it has been argued that firms increasingly will face pressure from those well-qualified employees recruited during the economic boom of the 1960s to deliver the explicit or implicit career promises through internal promotion, which militates against outside appointment to positions higher on the job hierarchy. This has resulted in greater emphasis on recruitment at the bottom with the result that greater attention must be paid to a prospective employee's "trainability":

> *Success in education provides some evidence that the training costs of these ... (better educated) ... employees will be lower than those related to training individuals who have not succeeded educationally. The basic educational theory behind this is that those who have the aptitude and the motivation to learn material whose relevance is not immediately clear to them are more likely to benefit from the training offered by firms, as some of these benefits are also likely to be long term.*

(OECD, 1977: 83-84)

The individual, for his part, is faced by a distinct Hobson's choice. If he pulls out of the educational process he must take a lesser job or face the increasing prospect of unemployment. If he continues on to the higher educational reaches he still ends up with a job he perceives as inferior, by past standard, to his new qualifications. In either event he is confronted with a second-best solution. But on the whole the individual usually finds it less painful to follow the second strategy, and goes on to acquire further education.

While there may be recent signs that interest in university education has slipped, the degree to which this has happened is much less than would be needed to return the education/occupation relationship to its pre-1960s arrangement. The fact that a trend toward lower university enrolment has emerged is, of itself, no evidence that credentials creep is on the wane. The magnitude of such a shift is the crucial point, and the recent adjustments are too slight to provide evidence that a self-correcting mechanism is developing.

The educational institutions themselves have faced funding formulae in which student numbers are paramount. Consequently they show little interest in a more restrained or balanced approach to recruitment. This applies between disciplines within an institution as much as between institutions. Consistent with the credentials creep hypothesis, though not necessarily proof of it, is the trend toward certain forms of higher degree study in Australia. It is now recognised that many bachelors degrees no longer guarantee a job, at least not one appropriate to the qualifications held. It follows that the first degree in itself is less persuasive for rapid career progression. Unable to distinguish himself sufficiently from near rivals, the ordinary graduate returns for further study. In many cases the added education can be relevant to task performance, as with a graduate in engineering who, finding himself involved with management tasks, returns to study business administration. But there are instances where the graduate program is at best only marginally justifiable in the task performance sense.

This trend is clearest in the numbers enrolled in coursework Masters degrees, as distinct from the Masters degree by research: between 1968 and 1976 enrolment in the research programs rose by 62 per cent to 5818, while enrolment in the coursework programs rose by 219 per cent, to 6482. "That it is the credential rather than the education itself which is considered important", as the OECD authors point out, is demonstrated:

> *by the fact that although in some countries there are 'diploma mills' which provide diplomas but virtually no instruction, there are no institutions of higher education which offer instruction but no diplomas. This has led to the suggestion that the proliferation of education certificates at all levels has been due not so much to the desire for equality in itself but to social pressures for educational credentials.*

(1977: 76)

While the credentials creep phenomenon is rooted in the expansion of mass education opportunities, its magnitude has been heightened by the onset of high unemployment levels, particularly among youth. Individuals with no job prospects remain in or retreat back into the educational process. This constitutes a type of hidden unemployment, which in time can convert to underemployment as the individual eventually acquires the educational training necessary to distinguish himself from near rivals and so get the job. Without detracting from the seriousness of problems created by unemployment, it should be recognised that underemployment can create a range of even more serious problems for society as a whole: it leads to frustration and disenchantment on the job; it is more difficult to detect and to measure than unemployment; and its remedy probably requires far more radical restructuring of society and its institutions.

In Australia we now have a situation where the output of higher credentialled individuals is apparently outpacing the ability of industry, commerce and the public sector to absorb them at what, by past standards, is an appropriate task level. While it is not easy to specify what constitutes harmony in the relationship between education or training qualifications and occupation or tasks to be performed, there is broad consensus that the relationship has certainly changed. Whether this is a desirable or undesirable development is much less subject to broad agreement. Indeed, the two main approaches to manpower planning draw their dividing line on this very point.

Approaches to Manpower Planning

In its broadest form, manpower planning implies action in the present to avoid a recurrence of problems in the future

The growing range of problems brought within the purview of manpower planning has extended the range of different approaches contemplated and attempted. In one dimension manpower planning can be seen as either diagnostic, where attempts are made simply to look ahead and chart the hazards likely to be encountered, or decision oriented where the aim is rather to achieve a specified goal. Here the purpose of the plan is to ensure that the supply of trained manpower is available in the right numbers at the right time. In a second dimension manpower planning may be cast at the enterprise level, or at the wider society level. In a third dimension the manpower plan may be essentially supply oriented or essentially demand oriented, although clearly both facets must be accommodated in any competent effort. The question is really whether the one or the other is seen to set the basic constraint. In a fourth dimension, some manpower planning may be designed to achieve essentially manpower goals, while other planning may rather be in the service of non-manpower goal achievement. In the former case manpower planning is not set as a servicing activity, while in the latter case it is. Overlying all this, the manpower plan may be cast along the lines of the Manpower Requirements Approach (MRA) or the Manpower Absorption Approach (MAA).

The Manpower Requirements Approach favours the idea of an "appropriate" level of training and qualification to perform certain tasks. Its aim is to ensure that education and training institutions will operate to provide the necessary manpower for meeting the economy's production, distribution and servicing requirements over the future. The emphasis is on avoiding bottlenecks, although there is also an implication that overqualification should be eschewed in the interests of preserving the historically established relationship between education/training and occupation/task.

The Manpower Absorption Approach, on the other hand, is much less concerned with the changing patterns of education and occupation. Indeed, for social as much as for economic reasons certain advantages in this are identified. For example, although a worker's qualifications may go beyond the primary requirements for the task at hand, he is nonetheless "able to do a better job altogether". Further, the new generation of workers with better educational backgrounds are seen to push for modification to older authority structures in industry, which may spill over into society generally. Hence, as Teichler puts it, the focus of the MAA is rather on the question: "Under what conditions can the occupation system absorb growing numbers of graduates and how would this affect recruitment, occupational structure, the development of occupational roles, etc.". The conceptual, perhaps even ideological, base of the Manpower Absorption Approach is that:

> ... *the traditional notion of 'demand' is too narrow a concept ... supply-induced effects need to be taken into consideration, and ... those who work with requirement forecasts have only a very vague idea of what they mean by 'qualification'. This indicates that there is a wider field for education policy than the Manpower Requirements Approach would lead one to assume.*
> (Teichler, 1976: 18)

Manpower planning cannot operate unless governments and other groups having influence on policy implementation determine whether the goal is to overcome credentials creep or to accommodate to it. Reducing this to a specific illustration, should a law degree, like an arts degree, be seen as one means of preparing for a career in commerce, industry, the Public Service, etc. (as is the tendency in the United States of America), or should it be mainly a preparation for practising as a solicitor or barrister (as was the case in Australia until recently)? This really amounts to a choice between the Manpower Requirements Approach on the one hand and the Manpower Absorption Approach on the other. Without such specification the manpower planner would be free to move in the same direction as in Britain, where there are said to be about 600 lawyers per million members of the population, or as in Israel where the ratio is 2200 lawyers per million members of the population.

The Feasibility of Manpower Planning

One of the intriguing features of manpower planning, particularly the MRA version, is that it enjoys stronger support among the potential user or client groups than it does among the potential producer groups. That is to say, the experts themselves are a good deal more sanguine about the scope for manpower projecting than those who would use the results of such effort (for an optimistic analysis, see Freebairn and Withers, 1977). The support that politicians and other policy makers give to the Manpower Requirements Approach is based largely on the view that it provides an electorally costless means of solving deep-seated problems. Hence the whole area of manpower policy attracts its share of rhetoric and political opportunism.

Scepticism about the feasibility of the Manpower Requirements Approach derives largely from the practical difficulties presented by inadequate data bases, the failure of governments to specify clearly their goals and constraints, the lack of necessary manpower and, perhaps most important, the uncertainty surrounding technological change and changing input/output ratios. In one of his more widely quoted observations Blaug stated that:

> ... *all the evidence shows that we do not yet know how to forecast beyond three or four years with anything remotely resembling the 10 per cent margins of error that are regarded as just tolerable in general economic forecasting ... indeed, so notorious is the unreliability of such forecasts that there is not a single country on record that has made a serious effort to implement comprehensive targets for manpower requirements.*
> (1967)

Little has occurred over the last ten years to warrant a more optimistic view. Indeed, good reason exists to be cautious even about the usefulness of many forecasts in the three to four year range.

Perhaps the most persuasive single indictment of the reliability of medium to long term manpower forecasts comes from Ahamad and Blaug's evaluation of ten major manpower forecasting exercises in eight countries. (Half of these focused at the macro level and half dealt with single occupations.) They found:

> *... that there was considerable variation in the errors of forecasts of employment by occupation, using models similar to the MRP approach. For example, many of the errors in French forecasts were smaller than 5 per cent but, in a few cases, the errors were greater than 20 per cent and in one case it even exceeded 60 per cent. The errors seem to have arisen partly because of the basic fixed-coefficient model that was adopted but there were also large errors in the projected levels of employment and productivity growth in the various sectors of the French economy.*

> *Likewise, for single occupation/education forecasts, we found that there were often large forecasting errors in both the coefficient (density-ratio) and the assumed exogenous variable (output). Swedish forecasts of engineers are a case in point. In some cases, the errors in the various sectors were in opposite directions and hence they partly cancelled one another in the aggregate, in other cases, the forecasting errors were in the same direction and hence there were no cancelling effects.*

(1973: 310-311)

Because of this type of experience the Manpower Services Commission in Britain, a body intimately concerned with the practical policy usefulness of manpower forecasts, has accepted that:

> *At the national level, the labour market is really much too complicated to allow accurate and precise forecasting of the demand for labour: the time lags and uncertainties are simply too great and the usefulness of such forecasts for detailed policy is very limited. No country has succeeded in making substantial headway on the basis of national manpower forecasts.*

(1976: 8-9)

The Australian position should be the same. The weight of evidence against national level comprehensive manpower forecasts, particularly in the long and medium term but sometimes in the short term, is so strong that it would be wishful thinking to imagine we could do better than other countries in this area. In fact our performance would be even less satisfactory, given that other countries have a stronger tradition of comprehensive manpower policy, a much better data base from which to work, and a much more substantial infrastructure of specialists to perform that work.

The Manpower Requirements Approach, on balance, is the more demanding, for the following reasons:
1. The Manpower Requirements Approach implies a bulls-eye focus, whereas the Manpower Absorption Approach deals more with the labour market as a sponge with fairly wide levels of tolerance.
2. The Manpower Requirements Approach would impose a greater strain on

institutions within a democratic framework than would the Manpower Absorption Approach.

3. The Manpower Requirements Approach focuses on the nature of demand, which is the more difficult to divine, and then manipulates supply to achieve balance. The manpower Absorption Approach rather accepts supply to occupations as the pacesetter, with the result that the purpose of the plan is to bring demand and utilisation into line.

4. Most important, the Manpower Requirements Approach generates forecasts whose accuracy and reliability will be very much influenced by the moving target of credentials creep. The Manpower Absorption Approach, on the other hand, accepts credentials creep as a legitimate process: indeed, the whole planning activity revolves around having other institutions and arrangements adjust to it.

While the Manpower Absorption Approach is the easier to implement, there are reasons that this path should not be followed. It has the effect of deferring to what has already happened which ignores the economic and social rationality of the basic arrangement forced upon us. The Manpower Absorption Approach provides no analysis of the absolute desirability of allocation of resources within society. The hidden cost of the MAA is its failure to consider the alternate uses to which funding could be put, such as for housing, transport, health services, etc. It is not suggested that the Manpower Requirements Approach provides a full benefit-cost analysis, but at least this approach in a general way has regard to alternate uses in the sense that it denies to education the *carte blanche* implied in the Manpower Absorption Approach.

A second piont is that the Manpower Absorption Approach ignores the longer term social cost of credentials creep. This can be reckoned primarily in terms of increased job dissatisfaction. In addition, the MAA ignores the fact that the individual is trapped in a vicious circle of credentialism from which he himself may very much like to escape.

Finally, and perhaps most importantly, the Manpower Absorption Approach represents at best a short term remedy. Absorption ultimately will have to confront saturation, which means that the Manpower Absorption Approach is simply delaying till later the application of some approach roughly consistent with the basic aim of the Manpower Requirements Approach.

Nothing put forward here should imply an argument against the importance of manpower planning *per se.* Clearly there is a growing need in Australia for governments, educationists, trade unions, firms, etc. to give much more constructive and integrated thought to what the various manpower goals and constraints should be. The critical emphasis has been rather on the impracticability of any planning which, through the application of manpower forecasting techniques, attempts to follow a rigid Manpower Requirements Approach and the application of output quotas implied therein. Similarly, the Manpower Absorption Approach has been rejected as unacceptable in a broad welfare sense, and as representing at best only a short term palliative.

Given all this, it can be argued that Australia's manpower policy should be based on an acceptance of the following propositions:

1. Imbalances between the education system and the occupation system will continue, probably growing worse until moves are made to confront the problem.

2. The problem is multi-faceted, although in essence it can be reduced to the phenomenon of credentials creep.

3. The Manpower Absorption Approach does not provide a satisfactory framework within which to develop manpower policy. The Manpower Requirements Approach, while conceptually more attractive (these propositions are normative, or ideologically based), requires a degree of skill in manpower forecasting that simply is unavailable. Accordingly, the policy should be a modified Manpower Requirements Approach in which the key aim is to wind back the credentials creep phenomenon.

4. Imbalances will continue and they cannot all be prevented through wise anticipatory measures, but we can reduce their severity and improve our ability to respond to them more effectively in the short term.

The modified MRA is offered essentially as an alternative to those who would promote the development and implementation of detailed manpower forecasts for educational planning purposes. The broad dimensions of this, together with the academic's role in it, are examined in the next section.

A Feasible Manpower Approach

A modified Manpower Requirements Approach, like the Manpower Requirements Approach proper, would accept that manpower planning should eschew credentials creep as a matter of principle. But rather than seeking to meet these problems by having a central authority impose funding cuts in line with target quotas, the modified Manpower Requirements Approach would concentrate the adjustment mechanism at a much more decentralised level, with "the market" playing a greater direct role than is the case with the Manpower Requirements Approach proper. The measures necessary to effect a modified MRA fall into two broad categories: the improvement of labour market intelligence and the modification to procedures and practices. A brief outline is provided below of the types of measures contemplated.

Labour Market Intelligence

A much more sophisticated labour market data base is essential for short term forecasting and for other manpower planning work. This type of data comes from more careful attention to census design, the establishment of longitudinal series through continuous work history sampling, special labour market surveys to link biographic, education and labour market experience variables, and so on. It is used mostly by planners and policy makers. The essence of labour market intelligence is somewhat different, for its main client-user groups are individual decision makers in society, such as school leavers selecting education/occupation streams and firms hiring new employees. Labour market intelligence thus requires the marketing of relevant education/occupation information to a mass audience of non-specialists.

One of the more pressing needs is for a full census survey each year of tertiary institution graduates—the annual survey conducted by the Graduate Careers Council of Australia since 1972 is a useful source of data on first destinations of university (and now college) graduates, and could well be expanded to provide the type of data referred to here. The purpose of such a survey would be to establish for each graduate

1. the type of job secured, particularly the level of task complexity in relation to educational qualifications gained; and

2. the time lapse between completing a program of study and securing full-time employment.

The first-mentioned feature would be rather resource intensive, requiring the establishment of a task evaluation facility similar to that developed and implemented by the Swedish Employers Federation (1977). Such a system would enable a monitoring of credentials creep, which in Australia is urgently needed.

Data on lapse time for placement, while less useful without additional information on the type of placement involved, is nonetheless crucial in itself. The series, once established, would help signal at an earlier stage probable market tightening for different occupations. For example, we might expect that such a series, had it been available for architects since 1970, could have shown in successive years that three months after the final examinations 10 per cent (say), then 15 per cent, then 20 per cent ... etc. of the previous year's graduates were still unemployed. Indeed a full census could easily be implemented by the tertiary institutions themselves if they made completion of the necessary questionnaire at the time of the graduation ceremony a prerequisite (along with a clean account on parking fees and library fines) to receiving the reward. This practice, it should be noted, is the main reason for the excellence of American data on Ph.D. manpower.

A proper labour market intelligence network would form the basis of an early warning system, enabling a range of manpower programs to respond far more quickly and more effectively to emerging imbalances as they are detected. Its importance rests on the fundamental proposition that much (though not all) of the emerging imbalance between the education system and the occupation system derives from poorly-informed decisions: fewer individuals would flow into the education/training streams of tightening occupations if they knew the occupations which were tightening. Focusing on another specific area, much of the present problem with teacher unemployment could have been avoided had manpower specialists—and educators—several years ago shared with prospective entrants to teacher training programs their emerging pessimism about the direction in which the teacher labour market was headed. That is, the clear signs of teacher oversupply were present to be read by manpower specialists several years before this situation became widely known among prospective new entrants.

Australia has no tradition of gathering labour market data. For one thing, most of the period since the Second World War has been free of unemployment problems. Another point is that there have been few, if any, special interest or pressure groups pushing for a more comprehensive labour market data base. In other countries the broader industrial relations system imposes on unions and employers a need for better data specific to certain industries and occupations. But in Australia the arbitration system tends to utilise much more aggregated data, and in any event our system is characterised by small, under-equipped trade unions that are not oriented toward research. Further, the number of academics interested in and working with labour market analysis has been small, particularly in comparison with the number in the United States and certain European countries. As is argued in the next section, the rank and file academic has a professional responsibility to push for much better data on the education-work interface.

Modifications to Practice and Procedure

A series of modifications to practice and procedure in tertiary institutions could help reduce credentials creep. This could be achieved where the individual can exercise greater flexibility in career preparation, where the employers' excessive use of educational attainment as a means of differentiating among job applicants can be overcome, and where tertiary institutions can be dissuaded from their growing scramble for students to maintain funding.

For the individual it is important to provide a more informed framework from which to make educational and occupational decisions. This could be aided by an arrangement in which an individual takes a break between completing secondary schooling and entering tertiary education. Education can be a habit-forming experience, and for many individuals the easiest thing is to continue straight on from secondary school to college or university. But the individual who takes a year off acquires a much better information base from which to make an education and/or occupation decision. Provided he is able to acquire some work experience during the period—and this can be difficult in times of high youth unemployment—he can also provide other employers with an alternate labelling mechanism, that is, performance and references in respect of that work experience.

Similarly, part-time study at the tertiary level should be much more encouraged than it is. The advantages of part-time work are that it delays the point at which an individual makes an irrevocable decision within a stream of study preparing for a specific occupation. Since part-time study is undertaken in the broader context of work, this is likely to lead to a more informed selection of subjects within the overall program of study.

Employers' excessive use of educational attainment as a means of differentiating among job applicants will be overcome only if this procedure either becomes more expensive or a better decision model can be established. This would require more sophisticated hiring tests. The ideal would be a battery of tests that made educational certification unnecessary since the certification could be easily established by the tests themselves. Indeed, just as it may become illegal for an employer to seek details on religion and sex, so too he could be precluded from seeking details on prior educational achievement in most cases. This would certainly inhibit the problem of credentials creep.

Perhaps the greatest potential for inhibiting credentials creep lies in the way universities and colleges acquire funds and recruit students. If governments want to follow the Manpower Absorption Approach there is little need for immediate attention to this area. In the event, however, that the Manpower Absorption Approach is unacceptable, the need to break the nexus between enrolments and funding is paramount. Obviously it will never be possible to ignore completely the number of students attached to an institution in determining the funding for that institution. What is argued here is the need for other factors to be given much more weight than has been the case to date.

The first essential step is for the Federal Government to declare, as part of its overall manpower policy, that the Tertiary Education Commission is free, indeed encouraged, to maintain funding levels to institutions where enrolment is curtailed in courses leading to occupations with employment problems. The Tertiary Education Commission, and its component Councils, could give effect to this policy through three specific devices. These are discussed here in terms of universities, but in a duly modified form could be implemented in other areas as well.

1. The Tertiary Education Commission should designate all degree programs as either:
   (a) occupation preparation specific, or
   (b) occupation preparation general.
2. Based on lapsed-time placement data and using other information provided by a to-be-established Australian Manpower Commission, the Tertiary Education Commission would take each of the degree programs in the occupation preparation specific category and rank them within the following scale:
   (a) demand falling—severe
   (b) demand falling—moderate
   (c) demand stable
   (d) demand growing—moderate
   (e) demand growing—strong.
3. Where degree programs are ranked into the demand falling—severe category, funding levels would be maintained provided the institution does not admit students whose matriculation score is lower than the average matriculation score of, say, the bottom 10 per cent of students admitted to that degree program in the previous year. Students admitted in contravention of this formula would not be counted for funding purposes, and indeed might impose on their institution actual funding cuts.

This scheme, obviously, would require a much more sophisticated data base than is at present available in Australia.

The Role of the Academic in Manpower Matters

The credentials creep problem is complex and not easily overcome. Certainly the individual academic does not have the power to throw the circuit-breaker. Indeed, as has been argued earlier, this is not really within the competence of any of the groups potentially accountable for credentials creep. But to the extent that some remedial action is possible the most likely effectiveness lies with governments through efforts to improve labour market intelligence; with employers through more appropriate personnel selection procedures; and through macro-level tertiary bodies revising student funding practices and procedures. The academic really has a secondary role in all this. Still, he does have clear responsibilities. He can and should be held accountable for failing in future to meet these responsibilities, which can be captured in two simple propositions.

First, the academic is obliged to consider and confront manpower issues. In earlier days when the main imbalance problem was undersupply of skilled manpower the academic's divorce from these issues could be more morally justified. But with the switch to problems of excess supply, underemployment and even unemployment, the academic is no longer entitled to ignore the labour market consequences of his professional action.

Second, the academic's growing awareness of manpower matters must be backed up with his own specific involvement in certain ways. A number of initiatives can be identified:

1. The academic has a professional responsibility to press for the collection of better data covering the linkage between education and work. This may be achieved through staff associations or through the institution structure proper.

2. The academic has an equal responsibility to help disseminate the labour market intelligence among his students, and to encourage in them an awareness of labour market data and details. This is less important where a student is pursuing a particular program purely for its inherent educational value. But most students, even those at university, eventually see their studies as preparation for the world of work. The academic should be held accountable for his students' ignorance of the labour market problems presented through credentials creep and underemployment. Responsibility for ensuring realistic work expectations among students rests primarily with the academic.

3. The academic should encourage those full-time students with labour market anxieties to switch to part-time study when appropriate job openings occur. This would help overcome the problem of large numbers of graduands from full-time study attempting to squeeze into the labour market during the December/February period. One implication of this for the academic is clear: he must accept growing responsibility for providing lectures and consultation during the evening.

4. The academic should develp stronger ties with professional bodies and work with his practitioner counterparts in attempting to understand the labour market conditions for graduates.

5. To encourage a greater use of independent testing devices among employers the academic should resist pressures from that group for more details on students' performance, such as exact marks, class rank and so on.

This hardly imposes an onerous load on the rank and file academic, particularly given that the problem to be confronted is in part the result of his own actions. Morally the academic should probably be called upon to account for much more than has been prescribed here. But, to be pragmatic, the most effective agents for change are the government, the employers and the bodies like the Tertiary Education Commission. What is distressing is that most academics will not willingly accept even their secondary role in manpower responsibility.

Chapter Ten

Accountability: Philosophy and Practice

N. A. Nilsson

My task was to give some sort of philosophical overview of the foregoing chapters for the sake both of theory and of practice. But not only do these papers show a great variety of concern; they arise out of a variety of specialised disciplines. What is more, all the writers seem to have different ideas about what exactly "accountability" means, although they certainly all have a fair idea what it *means*. On these substantive matters I am not competent to criticise the specialists in their own fields. And it would be pointless, even if I could, to summarise what they say. What I shall do is attempt to show how we can deploy their achievements to help us cope with a rapidly developing practical situation in which we are all to some extent personally involved. I shall look first at the notion of accountability itself, paying particular attention to the various ways in which the term is used in these papers. I shall then try to distinguish the substantive from the semantic issues and try to provide a map by which to locate and relate our treasures.

We are told that "accountable" is synonymous with "responsible" and "answerable". This is not so. Certainly "accountable" and "answerable" seem to mean much the same, but it requires a very special context for "responsible" to do duty for either of the other two. But as a way of getting started, I shall give an apparent counter-example to what I have just said. In this, "accountable" just means "responsible". It is from the *Edinburgh Review* for 1821 in which the Rev. Sydney Smith (the clergyman whom Lord Macaulay nicknamed "the Smith of Smiths") attacked the savage use of spring guns and man traps against poachers.

> Their object is to preserve game; they have no objection to preserve the lives of their fellow creatures also, if both can exist at the same time; if not, the least worthy of God's creatures must fall—the rustic without a soul—not the Christian partridge—not the immortal pheasant—not the rational woodcock, or the accountable hare.

(Smith, 1821: 128)

This apparent exception I shall attempt to explain later. For the moment it suffices to draw attention to the assumed uniqueness and supposed special worth of creatures like ourselves who can truly be said to be *responsible* for their actions. But responsibility and accountability are not the same things. There are many things I am responsible for which I am not, as it happens (but only as it happens), accountable for. Little things. Most of the things, perhaps, that I do. For example the choice of socks I made (*almost* without thinking) this morning. What *is* true is that anything at all that I am responsible for I may find myself accountable for as well. Something which might seem utterly trivial in one society or set of circumstances may be fraught with grave consequences in another. To be accountable I must be liable to be called to account for what I do—and the likelihood here must be a real possibility, even if I remain accountable (because of, say, another's neglect) only in principle. And I can only be called to account by a person—another person. (Self-accountability is an institutional concept and really means mutual accountability.) Moreover there are many things which are not trivial and for which I might be responsible but not accountable. There is a very imperfect fit, for example, between morals and the law. And there are other occasions, too, when a sudden shift of values may give a new significance to some action hitherto unnoticed. I might not only escape the attentions of the police, but of the neighbours as well, and even the conservationists. I do something, say, and there is no-one who would so much as dream that I ought to be called to account about this, nevertheless serious, matter. I have just eaten the very last great auk for supper, and no one cares. No one at all.

And just as we can have responsibility without accountability so we can have accountability without responsibility. I may be called to account because of actions which were unintentional or accidental. Indeed, I may be called to account (as head of a government department, say) because of actions which were not mine at all and of which I knew nothing and could have known nothing. It is possible for a baby in arms or a totally insane person to be legally accountable for some harm. And it is interesting to note here how the two words might retain quite different associations in the discussion of criminal responsibility. Attempts have been made, for example, to extend the notion of strict liability as a beneficent principle in criminal law. This repudiation of the doctrine of *mens rea* was described as "the elimination of responsibility", causing great scandal. As H. L. A. Hart (1968: 197) pointed out, however, there was no question at all that anyone was attempting to eliminate legal *accountability*.

There are two reasons why responsibility and accountability are often confused. The first is verbal and the second metaphysical.

1. Firstly, it is only persons who can be morally responsible. Persons are said to be responsible *for* all sorts of things—too many for convenience. I am responsible for the health of my children, and I am also responsible simply *for* my children (in respect of, say, the comfort of my unhappy neighbours). Much the same goes for my pet dog. What is more, I am responsible for seeing to these things (which is to say I am responsible for my actions), and I am also said to be responsible for the consequences of those actions. But there is worse to come. As far as ordinary language is concerned I can be responsible for the dent in the ground when I innocently fall off the roof in just the sense (a purely causal one) in which we can say that hailstones were responsible for the dents in that same roof. At least it seems to me that ordinary language will allow us to say all these things. Sometimes, admittedly, there is disagreement about some of them: as,

for example, whether it can be said quite naturally that someone is responsible for his actions (rather than, say, for the consequences of those actions) (see Pitcher, 1960; cf. Hart, 1968). But for all that there is no doubt that I can have many responsibilities *for* many things (which, by the way, does not necessarily make me a responsible person). And the notion in particular of an action freely chosen is a central one despite all these other cases. But in addition to the notion of being responsible for things, *as* someone, there is the rather different notion of being responsible *to* someone. Now "responsible to" *does* roughly mean the same as "accountable to" and "answerable to". Hence, perhaps, the mistaken belief that "responsible" *tout court* means the same as "accountable". But this is not so. One can be responsible without being responsible *to* anybody. To be accountable, on the other hand, one *must* be accountable to someone, at the very least in principle.

2.   But might there not also be a conceivable set of circumstances in which all cases of being responsible for our actions, however trivial, are cases in which we are responsible or accountable *to* someone? And I mean everything. He, whoever he is, keeps even *such* accounts. This situation is not merely conceivable; it has been quite familiar for centuries. God is supposed to do just this. And this explains the Sydney Smith quotation above. We have here the theological concept of Accountable Man, but it needs a very special context to sustain it. God notices and cares about everything done through an exercise of free will, however trivial it might seem to us. What is more, there is actually a *Day* of Accounting. God then, and the day of the trumpets. Which brings me to the chairman of the Tertiary Education Commission.

The groundwork for the present accountability movement as an exercise in the increasing governmental control of higher education was laid in the 1973 Report of the Interim Committee for the Australian Schools Commission (Karmel, 1973). But although educational accountability is an ancient idea— Socrates was executed because of it—in its present form it is an importation from America. In a famous statement on 3 March, 1970 President Richard Nixon told the United States Congress:

> *From these considerations we derive another new concept:* **accountability**. *School administrators and school teachers alike are responsible for their performances and it is in their interests as well as in the interests of their pupils that they be held accountable.*
>
> (Nixon, 1970: I,3.)

It was this particular notion of accountability which became firmly established in government circles in Australia in 1973 through the influential Karmel Report. In chapter 18 of that report, entitled "Administration and Accountability", the following statement occurred:

> *The Committee is concerned that there should be public accountability in respect of all grants recommended. Public accountability implies published evidence that funds have been applied properly.*
>
> (Karmel, 1973: 136)

Although it is possible, as D'Cruz (1977) has shown, to extract a broader (and actually conflicting) view of accountability latent in other more theoretical parts of the same Report (especially Chapter 2), it is difficult to think that this kind of educational slip-slop is anything more than a cosmetic exercise. Brian Crittenden has this to say of it:

> *I have taken the authors at their word when they say that financial decisions in education should be guided by criteria of educational theory and value, and I have tried to draw attention to important aspects of the report in which its statement of theory is vague or ambiguous or inconsistent, either within itself or with its practical conclusions.*

(Crittenden, 1975: 19)

And in my opinion he succeeds. It is this narrow public accountant's view of accountability which has prevailed and is now being extended into the post-secondary sector.

I have no doubt after reading the present collection of papers that we all know pretty accurately now what is going on, and even to some extent what might be in store for us. We have been very well briefed. The difficulty about a paper like Chippendale's is that after reading it there doesn't seem much more to be said on that particular topic. The only worry I have is that he might have put ideas into their heads. I shall try a little later to give a map of these achievements, for I think they are already considerable. At the moment, however, I am particularly concerned about the best way to discuss it all. And I should like firstly to try out the usefulness of my distinction between accountability and responsibility.

I have suggested that responsibility and accountability have been confused because "responsible to" means much the same as "accountable to" and "answerable to". But let us now ask why it is that in the ordinary affairs of men "responsible to" should have come to mean much the same as "accountable to" and "answerable to". It is not really all that surprising. By the time one of the multitude of actions and effects for which in a literal sense I am responsible reaches the dignity of provoking comment, I am already operating under the social constraints of likely blame and possible sanctions. "He is responsible for that", is something we might say a thousand times a day, but we don't. We save up such expressions for special occasions. In other words, the interesting cases for practical purposes are those in which someone is *held* responsible. What is significant here is not the proposition that someone is responsible for something but the utterance. To understand this better, let us turn to the wider notion of being held accountable. We bother to hold people accountable for the same reason that we hunt up any other causes in nature which might affect our well-being. We have a *right* to be interested in what others do when what they do (and even what their dog does) can have important effects on our lives. And the concept of accountability logically implies such a claim of legitimacy. To this extent we must often mind our neighbour's business in order properly to mind our own: and that is a basis for justification. But in a context of likely blame and punishment we are most interested in those things for which men are not merely accountable but for which they are also responsible. "Responsible to" is a shorthand way of referring to the particularly interesting cases when a person is "accountable to" another in a context of likely blame or punishment; when, that is to say, he is not merely accountable but personally responsible.

To be responsible for an action I must have done it, and done it freely. To be accountable, on the other hand, is to be liable to be called to account for such an action. And it is irrelevant whether I am *likely* to be called to account. To be actually called to account could be thought of as unpleasant, although not necessarily as bad. Like taking medicine. We might even believe that we deserve investigation. "Give an account of yourself!", says Dr. Arnold of Rugby, and Tom Brown trembles—but not Flashman. The logic of accountability is closely tied up with words like "authority", "respect", "power" and "punishment". But certainly the exhortation "Give an account of yourself!", even if not particularly frightening, is definitely threatening. But although this particular *use* of the phrase contextually implies disapproval, this is no part of the logic of the word. Some people are even encouraged to look forward to the Day of Judgement. They have nothing to hide (or so they think) and perhaps a great deal to gain. For we can only deserve praise or other rewards if the actions which attract them are our very own. We can acquire all kinds of responsibilities, then, and even acknowledge them as responsibilities without ever being called to account or even held accountable.

And then it happens. We are given a medal or the Order of Merit, and we know that there must have been an accounting. "This is your life", they say to us. Now it has been a bit like this with post-secondary education recently. Suddenly the government through its academic hacks has shown a particular interest in things which have hitherto gone unquestioned officially. And suddenly we find all sorts of things pinned on us.

Many of the present papers are concerned with the exercise of *power* over institutions in a variety of areas from staff conditions to curriculum. Universities and·colleges are to be coerced into doing this or that. And this exercise of power is taking place in an atmosphere of disapproval (deserved or undeserved). What is accountability, then? Obviously it's what they can do to us. Good Heavens!, it's what the *are* doing to us. But to refer to this simply as accountability is a great muddle.

There are two main classes of things which, it is alleged, they are doing or are likely to do to us. Firstly, what they do to us in the way of investigation; and secondly, what they do to us as a result of such investigation. Either or both of these could be completely justifiable. The question to ask is whether they *are* justifiable. We should also note that with careful management of public opinion and the orchestration of incipient institutional rivalries such an investigation could actually take on the complexion of a punishment. Peter Sheldrake has considered the idea that in a Gilbertian situation such as our present Enquiry War one could well (even without the help of Sullivan) present the inadequacies and arbitrariness of many current "enquiry" recommendations in terms of "the punishment fitting the crime". And certainly the foolishness of some of the reports is well matched by that of some of the submissions. Partly, of course, this remark of Sheldrake's is just a bit of fun. But it is also partly true. To call, say, the universities to account against a background of vote-catching scurrility could *literally* be described as punishment. To punish academics is currently very good politics. Thus Ramsey and Howlett quote Senator Rae's deprecatory but very significant remark during the Senate debate on the Annual Report of the Australian National University: "... we are not concerned with aggressive accountability, we do not operate on the basis that we require institutions to answer our queries as though they were malefactors of some sort". (Hansard, 10 March,1978). The paradigm of an action or activity falling under the concept "punishment" is the deliberate infliction by someone in authority, and according to rule, of something unpleasant on an offender because of something he has done or left undone. To inflict the Anderson Committee on South Australia because of certain particularly nasty border disputes might well be thought of as a punishment, and perhaps as thoroughly deserved, in just those terms. The results of their ineptitude, though, is better described as an affliction. It is the difference between the lash and the common cold.

Accountability is a concept closely connected with authority, and authority is[x] a very different thing from power. One can be in authority and have a right to demand information but have no power to give this effect. On the other hand one might possess the power to mount a Watergate break-in or enforce a search but without the authority to justify it. Or even if one is in authority this might still not be a proper exercise of that authority. A justification is necessary. We must not confuse accountability with burglary, or highway robbery (Stand, if you please, or sit—but deliver!).

Even when someone is legitimately accountable the procedures for calling that person to account can be objectionable (in their publicity, say, or in their frequency) and therefore to some extent self-stultifying. The concept of answerability—which as far as etymology is concerned underlies this little family of concepts—is delicately poised between answering questions and answering charges. Such demands could amount even to harassment: where a person's ability to accomplish the very things for which he is to be called to account is impaired. But worse: it could (as in the case of accountability as punishment) significantly diminish the area in which he exercises the freedom of choice on which his responsibility depends. Punishment is pressure, and pressure means reduced freedom. And reduced freedom implies diminished responsibility, and this (as some people wish to use the term) seems to mean that a person is less accountable. So more accounting means less accountable? Surely not. Hall and Willett are right when they point out that "a person whose decisions are checked frequently is less responsible than one whose decisions are untested ... for years, for example, a chief executive" (36; See also Ramsey and Howlett: 75). This is the crucial ambiguity in the notion of "more accountabie". Does it mean more importantly accountable because accountable for so much more or for things of so much more importance—or does it mean more subject to petty harassment by the self-important?

Accountability, then, requires some kind of justification in terms of rules and legitimate procedures. But of course these can conflict, and we are thrown back on disputes about values. Just think of the work of clarification and reconciliation to be done in a field which includes such concepts as duplication, freedom, coordination, diversity, rationalisation, autonomy, efficiency and relevance. We could make a start by redeeming some of them from their present status as mindless catch-words. Burke and McKenzie have made an important contribution here with their investigation of the notion of efficiency. They rightly point out that the demand for efficiency is a "common thread amongst all the pressures for accountability" (97), and they show very convincingly that this leads to muddled thinking and a narrow view of educational responsibility. But they also claim that the "notion of efficiency logically should be subsumed by that of accountability" (81). This however, is not the case. The connection with "efficiency" is a contingent, not a logical matter. Firstly, as Burke and

McKenzie know well, the notion of efficiency is neutral as between a number of conflicting values. In the present context, however, that unqualified use of the word which they warn us of (97) does tend to attract certain values of the production line sort. Efficiency unqualified could bring all sorts of horrors. As Fungus the Bogeyman's wife Mildew remarks first thing in the morning:

> *'I'll change the sheets today, drear. The dirt has almost worn off these.'*
> *'I know love, (he replies) the smell's all gone.'*
>
> (Raymond Briggs, 1977)

But in addition to such unusual efficiencies accountability can actually accommodate inefficiency as well. We can see this if we move from the realities of children's literature to the fantasy world of industry. One can be called to account (as every shop steward knows well) because one is not doing one's worst, or because one refrains from properly and decently "going slow".

Accountability is a verbal device for endorsing what people may do or try to do to us by implying that it is in some sense justified, usually by reference to certain reasonable duties. The range of justification which might warrant accountability is the same as that which warrants the authority. And it is a very considerable range raising all sorts of problems about:

> *Why be accountable? Who is accountable? Accountable to whom? Accountable for what? When is one accountable? How is one to be accountable?*
>
> (D'Cruz, 1977: 188)

There is no doubt that there are many things going on in the post-secondary sector for which we ought to be called to account, and for many of which we are also in fact responsible. There are also, however, many things which we ourselves are not responsible for. Nevertheless we are the ones who have to show them all in our accounts. Some of the worst of these are due to the mistakes of our masters. But then memories are short, and they keep changing their hats; and who cares anyway? It's just like them to make a mess and then start complaining a year or two later about the smell.

As D'Cruz has reminded us, when we get down to sorting out just what our responsibilities and accountabilities are the situation becomes fairly complicated. And some of the answers to his sensible questions are little short of irresponsible themselves. Hart helps here when he points out that the concepts "'responsible person', 'behaving responsibly' (not 'irresponsibly'), require for their elucidation a reference to role-responsibility"—a very complex business (Hart, 1968: 213). The subject is connected with that quaint talk of old-fashioned moral philosophers about "my station and its duties" (Bradley, 1935: 160). A moment's thought should provide us with the picture of a network of overlapping and conflicting duties and expectations which, if it doesn't alarm us, should certainly preserve us from complacency (see Harman and Johnson: 106). Or so you would think. But what do our New Accountabilists think about it all, and what guidelines do they offer? If we are to believe D'Cruz and Crittenden, the Interim Committee for the Schools Commission were so muddled that their advice wouldn't have been worth having. But worth having or not, there were some important people on that committee who as senior administrators were in a position to retail their two pennyworth of committee wisdom to their employees whether they wanted it or not. Thus A. W. Jones for example, then Director General of Education in South Australia, to his teachers in 1974:

> *To whom is the professional educator accountable? Teachers, for example, are accountable to their employers, their school principals, their staff colleagues, the parents of their pupils, their pupils, the teaching profession and they are also responsible to themselves. Increasingly, professional educators are being held accountable by an informed public who are demanding evidence ... etc. etc.*
>
> (Jones, 1977: 20)

It's not very clear. How far does accountable go? Is it merely the provision of information, and if so would that do for "their employers"? Does it mean a great deal more, and if so would that do for "the parents of their pupils", or, for that matter, "their pupils"? And what if these various accountability demands conflict? Has Mr. Jones as a senior administrator never encountered that? What do the teachers do then? Poor devils. And is the kindergarten teacher really to be *accountable to* her charges? (Five-year-olds often have quite bizarre preferences). Teachers "are responsible to themselves" too, we are told for good measure. But who is talking about responsibility? Does the writer think that responsibility and accountability are the same? Is it because he thinks that they are the same that he makes the foolish statements in the first part of the paragraph? Does he think at all? With nothing to go on but nonsense like this how could we ever find out?

The paradoxical accountability of the kindergarten teacher or the teacher of the mentally defective to her charges is part of the same pattern of rhetoric which lends plausibility to the withering away of the autonomy of tertiary institutions. But if we drive the wedge I have been recommending between accountability and responsibility we can rob this rhetoric of much of its strength. We might indeed have certain responsibilities to all and sundry, but that does not mean that we must be directly accountable to them all. One can *have a responsibility to* someone without *being responsible to* him in the sense of being accountable to him. The mistake is a verbal one, and it is as simple as that. One might indeed discharge this responsibility by refusing to be accountable to him. The relationship between a teacher and pupil or between a doctor and patient is a very subtle and complex one. There are things, for example, which it is necessary to know about one's student or one's patient but never to divulge to him. And if there are occasions on which our very responsibility forbids us even to make answer, how much less defensible is it for us to put ourselves under direction—as if this could come forward as accountability in any sense. It might well be irresponsible of academics *not* to act as critics of the society which pays them, or to provide their students with what they want rather than what they need. To defer to the lay opinions of our paymasters in genuinely academic matters is to betray the duty we owe to them. And this is so, even if they don't mind (cf. McDonell: 45). The well-known problems here are problems not of authority, but of power. There is a difference, incidentally, between the case of the pupil and that of the paymaster. We must refrain from deferring to the opinion of the former in certain matters because we have a *responsibility* to him, whereas we must avoid deferring to the opinion of the latter because we are *accountable* to him.

It is here that we can find a place, in the case both of CAEs and universities, for academic autonomy. There are aspects of professional responsibility requiring such freedoms throughout the whole tertiary sector. It is not a monopoly of the universities. But there are certain things, to do with research for example, which are peculiarly the province of universities and need special protection. And I believe these should be safeguarded for the sake of the whole tertiary sector. Peter Chippendale reminds us that one main contributory factor to the current pressures upon us is the "promotion by the State of new forms of post-school education which lack a tradition of autonomous government" (18). I certainly do not think, however, that the universities should have immunity from constraints on activities which they share with the CAEs—"shared" in many cases because of irresponsible poaching. Universities should be free not to do as they like but to do what they ought to be doing. But for these substantive positions I have not offered any arguments here. Nor do I think it is simple. Hall and Willett, for example, introduce (in sharp disagreement) the question of the independence of the notions of institutional autonomy and academic freedom, with the universities of West Germany as their example (41, 42). But I suppose we all know that an increase in autonomy is very welcome to the Mafia in some of our institutions of higher culture—although it's often a bit hard on the academics under their control. All I have undertaken to argue here is that for the sake of certain freedoms throughout the whole tertiary sector we must insist on the distinction I have indicated between accountability and professional responsibility. And with this, of course, we have raised the idea of self-regulation and accountability within an institution (see Harman and Johnson).

The pressures on academics caused by present methods of funding, with the consequent unseemly scramble for students, could give rise to another case of the improper use of power disguised as accountability. They will "vote with their feet" we are told, menacingly. We become "accountable" now to our customers. And with an imminent over-supply of medical practitioners there is the danger that something very similar might happen—perhaps is already happening—there. Doctors might more and more be tempted to give their patients what they want rather than what they need, dignifying this as accountability. And patients want all sorts of things besides pills. There is as great a challenge here to professional self-regulation as there is in those areas in which we academics are currently found wanting. Still they have made a start. The Australian Medical Association has already, I believe, amended the Hippocratic oath with the admonition: *Timeo Danaos et dona ferentis*—Watch out especially for Greeks bearing gifts.

I began by suggesting that although most of the writers seem to have different ideas about what "accountability" means they all have a fair idea what it *means*. This second sense of "meaning" brings us to a consideration of practicalities and strategies. It directs our attention to accountability as a movement, the import of which we may explore in devising our day to day procedures (if the demand is legitimate), or in devising strategies of defence (if it is only an exercise of political power). And we have an interest in this not only as educationists but as practitioners as well—workers (to quote a delightful parody by Ted Caddick) "in the grass roots at the coal face".

The exploration of these substantive questions lies, for example, with the theories of higher education and of public administration. But the most concerted and detailed efforts of this kind so far have been organised in the service of government by enquiry. This opens up two very interesting questions. Firstly, what responsibilities does this lay upon the members of the academic community, and how should they discharge them? And secondly, in the case of the members of these committees of enquiry (and especially of their "expert" chairmen who tend to remain behind in senior secretarial positions), to whom are *they* accountable?

Harry Medlin has a sharp answer to this. He is suspicious of us all:

> *The time has come to turn the tide and to demand answerability of the plethora of mediocre pedants flung up in and around higher education over the last five years or so ... Answerability must now be required of the trendies, sutlers and sycophants who smokescreen the contest by pretending that to 'prose on' about educating is the same or even better than doing it.*
>
> (Medlin, 1978)

The only disagreement I have with this is that I believe talking about education is important, and could be done better. Moreover I should like to suggest some ways in which we might improve it, or at least discredit some of the "prosing on" he refers to. I shall look first at the level of responsible educational theorising in the post-secondary sector today, and then at the enquiry industry itself.

One has only to look at the present collection of papers to be convinced that there is a great amount of responsible and effective work being done throughout the tertiary sector. There is, however, some want of coordination, and there is above all a want of disrespect for the inept pronouncements of educational experts in positions of great power. As to the former, it is interesting that one of the more important developments has occurred in the CAE sector with a series of influential conferences at the Darling Downs Institute in Toowoomba. The first organised response to the 1973 Karmel Report on Schools in Australia, with its emphasis on accountability, took place at one of those conferences. But the response overall in the tertiary education sector is still fragmentary and timid. Think of all those departments of Education eating their heads off in the nineteen universities, and the fifty educational research and development units scattered throughout the universities and colleges.

There are special problems about the university departments of Education. With some notable exceptions they are very timid when it comes to disagreeing with authority—especially when that authority is responsible for employing their graduates. This is a pity because certain members of the post-secondary sector are especially protected so that they can speak out when necessary, and when they do one always hopes that it will be for everybody. One would hope, for example, that in university departments, where it is so cheap to be brave, one could develop a resource for defending the defensible anywhere in the sector. But it hasn't happened significantly so far.

In addition to this, however, there is an intellectual failure. One of the freedoms of academic life is that you can choose your own problems, and you might well decide to exercise this freedom by choosing problems which you know you can manage using existing techniques. And no-one would deny that it is important to develop and extend such techniques in the social sciences. It is hard to find good sergeant majors to train students on the parade ground of the M.Ed. and Ph.D., and they should be cherished when they are found. Still it is not as easy to restrict oneself thus in an engineering discipline like Education as it is in some of the social sciences. In the social sciences you do have a certain latitude to explore possible worlds; but again and again in Education you are forced to pay attention to the one you are currently stuck with: the world, for example, of the Tertiary Education Commission. This is the world which obtrudes upon us when someone finishes a new report—on post-secondary coordination in South Australia, say, or on study leave. A large bundle of papers lands on somebody's table and the question arises about what to do with it. One of the things we can do, and ought to do, is look critically at such productions as pieces of educational theory.

Sometimes the university administration, say, will send such a document off to the university department of Education for a professional opinion. One of the more comical memories I treasure is of a senior academic caught in this way going around asking people how on earth to go about it. Where should he begin? There was no way that any of the familiar tricks in his post-graduate puzzle box could help him even to get started. Now I am not entirely unsympathetic with this. Consider, for example, if the bundle of papers happened to be the Karmel report on Tasmania, or the Anderson report on Darwin or an account of that long battle on shared funding between Senator Carrick (the Federal Minister for Education) and two of the State Ministers at the secret meeting of the Australian Education Council in June, 1977. The prospect of making sense of any of those documents would make anyone scared. Where indeed *do* you start? But for all that, start you must. The difficulty of course is that the educational cogitation which goes on when the important decisions are made is couched (if that's the word) in ordinary language. There is none of that carefully vetted stuff which is all that is allowed when a poor student is hammering out his thesis proposal. Senator Carrick has probably never put forward an M.Ed. proposal in his whole life. He skips around and ducks and weaves and keeps changing the rules because he has the power to do so. Some student. As for the report writers, they throw up a facade of tables and figures and academic looking prose, but again and again it is evident that the real weight behind the recommendations lies elsewhere. Some might suggest that these documents should not be seen as exercises in educational theory at all, and that we should only look at the conclusions and learn to duck or ride with the punches. But I think this is too cynical a view; and I also think it is gutless. I am all for parade ground drill, but one justification for such manoeuvres is that some time you might be expected to show what you can do on the battle-field.

One of the ways in which we might orchestrate some kind of responsible opinion about these matters is through administrative studies. Educational Administration is an area in which we might expect some output from university departments of Education. Although in some places a lot of it is little more than in-basket/out-basket prestidigitation, there is a real subject there somewhere. I know there is, because it is related to the subject of public administration and I have actually heard people talking sense in that subject. Roger Scott, for example, addressed himself to the problem of educational accountability in his inaugural lecture at the University of Queensland this year (1978). The task, he said, was "to bring to bear some of the recent studies in the general field of Public Administration upon the more tepid controversy about the efficiency and effectiveness of the tertiary sector of education" (Scott, 1978: 1). But what help have we had so far from Educational Administration itself in Australia? Consider, for example, W. G. Walker's paper "What On Earth Is Accountability?" at the 1973 conference in Toowoomba. As an orientation paper it was a disaster.

In this paper he offers to "look at a definition of the term; relate accountability to the concept of power"; and to place all this in the context of the real situation abroad and in Australia, supported by historical examples. But for Walker "accountability ... is simply responsibility". That is his first mistake. Therefore, he goes on, we must begin with "the concept of power". And that's his second. He shows no knowledge of the standard logic of these terms in elementary social and political philosophy. He makes no attempt to relate "power" to "responsibility", or even to distinguish it from "authority". He claims (as a basis for his historical examples) that accountability simply has to do with having a "*powerful* master" (my emphasis); and for this purpose "compassion" (of all things) can count as "a master". He believes that an early Governor of New South Wales actually held himself "accountable *to*" (my emphasis) not only the Colonial Office but also "the hordes of children ... who roamed the streets of" Sydney. He believes "that accountability is a multifaceted concept", and pictures it as a cube divided into nine segments on each of which he writes something like "child", or "Australian society", or "self-esteem". What is more, if the accountabilists get too menacing we can always say to them: but gentlemen, "education consists largely of a close human interaction relationship, almost mystical in character ..." (Walker, 1977). And in all this Professor Walker claims to be against accountabilism. No wonder. I wish he were on the other side.

In raising my second practical question about accountability I refer to the work of those whom Harry Medlin refers to as that "plethora of pedants flung up in and around higher education over the last five years or so". But it is connected of course with our previous question about the responsibility of educationists in universities. They don't come from Mars, these so-called experts. But they do have manifold responsibilities, and these generate a complex network of accountability relationships. One thing is certain: insofar as their work is peddled as academic (and there is no doubt that their ability to provide this kind of imprimatur is one of their main attractions for the politicians who employ them) they are of course accountable *to us*.

We must be very clear about that characteristic by which, for example, the post-secondary enquiries which have become such a feature of the academic scene during the last ten years are different from all other kinds of enquiry. An enquiry of this kind—into the knowledge industry itself—is entirely distinctive in that it is a part of the very enterprise it is investigating. Much of the respectability which invests some of the instruments (which I believe are being used to erode important values in tertiary education) is itself borrowed from the previous achievements of that sector. People have been put into positions of authority who are *academic* authorities—or have been. They are thought of as authoritative as well as authoritarian. But they are also *ipso facto* as vulnerable to challenge as we are. They cannot be accountable to their political bosses alone. Insofar as their work claims academic authority it becomes part of the very industry they are investigating, and they are as accountable to its standards of academic competence and honesty as are their victims. I recommend this as the best strategy currently available to us. In this connection I find myself very much in sympathy with Ernest House, talking about the American accountabilists: "I would like to suggest that we empower a federal agency to increase the accountability of business to the public and make an educator chairman of the advisory board" (House, 1974: 279). Of course we could never achieve such a thing, but this is just the rhetoric that is needed at the present time—the kind of rhetoric which Harry Medlin used. "The time has come", he said; and I really believe it has.

The Contributors

Dr. GERALD BURKE,
Senior Lecturer,
Faculty of Education,
Monash University,
Clayton, Victoria.

P. R. CHIPPENDALE,
Senior Lecturer,
Higher Education Policy Research and Evaluation Unit,
Darling Downs Institute of Advanced Education.

Dr. W. C. HALL,
Director,
Mount Gravatt College of Advanced Education,
Mount Gravatt, Queensland.

Dr. G. S. HARMAN,
Fellow,
Education Research Unit,
Australian National University,
Canberra, Australian Capital Territory.

JANFERIE M. HOWLETT,
Academic Assistant,
Adelaide College of the Arts and Education,
Underdale, South Australia.

J. T. HYDE,
Research Officer,
Committee of Enquiry into Post-Secondary Education
South Australian Council for Educational Planning and Research,
Kent Town.
(currently research scholar in political science, University of Adelaide.)

Professor RICHARD ST. C. JOHNSON,
Deputy Chairman,
School of General Studies,
Classics Department,
Australian National University,
Canberra, Australian Capital Territory.

Dr. RUSSELL D. LINKE,
Senior Lecturer,
Educational Research Unit,
Flinders University,
Bedford Park, South Australia.

Dr. J. A. McDONELL,
Director,
Department of Continuing Education,
Monash University,
Clayton, Victoria.

PHILLIP McKENZIE,
Research Officer,
Australian Council for Educational Research,
Hawthorn, Victoria.

Professor J. R. NILAND,
Professor of Economics,
Head, School of Economics and Department of Industrial Relations,
University of New South Wales,
Kensington, New South Wales.

Dr. N. A. NILSSON,
Senior Lecturer,
School of Education,
Flinders University,
Bedford Park, South Australia.

ALLAN PATCHING,
President,
Federation of Staff Associations of Australian Colleges of Advanced Education,
and Head, Mathematics Department,
Murray Park College of Advanced Education,
Magill, South Australia.

Dr. GREGOR RAMSEY,
Director,
Adelaide College of the Arts and Education,
Underdale, South Australia.

PETER F. SHELDRAKE,
Reader and Director,
Educational Research Unit,
Flinders University,
Bedford Park, South Australia.

Emeritus Professor F. J. WILLETT,
Vice-Chancellor,
Griffith University,
Nathan, Queensland.

Bibliography

Abbey, B. and Ashenden, D. (1976) "Book Review, Schooling in Capitalist America," *Australian Left Review*. 54: 30-34.

Academic Awards in Colleges of Advanced Education (1969) *Report of the Inquiry into Awards in Colleges of Advanced Education*. Melbourne: Government Printer.

Adams, W. (1974) "The State of Higher Education — Myths and Realities," *AAUP Bulletin*. 60.

Ahamad, B. and Blaug, M. (Eds) (1973) *The Practice of Manpower Forecasting*. San Francisco: Elsevier.

Allen, J. A. (1977) *Accountability in Higher Education in Australia—an Administrator's Viewpoint*. Conference on Accountability in Australian Higher Education: What Form Does it Take: What Form Should It Take? Darling Downs Institute of Advanced Education. 5-7 (an unpublished paper held in the Institute Library).

Anderson, D. S. (Chairman) (1978) *Post Secondary Education in South Australia*. Report of the Committee of Enquiry on Post-Secondary Education. Adelaide: Government Printer.

Anderson, D. S., Batt, K. J. and Rosenberg, K. J. (1976) *Communities and Colleges: Post-compulsory Education in Northern Australia*. Canberra: Australian National University.

Ashby, Sir Eric (1973) "The Structure of Higher Education: A World View," *Higher Education*. 2 (2): 142-151.

Australia. Academic Salaries Tribunal (1976) *1976 Review*. Canberra: Australian Government Publishing Service.

Australia. *Constitution*.

Australia. Department of Education (1977) *Report for 1975*. Canberra: Commonwealth Government Printer.

Australia. Hospitals and Health Services Commission (1975). *Report on Continuing Medical Education*. Canberra: Government Printer of Australia.

Australia. Hospitals and Health Services Commission (1976). *Second Annual Report for the Year 1974-75*. Canberra: Government Printer of Australia.

Australia. Laws, Statutes etc. *Audit Act, 1901-1973*.

Australia. Laws, Statutes etc. *Ombudsman Act* (No. 181), 1976.

Australia. Laws, Statutes etc. *Remuneration Tribunals Act, 1973-1975*.

Australia. Laws, Statutes etc. States Grants *(Tertiary Education Assistance) Act* (No. 25), 1977.

Australia. Laws, Statutes etc. *States Grants (Tertiary Education Assistance) Act* (No. 158), 1977.

Australia. Laws, Statutes etc. *Tertiary Education Commission Act* (No. 25), 1977.

Australia. Laws, Statutes etc. *Trade Practices Act, 1974* Memorandum showing the Trade Practices Act 1974—(a) As in Force Immediately Before the Commencement of the Trade Practices Act 1977; and (b) As Amended by The Trade Practices Act Amendment Act 1977.

Australia. *Parliamentary Debates* (1958) House of Representatives, Vol. 19: 1456, 6th May.

Australia. Parliament *Report of the Auditor-General* (1977) Parliamentary Paper No. 133/1977. Canberra: Acting Commonwealth Government Printer.

Australian Bureau of Statistics. 1977d *The Labour Force.* Canberra: Government Printer.

Australian Bureau of Statistics. 1977c *Schools.* Canberra: Government Printer.

Australian Bureau of Statistics. 1977b *University Statistics.* Canberra: Government Printer.

Australian Bureau of Statistics. 1977a *Colleges of Advanced Education.* Canberra: Government Printer.

Australian Bureau of Statistics. 1977d *Apprentices and Employees working as Tradesmen.* Canberra: Government Printer.

Australian Commission on Advanced Education (1973) *Teacher Education 1973-75.* Report of the Special Committee on Teacher Education (Cohen Report) Canberra; Australian Government Publishing Service.

Australian Conference of Principals of Colleges of Advanced Education (1977a) Memorandum and Articles of Association, 4.

Australian Conference of Principals of Colleges of Advanced Education (1977b) *Submission to the Committee of Inquiry into Education and Training.* Mimeo.

Australian Education Council. (1978) *The Supply and Demand for Teachers in Australian Primary and Secondary Schools.* Report of the Australian Education Council Working Party. Canberra: Australian Government Publishing Service.

Australian Vice-Chancellors Committee (1971) *Chairman's Report, 1967-70.*

Baldridge, J., Curtis, D., Ecker, G., and Riley, G. (1977) "Alternative Models of Governance in Higher Education" in Riley, G. and Baldridge, J., *Governing Academic Institutions.* California: McCutchan Publishing Corporation, 2-25.

Barker, L. J. and McNulty, L. J. (1978) 'A Practical Model for Accountability in Higher Education—The Darling Downs Institute of Advanced Education Experience', paper presented at the Fifth Annual Conference of the Higher Education Research and Development Society of Australasia, 2-4 June. Adelaide.

Batt, K. J. "Post School Education and Community Relationships," *Unicorn.* 2 (2) 38-44.

Beare, H. "The Beare Eleven." Canberra: Australian Capital Territory Schools Authority.

Beazley, K. (1977) "The Labor Party in Opposition and Government". In I. Birch and D. Smart (Eds) *The Commonwealth Government and Education 1964-1976:* Political Initiatives and Development. Victoria: Drummond.

Birch, L. K. F. (1975) *Constitutional Responsibility for Education in Australia.* Canberra: Australian National University.

Birch, I. K. F. (1977) "The Commonwealth Parliament and Education," *Educ. News.* 16: 25.

Blaug, M. (1967) "Approaches to Educational Planning," *The Economic Journal* June, 262-287.

Blaug, M. (1969) "The Productivity of Universities," in Blaug, M. (Ed) *The Economics of Education 2.* Harmondsworth: Penguin.

Bok, D. C. (1973) "Defining the Aims of Liberal Arts," *Times Higher Education Supplement:* London.

Bowden Lord (1967) "The Universities, the Government and the Public Accounts Committee," *Minerva.* VI.

Bowens, C. A. (1971) "Accountability from a Humanist View," *Educational Forum.* XXXV: 4.

Bowles, S. and Gintis, H. (1976) *Schooling in Capitalist America.* New York: Basic Books Incorporated.

Bradley, F. H. (1935) *Ethical Studies.* Oxford: Clarendon Press.

Briggs, Raymond, (1977) *Fungus the Bogeyman.* London: Hamish Hamilton.

Brimblecombe, E. M. (1976) "Community Involvement in Education from the Point of View of a Member of the Community," *Unicorn.* 2 (2): 7-10.

Bureau of the Census (1975) United States Department of Commerce, Current Population Reports, series P-20, No. 278. U.S. Government Printing Office.

Burke, J. C. (1977) "Coping With the Role of College or University President" Educational Record, American Council of Education, 58 (4): 388-402.

Campbell, R. (1978) "Universities and the Future," *Australian Quarterly.* 50 (1): 51-66.

Campbell, W. B. (1976) Academic Salaries Tribunal 1976. *Federation of Professionals 1976 Review.* Canberra: Australian Government Publishing Service.

Carlson, R. O. (1977) *Accountability in Higher Education: An Overview.* Conference on Accountability in Australian Higher Education: What Form Does It Take: What Form Should It Take? Darling Downs Institute of Advanced Education. (Sound tape of address delivered to the conference, held in the Institute Library).

Carnegie Commission, 1973, *Report into the Governance of Higher Education.* New York: McGraw Hill.

Carter C. (1969) "Can we get British education cheaper?" in Blaug, M. (Ed) *The Economics of Education 2.* Harmondsworth: Penguin.

Chippendale, P. R. and Wilkes, P. V. (1977) *Accountability in Education.* St. Lucia, Queensland: University of Queensland Press.

Clark, B. R. (1977) "Faculty Organisation and Authority," in Riley, G. and Baldridge, J. *op.cit.* 64-78.

Committee on Open University (1974) *Open Tertiary Education.* Canberra: Australian Government Publishing Service.

Crittenden, B. (1975) "Arguments and Assumptions of the Karmel Report: A Critique," in J. V. D'Cruz and P. J. Sheehan, *The Renewal of Australian Schools.* Richmond Victoria: Primary Education Pty. Ltd. 3-20.

Cutt, J. (1972) *Program Budgeting and Higher Education.* Canberra: Public Finance Monograph No. 1, Australian National University.

Cutt, J. (1976) 'Planning-Programming-Budgeting Systems in Tertiary Education,' Canberra, unpublished paper.

Cutt, J. and Tydeman, J. (1976) *A General Approach to the Analysis of Public Resource Allocation.* Canberra, Mimeo.

Dale, R. Esland, G. and MacDonald, M. (Eds) (1976) *Schooling and Capitalism.* London and Henley: Routledge and Kegan Paul in association with the Open University Press.

Davies, A. J. (1972) "Bureaucracy in Educational Organisation: The University," in Walker, W. G. (Ed) *School, College and University: The Administration of Education in Australia.* University of Queensland Press: Queensland.

Davis, R. H. Abedor, A. J. and Witt, P. W. F. (1976) "Commitment to Excellence: A Case Study of Educational Innovation." Michigan: Michigan State University.

D'Cruz, J. V. (1977) "Towards an Inclusive Notion of Accountability," in P. R. Chippendale and P. V. Wilkes, *Accountability in Education.* St. Lucia Queensland: University of Queensland Press, 183-205.

Dennison, J. (1976) "The Concept of the Community College," in *Lifelong Education and Poor People: Three Studies.* Australian Government Commission of Enquiry into Poverty: Australian Government Printing Service.

Department of Education and Science (1970) *Output Budgeting for the Department of Education and Science.* HMSO, London.

Derham, D. P. (1975) "Universities, Governments and the Assumption of Federal Responsibility for Higher Education in Australia," *Australian University.* 13 (3) 201-213.

Directors of Central Institutes of Technology (1976) Annual Report: 1976.

Drucker, P. (1974) *Management.* New York: Harper and Row.

Dufty, N. F. (1976) "Some Notes on Resource Allocation in Tertiary Institutions," *The Journal of Educational Administration.* 14 (2) 220-235.

Elliott, O. (1970) "Accountability," *Newsletter* LXXV (24).

Epstein, L. D. (1974) *Governing the University.* San Francisco: Jossey Bass.

Federation of Australian University Staff Associations (1976) Annual Report of Executive: August.

Federation of Australian University Staff Associations (1977) Submission to the Committee of Inquiry into Education and Training, June: Mimeo.

Freebairn, J., and Withers, G., (1977) "Manpower Forecasting for the Australian Labour Market," presented to the 48th ANZAAS Congress, Melbourne: August.

Freeman, R. B. (1976) *The Overeducated American.* New York: Academic Press.

Fuchs, R. F. (1963) "Academic Freedom: Its Basic Philosophy, Function and History," *Law and Contemporary Problems.* 28.

Gordon, A., and Williams, G., (1976) "Individual Demand for Education," Case Study: United Kingdom. Paris. OECD: Mimeo.

Graycar, A. (1975) "Power and Influence in Professional Education," in D. E. Edgar (Ed) *Sociology of Australian Education: A Book of Readings.* New York: McGraw-Hill.

Gubser, M. M. (1973) "Accountability as a smokescreen for political indoctrination." *Phi Delta Kappan.*

Hagan, J. S. (Chairman) (1978) Working Party for the Establishment of an Education Commission, Final Report. Sydney: Government Printer.

Hameister, D. R., and Hickey, T., (1977) "Traditional and Adult Students: a Dichotomy." *Lifelong Learning: The Adult years.* 1 (4) 6-8 and 18.

Harman, G. S. (1977) "The Political Environment of Australian Higher Education." Paper delivered at a Seminar, Department of Anthropology and Sociology University of Queensland, April. Mimeo.

Harman, G. (1978) "Provisions for Co-ordinating Post-Secondary Education at Federal and State Levels." Paper prepared for the Enquiry into Post-Secondary Education in South Australia.

Harman G. S. and Selby Smith C. (Eds) *Australian Higher Education.* Sydney: Angus and Robertson. (1972).

Harman, G. and Selby Smith C. (1976) "Current Trends and Issues in the Governance of Australian Colleges of Advanced Education." *The Australian Journal of Education.* 20 (2) 129-148.

Harrold, R. (1974) "Economic Thinking in Education," Western Australian Institute of Technology.

Hart, H. L. A. (1968) *Punishment and Responsibility.* Oxford: Clarendon Press.

Hawkins, C. A. (1975) "An Evaluation of Performance in Administrations of Higher Education," *Australian Journal of Advanced Education.* 5 (2) 29-32.

Hore, T., Linke, R. D., and West, L. H. T., (Eds) (1978) *The Future of Higher Education in Australia.* South Melbourne: MacMillan.

Hospitals and Health Services Commission (No. 211) (1973) *Act* (211).

House, E. R. (1974) "Accountability: An Essay Review on Three Books," *American Educational Research Journal.* XI (3) 275-279.

Houston, H. S. and Harman, G. S. (1978) "Course Accreditation in Australian Colleges of Advanced Education," *South Pacific Journal of Teacher Education.* 6 (1).

Hudson, H. R. (1976) "The Political Economy of Educational Advancement," in *New Directions in Australian Education.* Melbourne: Australian College of Education, 45-89.

Jones, A. W. (1977) "The Professional Educator," in *Ebb and Flow.* Adelaide: Education Department of South Australia.

Jones, K. N. (1977) "Accountability in Education: A National Viewpoint," in P. R. Chippendale and P. V. Wilkes (Eds) *Accountability in Education.* University of Queensland Press: St. Lucia Queensland.

Karabel, J. "Community Colleges and Social Stratification," *Harvard Educational Review.* 42 (4) 521-562.

Karmel, P. H. (Chairman) (1971) *Education in South Australia.* Report of the Committee of Enquiry in Education in South Australia, 1969-70. Adelaide: Government Printer.

Karmel, P. (Chairman) (1973) *Schools in Australia: Report of the Interim Committee for the Australian Schools Commission, May 1974.* Canberra: Australian Government Publishing Service.

Karmel, P. H. (Chairman) (1976) *Post Secondary Education in Tasmania.* Report of the Committee on Post-Secondary Education in Tasmania. Canberra; Australian Government Publishing Service.

Karmel, P. (1978b) "Education and Unemployment." Paper delivered to the Annual Summer School, University of Western Australia, 23 January 1978.

Karmel, P. (1978a) "Higher Education in a Steady State," *New Journal of Advanced Education.* 1 (1).

Kerr, E. (1975) *Report on a Visit by Dr. Edwin Kerr, Chief Officer, CNAA to Australia, September 21-October 22, 1975.* London.

Knight, S. and McDonald, R. (1977) *Adult Learners in University Courses.* Educational Services and Teaching Resources Unit, Murdoch University.

Knowles, M. (1970) *The Modern Practice of Adult Education: Andragogy vs. Pedagogy.* Association Press.

Landers, J. (1973) "Old Ideas In New Bottles," *Phi Delta Kappan.*

Leslie, L., and Johnson, G., (1974) "The Market Model and higher education," *Journal of Higher Education.* 45 (1) 1-20.

Lessinger, L. M. (1970) "Every kid a winner: Accountability in Education." S.R.A.: Palo Alto.

Levin, H. M. (1974) "A Conceptual Framework for Accountability in Education," *School Review,* 82.

Lumsden K. G. (Ed) (1974) *Efficiency in Universities.* Amsterdam: Elsevier.

Mackie, R. (1976) "Education for Liberation," *Australian Left Review.* 54: 26-29.

Manpower Services Commission (1976) *Towards a Comprehensive Manpower Policy.* Manpower Services Commission: London.

Marland, S. P. (1972) "Accountability in Education," *Teachers College Record.*

Martin, L. (Chairman) (1964-6) *Tertiary Education in Australia.* Report of the Committee on the Future of Tertiary Education in Australia. 3 Vols., Canberra: Commonwealth Government Printer.

Matthews, R. L. "Patterns of Educational Finance," *Australian Economic Papers.* 12: 145-161.

Maynard, A. (1975) *Experiment with Choice in Education.* Institute of Economic Affairs: London.

McCaig, R. (1972) "Communication in Educational Organization: The University," in Walker, E. G. *op. cit.* 102-111.

McLaren, J. (1974) *A Dictionary of Australian Education.* Ringwood: Penguin.

Medlin, E. H. (1978) "Accountability in Higher Education." Proceedings of the 5th Annual Conference, Higher Education Research and Development Society of Australasia, Educational Research Unit, Flinders University, Bedford Park, South Australia.

Medlin, E. H. Miscellaneous Papers, Barr Smith Library Special Collections, University of Adelaide.

Merrett, S. (1967) "Student Finance in Higher Education," *The Economic Journal.* 77: 288-302.

Mishan, E. (1969) "Some Heretical Thoughts on University Reform," *Encounter.* 32: 3-15.

Murray, K. (1957) (Chairman) *Report of the Committee on Australian Universities.* Canberra: Commonwealth Government Printer.

Niland, J. (1977) "Education, Work and Industrial Relations," *Australian Quarterly.* March 63-74.

Niland, J. (1978) "The Prospects for Manpower Planning and Forecasting in Australia," prepared for the Committee of Inquiry into Education and Training, March.

Nixon, R. M. (1970) *New York Times.* March 4, 18.

Nixon, R. M. (1970) "Message on Education Reform to the Congress of the U.S." March 3.

Organisation for Economic Co-operation and Development (1977). *Selection and Certification in Education and Employment.* Paris: OECD.

Organisation for Economic Co-operation and Development (1972) *Institutional Management in Higher Education.* Paris: OECD.

Ornstein, A. C. (1976) "The Politics of Accountability," *The Educational Forum.* November.

Partridge, P. H. (1976) *Post-Secondary Education in Western Australia.* Perth: Government Printer.

Partridge, P. H. (Chairman) (1978) *Report of the Committee of Inquiry into Post-Secondary Education.* Melbourne: Government Printer.

Pickford, M. (1974) "Costing University Resources." *Universities Quarterly.* 28: 349-361.

Pine, G. J. (1976) "Teacher Accountability," *The Educational Forum.* November.

Pitcher, G. (1960) "Hart on Action and Responsibility," *The Philosophical Review.* LXIX: 226-235.

Prest, A. (1966) *Financing University Education.* Institute of Economic Affairs, London.

Ramsey, G. A. (1978) "The Curriculum Function—Course Development and Accreditation" in *The Future of Higher Education in Australia:* T. Hore, R. Linke and L. West (Eds), Melbourne: MacMillan, 199-221.

Samuel, P. (1977) "The Scandal of our Universities," *The Bulletin.* March 12.

Schon, D. (1973) *Beyond the Stable State.* Harmondsworth: Pelican.

Scott, R. (1978) "Education and Public Accountability," *Journal of Advanced Education.* 1 (4): 4-7.

Skertchly, A. (1974) "Democratization of College Governance: The All-Campus Assembly," *Australian Journal of Advanced Education.* 4 (2): 4-9.

Skertchly, A. (1976) "Institutional Self-Renewal in Australian Universities," *Vestes.* 19 (1): 14-22.

Smart, D. (1976) "Federal Government Involvement in Australian Education, 1964-1975," *The Journal of Educational Administration.* XIV (2): 236-251.

Smith, Reverend S. (1821) "Spring Guns and Man Traps," *Edinburgh Review.* XXXV March, 123-134.

South Australian Board of Advanced Education (1977) *Report on Co-ordination of Colleges of Advanced Education in South Australia.* S.A. Board of Advanced Education: Adelaide.

Spann, R. N. (1973) *Public Administration in Australia.* Sydney: Government Printer of New South Wales.

Spaull, A. D. (1978) "The Academic Staff Associations" in Hore, T. Linke, R., and West, L. (Eds) *"The Future of Higher Education in Australia."* Melbourne: MacMillan, 84-100.

Sperry, J. (1975) "An accounting view of management in higher education," *College and University.* 50: 254-262.

Sperry, J. (1977) "Shifting State Aid from College to Student: A New Plan for Higher Education," *Carnegie Quarterly.* XXV (3).

Swedish Employers Federation (1977) *Tender och prognoser 1977.* (Trends and forecasts—population, education and labour market in Sweden.) Stockholm: SCB.

Tannock, P. D. (1975) *The Government of Education in Australia.* University of Western Australia Press: Nedlands.

Tannock, P. D. and Birch, I. K. (1973) "Defining the Limits of Commonwealth Education Power," in *Melbourne Studies in Education, 1973.* S. Murray-Smith (Ed) Melbourne: Melbourne University Press.

Teichler, U. (1976) *On the Changing Relationships Between the Educational and Occupational Systems: Conceptions and Recent Trends,* unofficial translation of paper presented to the International Labour Office World Employment Programme, Berlin, December.

Tertiary Education Commission (1977) *Recommendations for 1978.* Canberra: Australian Government Publishing Service.

Tertiary Education Commission (1978) *Report for 1979-81 Triennium.* Canberra: Australian Government Publishing Service.

Tertiary Education Commission (1978) *Report for 1979-81 Triennium. Vol. 1: Recommendations on Guidelines.* Canberra: Australian Government Publishing Service.

Tertiary Education Commission (1978) *Draft Report on Study Leave.* Canberra: Tertiary Education Commission.

Thompson, N. (1974) *Economics of Student Loans.* Canberra: Australian Government Publishing Service.

Topley, J., and Willett, F. J. (1976) "The Organization of a New University," *The Journal of Educational Administration.* 14 (1): 54-69.

Universities Commission (1975) *Sixth Report.* Canberra: Australian Government Publishing Service.

The University of Adelaide, (1977) Submission to the Committee of Enquiry into Post Secondary Education in South Australia. Adelaide: Mimeo.

United States Department of Health, Education and Welfare, Office of Education, H.E.W. (1971) *Report on Higher Education.* Washington D.C.

Van Lennep, E. (1974) Opening Address to the Conference on Future Structures in Higher Education, in *Policies For Higher Education.* Paris: OECD.

Walker, W. G. (1977) "What on Earth is Accountability?" in P. R. Chippendale and P. V. Wilkes, *Accountability in Education.* St. Lucia Queensland: University of Queensland Press, 3-20.

Walker, W. G. (Ed) (1972) *School, College and University: The Administration of Education in Australia.* Queensland: University of Queensland Press.

Wark, I. W. (1977) "Colleges of Advanced Education and the Commission on Advanced Education," in I. K. Birch and D. Smart (Eds) *The Commonwealth Government and Education 1864-1976: Political Initiatives and Development.* Melbourne: Drummond.

Watts, A. G. (1972) *Diversity and Choice in Higher Education.* London: Routledge and Kegan Paul.

Weller, P. (1976) "The Schools Commission, Political Resources and Federal-State Relations," in R. M. Burns *et al. Political and Administrative Federalism.* Canberra: Centre for Research on Federal Financial Relations, Australian National University.

Weller, P. and Cutt, J. (1976) *Treasury Control in Australia.* Sydney: Ian Novak.

Williams, B. R. (1976) "Resources Per University Student, 1957-75," *The Australian University.* 14: 7-14.

Williams, B. R. (1978) "Why all These Inquiries into Education?" *Search.* 9: 87-91.

Wood, P. (1977) "What Accountability Means to Governments," in *Accountability in Education,* Chippendale P. R. And Wilkes P. (Eds). St. Lucia, Queensland: University of Queensland Press, 103-117.

Woodhall, M. (1970) Student Loans: *A Review of Experience in Scandinavia and elsewhere.* London: Harrap.

Woodhall, M. (1974) *Distributional Impact of Methods of Educational Finance.* Organisation for Economic Co-operation and Development: Mimeo.

Wynne, E. (1976) "Accountable to Whom?" *Society.* 13 (2): 30-37.

Index

ACAAE, *see* Australian Council on Awards in Advanced Education
AEC, *see* Australian Education Council
AUS, *see* Australian Union of Students
AVCC, *see* Australian Vice-Chancellors' Committee
Abbey, B., 14
Abedor, A. J., 121
academic freedom, *see* academic staff
Academic Salaries Tribunal, 9, 24-5, 73
academic staff: academic freedom, 2-3, 30, 40-2, 44-5, 65-6, 73, 90, 125, 147; appointments, 32, 70, 82, 90, 107-9; associations, 8-10, 124; fixed term appointments, 65, 90, 94, 123; industrial matters, 9, 25; long service leave, 90; outside earnings, 25; promotions, 64-5, 72-3; quality, 38, 64, 70, 90, 107-8; redundancy, 59, 63, 65, 123-4; research, 2-3, 44-5, 61, 65, 72-3, 93, 97, 99, 105, 123-4, 146; salaries, 24-5, 89-90, 94; standards, 26, 63, 72-3, 90, 107, 109-10; study leave, 27, 65-6, 94, 97-8, 120, 123, 148; superannuation, 90; teaching, 2, 68, 72-4, 95, 98, 105, 108, 123-4; tension between administrators and, 68-72; tenure, 59, 65, 73, 80, 90, 93, 124; *see also* accountability; colleges of advanced education; tertiary institutions and education; universities
academic support staff, 89, 102
accountability, 17, 44, 77-8, 80-1, 119, 138-50; approaches to, 1-2, 11, 17-19, 120-1; community, 11-13, 15-16, 46, 50, 52-3, 55-7, 59, 62-3, 73, 79, 103-6, 110, 112, 115-17, 121-5, 145; educational, 20, 23-6, 45, 50, 62, 79, 97-9, 101-3, 107-17, 122-3, 150; fiscal, 11, 13-17, 21-2, 24-6, 29, 46, 58, 60, 66-7, 91, 96, 102-3, 120-1, 141; input/output, 18-19, 26-7, 37, 46-7, 66-7, 81, 94, 120-1; internal, 2-3, 11, 19, 59-62, 65-6, 70-1, 73-4, 76-7, 105-10, 136; international, 2, 12, 37-8; political, 11-12, 46, 57, 60-1, 95, 121, 142, 149; pressure groups, 8-10, 12, 111-12; questioned by the press, 12, 46, 58-9, 100-2; social context of, 12-14, 18, 20, 53-5, 62, 94; to the Commonwealth, 19-31, 37; to the States, 24-5, 29-30, 32, 36-8; to the students, 10-11, 18, 26, 47-8, 50-2, 63-4, 92, 102, 104, 110, 117, 122, 137, 146; *see also* academic staff
Adams, W., 123
Advanced Education, Board of (Qld.), 6, 21, 25, 102
Advanced Education, Board of (S.A.), 7, 35
Advanced Education Council, 63
Advisory Committee on Advanced Education, 87
agricultural colleges, 3-4
Ahamad, B., 131
Allen, J. A., 19, 21, 25, 28
Anderson Committee, *see* Committee of Enquiry on Post-Secondary Education
Anderson Report on Darwin, 148